CAMBRIDGE LIBRARY COLLECTION
Books of enduring scholarly value

Cambridge
The city of Cambridge received its royal charter in 1201, having already been home to Britons, Romans and Anglo-Saxons for many centuries. Cambridge University was founded soon afterwards and celebrates its octocentenary in 2009. This series explores the history and influence of Cambridge as a centre of science, learning, and discovery, its contributions to national and global politics and culture, and its inevitable controversies and scandals.

The Cambridge Songs
The Cambridge Songs are preserved - many of them uniquely - in a famous eleventh-century manuscript held in Cambridge University Library. Composed in Germany, mostly in Latin but with some vernacular sections, these lyrics are most notable for the variety they display in both genre and form. As one of the earliest examples of medieval secular song-writing they are a key part of the canon of European literature. This 1915 edition was the first to reproduce the complete text with facing-page transcriptions. Karl Breul, originally from Berlin, became the first university lecturer in German in 1884, and remained the most eminent Germanist at Cambridge until his death in 1932. His edition continues to be of value to medievalists today both as a source for the study of these remarkable poems and as a record of Breul's achievement in scholarship and palaeography.

Cambridge University Press has long been a pioneer in the reissuing of out-of-print titles from its own backlist, producing digital reprints of books that are still sought after by scholars and students but could not be reprinted economically using traditional technology. The Cambridge Library Collection extends this activity to a wider range of books which are still of importance to researchers and professionals, either for the source material they contain, or as landmarks in the history of their academic discipline.

Drawing from the world-renowned collections in the Cambridge University Library, and guided by the advice of experts in each subject area, Cambridge University Press is using state-of-the-art scanning machines in its own Printing House to capture the content of each book selected for inclusion. The files are processed to give a consistently clear, crisp image, and the books finished to the high quality standard for which the Press is recognised around the world. The latest print-on-demand technology ensures that the books will remain available indefinitely, and that orders for single or multiple copies can quickly be supplied.

The Cambridge Library Collection will bring back to life books of enduring scholarly value across a wide range of disciplines in the humanities and social sciences and in science and technology.

The Cambridge Songs

A Goliard's Songbook of the Eleventh Century

KARL BREUL

CAMBRIDGE UNIVERSITY PRESS

Cambridge New York Melbourne Madrid Cape Town Singapore São Paolo Delhi

Published in the United States of America by Cambridge University Press, New York

www.cambridge.org
Information on this title: www.cambridge.org/9781108003483

© in this compilation Cambridge University Press 2009

This edition first published 1915
This digitally printed version 2009

ISBN 978-1-108-00348-3

This book reproduces the text of the original edition. The content and language reflect the beliefs, practices and terminology of their time, and have not been updated.

THE CAMBRIDGE SONGS

CAMBRIDGE UNIVERSITY PRESS
C. F. CLAY, Manager
London: FETTER LANE, E.C.
Edinburgh: 100 PRINCES STREET

New York: G. P. PUTNAM'S SONS
Bombay, Calcutta and Madras: MACMILLAN AND CO., Ltd.
Toronto: J. M. DENT AND SONS, Ltd.
Tokyo: THE MARUZEN-KABUSHIKI-KAISHA

All rights reserved

THE CAMBRIDGE SONGS

A GOLIARD'S SONG BOOK OF THE XIth CENTURY

EDITED

FROM THE UNIQUE MANUSCRIPT IN THE UNIVERSITY LIBRARY

BY

KARL BREUL

Hon. M.A., Litt.D., Ph.D.

SCHRÖDER PROFESSOR OF GERMAN IN THE UNIVERSITY OF CAMBRIDGE

Cambridge:
at the University Press
1915

Cambridge:
PRINTED BY JOHN CLAY, M.A.
AT THE UNIVERSITY PRESS

IN MEMORIAM HENRICI BRADSHAW
ET IN HONOREM FRANCISCI JENKINSON
HOC OPVSCVLVM DEDICATVM EST

PREFACE

THE remarkable collection of Medieval Latin poems that is known by the name of 'The Cambridge Songs' has interested me for more than thirty years. My first article 'Zu den Cambridger Liedern' was written in the spring of 1885 and published in Volume xxx of Haupt's *Zeitschrift für deutsches Alterthum*. The more attention I paid to the songs and the more I corresponded with scholars about some of them, the stronger became my conviction of the importance of having the ten folios of this unique manuscript photographed and of thereby rendering this fascinating collection in its every aspect readily accessible to the students of Medieval literature. It is in truth necessary to invite the co-operation of all such students, whether their subject be Medieval theology, philology, philosophy or music, in the interesting task of elucidating the more difficult poems of what may be regarded as the song book or commonplace book of some early Goliard. Poems such as *Rachel, De Musica, De tribus symphoniis et de littera Pithagore*, and others must of necessity be dealt with by specialists. For years I have wished to take this work in hand, but till quite recently it proved impossible to find the necessary leisure for the execution, however inadequate, of the task. Now, in the very saddest year of my life, when so much for which I have lived and worked is crumbling to pieces, I have at last carried out my old plan as best I could under the present anxious conditions. Sad too is the thought that so many of the eminent scholars who would have welcomed the publication of a compact edition of the 'Cambridge Songs' have passed away from among us, notably Henry Bradshaw, Wilhelm Scherer, Ludwig Traube, and Paul von Winterfeld.

The purpose of the present edition is first and foremost to place this remarkable collection within easy reach of British and foreign scholars; to provide, together with the photographic reproduction of all the folios, a trustworthy transliteration

and a serviceable text of the songs, methodically arranged and properly indexed; and to give, in the introductory chapters and in the notes, a survey of the critical literature that has so far appeared, in England and abroad, on each of the 47 pieces, with some additional elucidation of either the text or the subject-matter.

In the transliteration (Chapter I) all abbreviations have been written out in full, but the letters substituted for the abbreviation marks have been printed in italics. Piper's reproduction of the abbreviation marks is not invariably accurate, as a comparison of his text with the photographs will show. In Chapter V the spelling has in a few cases been slightly standardized (e.g. the more usual letters *e* and *i* have been substituted for the occasional *ae*, *ę*, *oe* and *y*). The actual spelling of the manuscript can easily be ascertained on pages 3–22, and certain inconsistencies are all the more easily explained if we are justified in assuming that there were several copyists of the songs whose habits of writing were not quite the same. This assumption is, however, not absolutely necessary, for it is not likely that even the same scribe would be entirely consistent in his manner of writing.

In the introductory chapters, and also in the notes, the titles of books and periodicals are quoted in full, because these references are intended not only for advanced students of Old German literature, but also for students of Medieval history, theology, philosophy and music, as well as for students of Medieval literature generally in English-speaking countries, all of whom are naturally less familiar with the abbreviated forms in which these periodicals and the older discussions are usually quoted in German books. As the chief aim of the Introduction and Notes is to indicate as clearly as possible the 'literature' to be consulted on the subject, I have preferred to give such references in too explicit rather than in too concise a form. The very valuable notes contained in the third edition (by E. Steinmeyer, 1892) of Müllenhoff and Scherer's *Denkmäler* have purposely not been reproduced here. This scholarly work is still indispensable, and as it is easily accessible students should make a point of consulting it; but attention is called in the notes to all later publications in which the commentary of the *Denkmäler* is either supplemented or corrected. The notes vary considerably in ·length. While in the case of some very small, fragmentary and unimportant pieces, little could be said with any profit, and while, in the case of several poems of considerable importance, a reference to the third edition of the *Denkmäler*, followed by a short indication of the latest contributions to the subject, was all that seemed to be needed, in other instances much fresh

PREFACE

material has been supplied that had not been used for the elucidation of the poems. Specimens of English and German translations have been given, wherever possible, in the hope that they may tempt and show the way to future translators. There is still much fruitful work to be done for the 'Cambridge Songs,' more especially at the hands of English translators, who have so far almost entirely ignored them and whose attention may be particularly invited to Nos. 22–32.

The Essay on 'De Heinrico' (Chapter VII) has been reprinted, with additions and corrections, from 'The Modern Quarterly of Language and Literature' (1898), where it was, perhaps, not very generally accessible.

The General Index has been made as full and as useful as possible. There is also an alphabetical table of the first words of all the pieces, together with full references to the works in which the individual poems have already been printed.

I desire gratefully to acknowledge my indebtedness to several friends and colleagues who have very kindly helped me with references and suggestions. These are Dr James (Provost of King's College and in the present year Vice-Chancellor of the University), Professor Burkitt, Professor Priebsch, Professor Reid, Professor Rippmann, Dr Ezard, Dr Latimer Jackson, Dr Naylor, Dr Nicholson, Dr Rootham, Dr Charles Wood, the Rev. W. A. Cox, Mr A. B. Cook, Mr G. G. Coulton, Mr N. McLean, Mr A. Rogers, and, above all, our Public Orator, Sir John Sandys.

The photographs were taken by Mr W. F. Dunn of the University Library with his usual care and success. They are in size and, as far as possible, in other respects, exact reproductions of the manuscripts.

I am dedicating this book to Henry Bradshaw (of unforgettable memory) and Francis Jenkinson, those two learned custodians of the treasures of our University Library in recent years, to whom no student, young or old, British or foreign, has ever applied without finding the most ready and generous help. They have taken the most lively interest in all research upon our Cambridge manuscripts and early printed books, notably in that upon our priceless Codex Gg. 5. 35, and have on several occasions rendered me valuable assistance in my own work upon the 'Cambridge Songs.'

In conclusion, if it is inevitable that the sad and anxious months during which this edition has been prepared should have left their trace upon its pages, yet my work upon this book of all others has truly sustained and consoled me during the present crisis. For the 'Cambridge Songs' are one of the very earliest

instances of genuine interest taken by Englishmen in the literature of Germany. The work hitherto devoted to our manuscript has been marked again and again by a whole-hearted, generous and fruitful co-operation on the part of eminent English, French, and American scholars with the most distinguished scholars of Germany in the elucidation of these attractive, and often unique, poems. May we not hope that, when the clash of arms is hushed and men again turn their thoughts to the pursuits of peace, scholars on both sides of the North Sea will once more join in the common search, as of old, for the good, the beautiful and the true?

K. B.

10, CRANMER ROAD,
  CAMBRIDGE,
    July 10, 1915.

TABLE OF CONTENTS

		PAGES
	PREFACE	vii—x
I.	MANUSCRIPT AND TRANSLITERATION	1—22
II.	DESCRIPTION OF THE CAMBRIDGE MANUSCRIPT WITH SPECIAL REFERENCE TO THE 'SONGS'	23—29
III.	THE WORK HITHERTO DONE ON THE 'CAMBRIDGE SONGS' (1720—1914)	29—34
	A. Editions and Discussions	29—34
	B. Photographic Reproductions	34
	C. Translations	34
IV.	MEDIEVAL LATIN LYRICS IN GERMANY AND THE 'CAMBRIDGE SONGS'	35—38
V.	THE GOLIARD'S SONG BOOK	38—69
	A. General Discussion	38—41
	B. Carmina in Codice Cantabrigiensi scripta	42—69
VI.	NOTES	70—101
VII.	A CONTESTED PASSAGE IN 'DE HEINRICO'	102—111
	INDEXES	112—120
	A. Alphabetical Index of the First Words of all the Songs	112—113
	B. Synopsis of the Contents of the Goliard's Song Book	114—115
	C. General Index	116—120

CHAPTER I

THE CAMBRIDGE SONGS

MANUSCRIPT AND TRANSLITERATION

Gratuletur omnis caro xpo nato
dño, qui p culpa protoplasti
carnem nostram induit, ut sal-
uaret q plasmauit di sapientia. Caute cane, caute cane,
conspira karole.

Melos cuncta concinnantes grā-
tiarum actiones soluimus aciem qui no-
stras roborauit ad cernendum summi patris coeternum uerbum p quod cuncta
restaurantur & reguntur clementia
mira cuius bonitate atq; dono salu-
te haurimus.

Uoces laudis humane cuius carnis
rauce nodium maiestati tantum
sufficiunt. ſſ

Que angelica sibi militia in excelsis
psallere sciam uisit simphonia.

Hec trinaria mundi discordia se mo-
uendo concordare fecit armonia.

Qui in impium confirmando romanum
suos agnos forte lotos a luporum
morsibus pia pace custodiuit.

Hos cuonradus pius unctus dñi
iam defendit impando.

Quem prudentia di pelagi p destinauit
& elegit regere gentes
strenue dauidis exemplo messi-
que triumpho.

O romanorum stemate regum primo-
nis gradus eratis p ficiebat regius
moribus & factis ut p bauit euentus.

Tuus forās & fidelis passus plures
mundi labores p pinquorum
causas & amicorum haud secus
ergo suas desiderauit cunctis uma-
niuare p possibilitate.

Pater uti sciui nutrit natum ne
adolando nunc flagellando
repetitas mundi puarias pepe

hunc p bauit ut didicisset pna pietatis scala de descendere reis. ſſ catholicor.

Post heinrici morte omni deflendā greg
unc rex regum fidum ecclesiarum uisit
fore patronum.

Hunc romani principatus cuncti mox
elegere sibi defensorem & ppugnatorem
fortem orthodoxorum.

Gaudete omnes circumquaq; gentes grās
xpo dñs q uiduarum atq; pupillor
audit uoces suorum.

Age gaude roma urbium domna cum consensu
cleri deuoto te cuonradi p cepto subdi
qui tuam tua suas sed affectiue omnium
subditor querit utilitates.

Ad haec publicarum principi rerum & p uate
dedita uite iure tenet familiari uita
& saluti imparator nostro poscite
cuonrado xpo di electo.

Laus sto regi scor patri nato pneumati sco cui soli manet impium
honor & potestas quem angelor laudes
hōnū & uoces laudare suē p uenit.

Grates usiae soluimus
supreme cui nihil accedit neq; recedit omnia cauenti tū continenter inuisi-
bili dño. Ziruis decimi.

Uncta qui tno creauit ex nihilo
sua & hōnē formauit ad imaginem
uice dampnatorum angelor sui ord-
inc stimulatus serpens antiquus
suasit a ma pm mandere pomum
quo nos omnes heu mortales subim-
us dire mortis imperio.

Tacuit sed suę condolens facturę
misit huc filium sibi coeternum
forma subseruili rem mendati.

Urgo maria maris stella feta de sco
pneumate sco edidit salo ce pestuosi
lucem sempiterna salutem q xpm dñm
scissimum.

THE CAMBRIDGE SONGS

fol. 432 r

Gratuletur omnis caro. christo nato
domino. qui proculpa protoplasti
carnem nostram induit. ut sal
uaret quod plasmauit dei sapientia. Caute cane. caute cane
conspira karole.

Melos cuncti concinnantes gratiarum
actiones soluimus aciem qui nostre
mentis roborauit adcernendum summi
patris coeternum uerbum perquod cuncta
restaurantur et reguntur elementa
mira cuius bonitate atque dono salu
-tem haurimus.

Uoces laudis humane curis carneis
rauce nondiuine maiestati tantum
sufficiunt.

Que angelicam sibi militiam inexcelsis
psallere sanctam iussit simphoniam.
Nec non uariam mundi discordiam semo-
-uendo concordare fecit armoniam.

Qui imperium confirmando romanum
suos agnos fonte lotos a luporum
morsibus pia pace custodiuit.

Hos cuonradus pius unctus domini
iam defendit imperando.

Quem prouidentia dei preclara predesti
nauit et elegit regere gentes
strennue dauidis exemplo messie-
-que triumpho.

Ortus auorum stemmate regum periunio-
ris gradus etatis proficiebat regiis
moribus et factis ut probauit euentus.

Tiro fortis et fidelis passus plures
mundi labores propinquorum
causas et amicorum haud secus
ergo suas desiderauit cunctis uiribus
iuuare propossibilitate.

Pater ut suum nutrit natum nunc
adolando nunc flagellando
tempestates mundi peruarias christus

hunc probauit ut didicisset prona pietatis scala condescendere reis.   [catholicorum.
Post heinrici mortem omi deflendam gregi
Hunc rex regum fidum ecclesiarum iussit
fore patronum.
Hunc romani principatus cuncti mox
elegere sibi defensorem et propugnatorem
fortem orthodoxorum.
Gaudent omnes circumquaque gentes gratias
christo dantes qui uiduarum atque pupillorum
audit uoces suorum.
Age gaude roma urbium domna cum consensu
cleri deuoto te cuonradi precepto subdi
qui nontantum suas sed affectiue omnium
subditorum querit utilitates.
Adhaec publicarum principi rerum et priuate
dediti uite iure tenti familiari uitam
et salutem imperatori nostro poscite
cuonrado christo dei electo.
Laus sit regi seculorum patri nato pneumati. sancto cui soli manet imperium
honor et potestas quem angelorum laudes
hominum et uoces laudant rite per euum.

Grates usiae soluimus
subremae cui nihil accedit neque recedit omnia continenti non conitente inuisi
bili domino.   [-nis decimi.
Cuncta qui initio creauit exnihilo
suam et hominem formauit adimaginem
uice dampnatorum angelorum sui ordi-
Hinc stimulatus serpens antiquus
suasit amarum mandere pomum
quo nos omnes heu mortales subiace
mus dire mortis imperio.
Factor sed sue condolens facture
misit huc filium sibi coeternum tectu
forma subseruili rem mendatii.
Uirgo maria maris stella feta decelo
pneumate sancto edidit salo tempestuoso
lucem sempiternam saluatorem christum dominum
                        [sanctissimum.

THE CAMBRIDGE SONGS

Postquam innumera fecit signa tollerat
   sputa alapas flagella crucis inhonestam
   patitur mortem ponitur insepulchrum adit
   infernum frangit mortis imperium.
5 Tertia die surgit amorte trahens mi
   crocosmum adsemet ipsum scandit omnes
   super celos nunc adextris sedet patris altithroni.
Inde uenturus potens est deus oues saluare hedos
   dampnare has in celis gauisuras hos in penis
10 luituros promeritis. ℭtrinitatis fidelium.
Nonlongo post cum discipulis inconclaui congregatis spiritus
   etherea imbuit aula pectora beatorum indiuidue
Qui pergentes predicabant pater natus sanctus spiritus ſim-
-plex usia personis distincta unus est hic deus
15 temporis expers sumens matre principium.
Unum baptisma fides et una deus et hominum
   pater cunctorum qui super omnes est potentes ex
   altatus et benedictus insecula.
Hinc uos omnes precor fideles mecum eternum
20 psallite deum sono tantum nonchordarum
   sed canoro iubilo. ℭpotentia.
Quo nos omnes se laudantes semper saluet
   et conseruet adhonorem sui nominis incliti
   hic et ineterna maiestatis triumphali
25 Nunc osummi ciues celi nec non sancti uos pro
   phete et bisseni principales apostoli marti
   res confessores uirgines omnes adiuuate
   nos precibus   -pneumati sancto nunc et in-
Sit prepotenti laus creatori patri filio-
30 -eternum sempiterna creature letitia.
   nclito celorum
   laus sit digna deo. ℭsuasione uermis.
Qui celos scandens soli regna uisitauit
   redempturus hominem maligni seductum
35 Quem quis qualis quantus quid sit ratio
   ne gestiens rimari inmensum quem
   scias benignum potentem.
Patris uerbum caro factum mundi lumen tene
   bras superans puellam regalem matrem fecit mariam.
40 Castam intrans carnem sumpsit qui

peccati maculam nonnouit ut unus regnaret
   factus homo deus.
Ioseph iustus quem accepit anglico doctus
   uerbo regem regum agnouit maximum angelus
   pastorum monstrat gregi deum.
Celum torquens astra regens inuolutus
   pannis plorans rusticorum tecmina
   pannorum pertulit qui cuncta potestate protulit. ℭhunc magi munere querebant.
Quem herodes rex regno timens seductorem se
   suadente instrumentis bellorum quesiuit perdendum
Stella duxit quos dux fidelis sic doctorem
   tunc iubente donec puer erat ubi
   contulit intrantes dederunt munera
   supplices. ℭbuere domini.
Monstrant auro regem esse presulem designant
   thure. mirra signum tumulo tri-
Tunc herodes iussit cunctos iugu-
   lari masculos quos natura produxit
   binis quoque annis.
Hunc iohannes baptitauit unda pulchri
   iordanis et uox patris natum
   iussit exaudiri populis.
Hic clara natusque matre dedit signa
   celorum demonstrans se fore
   deum aqua suam gaudens mutat naturam
   et conuiuis unda mitis uersa in
   uinum placuit.
Lazarum terre tenebris conclusum amissu
   sumere precepit ut qui seua committat piacula dum laborat emendan
   -do mortis surgit tumulo.
Iuuenem quem reliquit uite flamen
   dum turba urbe portat luctuosa
   surgere iubet mortis uicta lege quo
   loquele det iniuste hoc exemplum uenie.
Puellam uite lumine priuatam in domo
   uite restauit uerbo cogitando qui
   peccauit animo discat deo confiteri
   tecta mente crimina.

Postquam innumera fecerit signa tollerat
spută alapas flagella crucis inhonesta
patitur mortem ponitur in sepulchrum adit
infernum frangit mortis impium.

Tertia die surgit a morte trahens in
evo cosmū ad semet ipsū scandit om̅s
sup celos n̄ redeuntis sedet pr̄s a dextris.

Inde venturus potens dc̄ oues saluare hedos
dampnare hā r̄et gauisuras hos penis
luctuos pmeriturs. Et unitas fidelium.

Hon longo p̄ cū discipulis in celaui eggans sp̄s
etherea imbuit aula pectora beatoru individue.

Qui pergentes p̄dicabant pater natus sc̄s sp̄s simplex usia p̄sonis distincta un̄e hic d̄s
tēporis expers sum̅s m̄e principiū.

Unū baptisma fides & una d̄s & hominū
pater cunctoru q̄ sup om̅s 4 potentes ex
alt et us e benedict̄ in secla.

Hinc uos om̅s p̄cor fideles mecum et m̄
psallite d̄m sono cantu n̄ chordarū
sed canoro iubilo. potentia

Quo nos am̅s se laudantes semp saluet
& conseruet ad honore sui nōis inclita

hic et in eterna maiestatis triumphat

Nunc o sum̅i ciues celi nec n̄ sc̄i uos pro
phete & bis se̅i principales apti martires c̄fessores uirgines om̅s adiuuate
nos p̄cib: pneumati sc̄o n̄e & in

Sit potentia laus creatori p̄ri filio-
et n̄i sempiterna creature lector
in etern celorum.

...ses digna deo. Suasione uermis
...scandens soli regna uisitauit
tempturus hōe maligni seductū
quis qualis quantus qd sit ratio
...tiens rimari immensum quem
...benignu potentem.

Uerbū caro factū mundi lumen tenē
supans puella regale m̄re sc̄i mana
astū intrans carnē sumpsit qui

peccati maculā n̄ nouit ut uiri regnaret
factus homo d̄s.

Ioseph iustus quē accepit anglico doctus
uerbo regē regū agnouit maximū angst
pastorum monstrat gregi deum.

Celum corq̄ns astra regens inuolutus pannis plorans rusticor cremina
puinoru oculis qui cuncta potestate pallet. Et magi munere q̄rebant.

Que̅ herodes rex regnantis seductoris se
suadente iustruuit bellor q̄ suit p̄pendū.

Stella duxit & dux fidei sic doctore
te rubente donec puer erat ubi
c̄tulit intrantes deder munera
supplices. buere dn̄i

Monstrant auro rege ee p̄sule designant
thure mirra signū tumulo tri-

Tunc herodes iussit cunctos iugu-
lari masculos quos nat̄a p̄duxit
binis quoq; annis.

Hunc iob̅s baptizauit unda pulch̄
iordanis & uox p̄ris natum
iussit exaudiri populis.

Hic clara nat̄q; m̄re dedit signa
celor demonstrans a se fore
d̄m aq̅ sua gaudens mutat nat̄a
& c̄turis unda m̄tis uersa in
uinū placuit.

Lazarū ore tenebris celusū amiss
sumere p̄cepto ut q̄ seua comit-
tat piacula du̅ laborat emendando moras surgit tumulo.

Iuuenē que̅ reliq̅ uite flam
dū ē ba urbe portat luctuosa
surgere iubet morti uicta lege q̄
loquele dedit iuste h̄ exemplū nomen

Puellā uite lumine p̄iuata in domo
uite restauit uerbo cogitanda qui
peccauit animo discat d̄o c̄ fit
tecta m̄re crimina.

Hic in cruce pendens q̄s creauit princeps
regū redemit inferni confregit
uertice alligando principē.

Rex resurgens morte uictor fulget
ascendendo thronū tenet & coronas
imponit scīs coronandis.

Spm̄ dm̄ sacrū sibi coetnū nuntios trans
misit consolari bis senos quo linguis
loquendo nob̄ gent̄ab: intimidi uerba
uite p̄dicarent que iudea sperneret.

Agmina celor̄ gaudeant q̄ incola
quem gignebat uirgo p̄sidens īcelo
sancta ueste debosra gentiū redēpto
tr̄a poli igne pontū rex impace com
ponit. Splendet nobile celo sedens

Regnū cuius fine nescit sceptrū
mundū implens factor facta con
-tinens.

Omnis sonus cantilene trifariā fit.
Uā aut fidiū concentūs sonus con
-stat pulsu plectro manuq̄: ut sunt
discrepantia uocū uariis chordarū
generibus.

Aut tibiarum canorus redditur
flatus fistularū ut sunt disimi
-na queq̄: folle uentris orisq̄: tu
-midi flatu p̄strepentia pulchre
mentem mulcisonant

Aut multimodis gutture canoro
idē son̄ redditur plurimarū
faucium hom̄ uolucrū animan
tiumq̄: sicq̄ impulsu gutteq̄: agit̄.

His modis canamus oxor̄ socior̄q̄:
actus quor̄ honorem p̄timlat̄
phemiū hocce pulchre lantfridi
cobbonisq̄: p̄nobili stēmate.

Quāuis amicitiarū genera pluri
legant n̄ sunt adeo p̄clara ut
istor̄ sodaliū q̄ cōmunes exstatex
itarcū ut neuter horum

suapte q̄ possideret gazarū nec ser
uor̄ nec alicuius suppellectilis altor̄
quicquid uellet ab altero n̄atū foret
more ambo coequales inullo umqā
dissides quasi duo unus ē̄ent inom
nib: similes.

Porro prior orsus cobbo h̄ dixē frī socio
diu mihi hic regale incumbit ser
uitiū q̄ frī affinesq̄: uisendo n̄ adeā
imemor meor̄ ideo ultra mare
reuertar unde huc adueni illor̄
affectū ueniendo adilles ibi satisfactū.
edet me lantfridus inqt ut te p̄pne
tam dire ut absq̄: te scīs hic dega
na arripiens cū uig̃ tecū p̄grām exul
ātcū ut tu diu fact̄ mocū uice p̄
pendens amori sicq̄ p̄gentes litora
mans applicar parte aū insit cobbo
sodali hortor frī redeas redeā uisen
do eū utta comite unū memo
riale frī frī facias.

Uxorem quam tibi solam uendicasti
p̄pria m̄ dedas ut licentē fruar eius
amplexū nihil hesitando manū
manui ei tribuens Inlare fruere
ut libet. frī ea ne dicat̄ q̄ semotim
fisus sim q̄ possidere. Classe tunc
apparata ducto secū inequor.
Stans lantfridus sup litus cantab.
chordarū actū cobbo frī fide tene
hacten̄ ut feceras nā idetens est
affectū seq̄ndo uota honor̄ p̄ter
dedecus frī frī ne fiat sicq̄
canendo post illum intuit̄
longius eū n̄ cernens fregit rū
tīmpanū.

At cobbo collisū hīem n̄ ferens
uertendo mulcet en habes p̄
amor q̄ dedisti tractū ant
n̄s expirat̄u iā n̄ seq̄ expiat ut

THE CAMBRIDGE SONGS

fol. 433 r

Hic incruce pendens q*uos* creauit p*r*inceps
   regu*m* redemit inferni confregit
   uectem alligando principe*m*.
Rex resurgens morte uictor fulget
5   ascendendo thronu*m* tenet q*uo* coronas
   *im*ponit sanc*t*is coronandis.
Sp*iritu*m du*m* sacru*m* sibi coete*r*nu*m* nuntios trans
   misit consolari bis senos quo linguis
   loquendo nob*is* gentib*us* no*n*timidi uerba
10 uit*ae* p*re*dicarent que iudea sp*er*neret.
Agmina celo*rum* gaudeant q*uod* incola
   quem gignebat uirgo p*re*sidens i*n*celo
   tincta ueste de bosra gentiu*m* rede*m*ptio
   te*r*ra polu*m* igne*m* pontu*m* rex inpace com
15 ponit. ℭ-splendet nobile celo sedens
Regnu*m* cuius fine*m* nescit sceptru*m*—
   mundum implens factor facta con
   -tinens.,
O*m*nis sonus cantilene trifariam fit.
20 Na*m* aut fidiu*m* concentu sonus con
   -stat pulsu plectro manuq*ue* ut su*nt*
   discrepantia uocu*m* uari*is* chordaru*m*
   generibus.
Aut tibiarum canorus redditur
25 flatus fistularu*m* ut sunt discrimi
   -na queq*ue* folle*m* uentris orisq*ue* tu-
   -midi flatu p*er*strepentia pulchre
   mentem mulcisonant
Aut multi modis gutture canoro
30 ide*m* son*us* redditur plurimaru*m*
   faucium ho*m*inum uolucrum animan-
   tiumq*ue* sicq*ue* inpulsu gutt*ur*eq*ue* agit*ur*.
His modis canamus caro*rum* sotio*rum*que
   actus quo*rum* honorem p*re*titulat*ur*
35 p*ro*hemiu*m* hocce pulchre lantfridi
   cobbonisq*ue* p*er*nobili ste*m*mate.
Qua*m*uis amicitiaru*m* genera plura
   legant*ur* no*n*sunt adeo p*re*clara ut
   isto*rum* sodaliu*m* qui co*m*munes extiteru*nt*
40 i*n*tantu*m* ut neuter horum

suapte q*uid* possideret gazaru*m* nec ser
   uo*rum* nec alicuius suppellectilis alte*rorum*
   quicquid uellet ab altero ratu*m* foret
   more ambo coequales i*n*nullo umqua*m*
5   dissides. quasi duo unus *es*sent inom
   nib*us* similes.
Porro prior orsus cobbo dix*it* frat*ri* sotio
   diu mihi hic regale incumbit ser-
   uitiu*m* q*uod* frat*re*s affinesq*ue* uisendo n*on* adea*m*
10 inmemor meo*rum* ideo ultra mare
   reuertar unde huc adueni illo*rum*
   affectui ueniendo adillos ibi satisfacia*m*.
Tedet me lantfridus inq*uit* uite p*ro*prie
   tam dire ut absq*ue* te scis hic dega*m*
15 na*m* arripiens c*on*iuge*m* tecum pergam exul
   tecu*m* ut tu diu fact*us* mecum uicem re
   pendens amori sicq*ue* p*er*gentes litora
   maris applicaru*nt* pariter tu*m* infit cobbo
   sodali. hortor f*rate*r redeas redeam uisen-
20 -do en uita comite unu*m* memo
   riale f*rate*r frat*r*i facias.
Uxorem quam tibi solam uendicasti
   p*ro*pria*m* mihi dedas ut licent*er* fruar eius
   amplexui nihil hesitando manu*m*
25 manui ei*us* tribuens hilare*m* fruere
   ut libet. f*rate*r ea ne dicat*ur* q*uod* semotim
   fisus sim q*uid* possidere. classe tunc
   apparata ducit secu*m* inequor.
Stans lantfridus sup*er* litus cantib*us*
30 chordaru*m* ait. cobbo f*rate*r fidem tene
   hacten*us* ut feceras. na*m* i*n*decens est
   affectu*m* sequendo uoti honore*m* p*er*dere
   dedecus f*rate*r frat*r*i ne fiat. ficq*ue* diu
   canendo post illum intuitus
35 longius eu*m* n*on*cernens fregit rup
   timpanum.
At cobbo collisu*m* frat*r*em n*on* ferens mox
   uertendo mulcet en habes p*er*dulcis
   amor q*uod* dedisti i*n*tactum ante amo
40 ris experime*n*tu*m* ia*m* non *est* q*uod* experiatur ultra

ceptum iter relinquam alicubi pretermittam
absque me.
Qui principium constas rerum faue nostris
piis ceptis atque mentis plectrum rege
precamur rex regum. Etate.
Pater nate spiritus sancte te laudamus ore
corde.   uite siti fragili
Inmortales celi ciues pia prece nos
mortales iam conciues uestros commen
date redemptori. Pater.
Fibris cordis caute tentis melos
concinamus partim tristes par
tim letas causas proclamantes
de pastore pio ac patrono
heriberto. Pater.
Quem etate iuuenili deus preelegit
sibi seruum ualde fidum bona
super pauca supra multa tandem
ministrum constituendum. Pater.
Mane etatis puer bone indolis
sarculo uerbi uinea christi libens
studuit sciens sibi tandem
denarii premia dari scolis sub
latus fit cancellarius
    imperatoris omnium morum
speculum bonorum placuit clero
simul et populo mitis atque pius
omni egenti largus census sui
tiro fortis christi pollens omni
karitate scandit dextram note
uiam phitagorace. Pater
Post non magnum temporis curri
culum summo pontifice largi
ente miles domini sublimari
meruit insedem pontificalem tunc
sibi subditus clerus et populus
uiuere patronum optant pium
cui christo talem auxit honorem
ouis et ouilis sibi commissi belli
tempore longo non pateretur pene

damna rerum nec ullum exscidium
sed summi pastoris subquiete con
gaudentes uocem sanctam audierunt. Pater
Circumquaque ministrauit ecclesiis
magno sumptu tempestate bellicosa tunc
temporis deuastatis seueritatem facie
tristem monstrans letum toto corde
spreuit mundum pectore pio iugem
compassionem gerit omni mala mundi
patienti. Pater.
Aduentantes longe plures conso
latur peregrinos incensanter alimenta
pauperibus erogauit fouit infirmos
atque uestiuit nudos munia diuina
complens rite cuncta tantum uacans
uitae contemplatiuae sanxit cunctis se
uirtutum ornamentis. Pater.
Augens demum cumulum bonorum summa
sancitatis rexit templum sancte dei genitrici
speciosum rehni littore situm inquo
defunctam carnis sue sanctam iussit
condere glebam uti resurrectionis
diem magnum actremendum hic secure
expectaret. Pater.
Postquam mundus fuerat indignus
tantum cernere domnum christus plura
loco sue sepulture fecerat signa
sui ad honorem nominis sancti. et
ut magis sanctam confirmaret fidem
premia daturum se incelis propter
eum hic interris laboranti. Pater.
O cunctipotens mundum regens
finis rerum creatarum omnem
finem nostrum fac finiri inte
solum. Pater.
Nunc corda pange melos deuote
filio sancte uirginis marie honor
et uita salus et letitia pax in
remota altitudo inclita lux
permansura laus indificua sancto sit

cepṭū tū reliquā alicubi pꝛmittā
absq; moꝛ

Qui principiū constat rerū saue nr̄is
quis cepꝛas atq; mꝛas plectꝛū rege
pꝛeamur rex regum. Grate.

Pate nate sp̄s sc̄e te laudamus ore
corde   uite sm̄ fragili

Inmortales celi ciues pia p̄eo nos
mortales ia conciues uros com-
dare redemptori. Pat.

Fibris cordis caute tenras melos
concinamus partim tristes partim letas causas p̄clamantes
de pastore pio ac patrono
heriberto. Pat.

Quē etate iuuenili deus pelegit
sibi seruum ualde fidū bona
sup pauca supra multa tandē
ministrū c̄stituendū. Pat.

Mane etatis puer bono indolis
sarculo uerbi uinea xp̄i libens
studuit sciens sibi tandem
denariū p̄mia dari scolis sub
latus fit cancellarius
      imperatoris omīū moꝛ
speculū bonoꝛ placuit clero
simul e poplo mitas atq; pius
omi egena largus census sui
tato fortis xp̄i pollens omi
karmate scandit dextra uoce
usa phitagorace. Pat.

Poꝛt̄n magnū temporis curre-
culum sūmo pontifice largi-
enus ruler dn̄i sublimari
meruit i sedē pontificatē tū
sibi subditus clerus & popts
uniere patronū optant piū
cui ap̄o dale auxit honorē
ouis & ouilis sibi comissi belli
tempore longo ꝓ pacetur pene

damna rerū neꝛ ulla exeidiū
sed sūmi pastoris subquiete congaudentes uoce sc̄am audier̄. Pat.

Circūquaq; ministrauit exitus
magno stipeu tempestate bellicosa tē-
pꝛis deuastans seuerrtate facit
eꝛistem monsbans lecū toto corde
spreuit mundū pectore pio iuge
compassione gere omī mala mundi
paciēt. Pat.

Aduentantes longe plures consolatur pegrimos incensant̄ aliorū
paupibꝰ erogauit souit infirmos
atq; uestuit nudos munia diuina
complens rite cuncta tantū uacans
uite complecaug sanxit cunctis se-
uiractū ornamus. Pat.

Augens demū cumulū bonoꝛ sūma
scitatus rex templū sc̄e di genitrici
speciosū rehui lucore situ iquo
defuncta carnis sue sc̄am iussit
edere glebā ita resurrectionis
die magnū actremdū hic secure
expectaret. Pat.

Postquam mundus fuerat indignus
tantū cernere donū xp̄s plura
loco sue sepulcure fecerat signa
sui ad honorem nominis sc̄i. &
ut magis sc̄am c̄firmaret fidē
p̄mia daturū se meelis p̄ter
eum hic tēns laborantī. Pat.

Omnipotens mundū regens
finis rerū creatarum omnem
finem nr̄m fac finiri uite
solū. Pat.

Nunc corda pango melos deuote
filio sc̄e urginis marie honor
& uita salus & letitia paꝛ iu-
remota altetudo melita luꝛ
p̄mansura laus indificua sc̄o sp̄u

cuncta uictor psla.
Aue recolende uictor & amande
semp meuu͂ honor sanctens͂.
Tibi nunc canoris modulemur
chordis certior q̃ tua nob
sto gr̃a sis & intecessor fortis
& adiutor tutela fidelis.
Ste benedict͂ pat̃ et͂nus q̃ te
insortem sublimauit ppria͂
militib: adhibitis. xxx. ccc.
teq: ductore͂ miltę ac p͂ncipe͂
miscete͂ fecit atq. humilem
p͂ces ut tuoru͂ audias ser-
uoru͂ quotiens tuam implo
rent clementiam hic & ubiq.
uictor inuictissime.
Stę: colendus summi dĩ filius
missus apr̃e incarnatus uir
gine q͂ moriendo uiuere nos
fecit ac resurgendo resurgere
precepit. & te longinq̃ misit
huc de pr̃ia n̄r ut fautor sis
& intecessor fidus. & in iudicio
dux indistricto cum uel in
discusso͂ nec erit absconsum.
Ste uenerandus sp̃s uigro para
clitus cuius iam uigore floreat
undiq: qui teu͂ dira sumpserunt
tormenta trinitatis munere
& luce scientię quineth͂o beator͂
regno uirgin͂ agnum laudent͂
meum.
Uictor adiecta dĩ diuina͂ gr̃a͂ iugit̃
pnob ora miseris una quo deitas ac ueneranda trinitas in
corde orescat n̄ro & floreat
& ut ualeamus sub p͂sent
curriculu͂ cernere xp̃m intra
uiuentium.
Mundi redemptor spes & p͂cator

S nate amarie uirginis alme.
Sit tibi su͂ma anglor͂u gloria qui
patri coeternus uiuus & uerus pneu
mate cu͂ sc̃o regnas in celo laus secu
lor͂u nc & in euu͂.
Iudex su͂me medię rationis & infimae.
Magnę rector celi pie redemptor seculi.
Imperatoris heinrici catholici magni
ac pacifici beatifica anima͂ xp̃e.
Qui heu paucis annis rexerat summa
imperii. Z mediocris. Imperatoris.
Sciens modum iuris reb: cunctis
ultu claro monstrauit cordis clementia͂.
Celeru͂ ptin͂ p posse sep̃ letificans. Imp.
Summo nisu catholicas auxit ecclas.
Subuenit pupillis clen͂s & uiduis Imp
Gentes suo plurimas sepius impio
subdit barbaricas.
Hostes ciuiles strennue animi con
silio uicit non gladio. Imp̃at.
Iuuit donu͂ su͂ma uiuit & de
missa regni potentia.
Mundi gazas tributi sic celi diui
tiis ita p͂ meruit. Imp̃at.
Heu o roma cu͂ italia caput mundi
quartu͂ decus p͂ didens.
Heu o franci heu bauuari-
uru͂m damnu͂ nulli estat in
cognitum.
Mons bauonis nimius felix seru͂
xp̃o regi pignus trepidum.
Hoc anglica posc̃it or̃a apl̃icis
poscit ordo prelucidus.
Hoc eterna uirgo maria fin͂
mundi posc̃it beati.
Dicant oms p͂cor fideles reg͂
regum nc dep͂cantes. Imp.
Audi nr̃as melos utrogam͂ athan̄
Sic te uocis n̄ro claudabunt
niae. Imp̃a.

THE CAMBRIDGE SONGS

cuncta uictori perscla.
Aue recolende uictor et amande
semper ineuum honor sanctensium.
Tibi nunc canoris modulemur
5   chordis certior quo tua nobis
sit gratia sis et intercessor fortis
et adiutor tutela fidelis.
Sit benedictus pater eternus qui te
insortem sublimauit propriam
10   militibus adhibitis. triginta. trecentis.
teque ductorem mitem ac principem
misericordem fecit atque humilem
preces ut tuorum audias ser
uorum quoties tuam implo
15   rent clementiam hic et ubique
uictor inuictissime.
Sitque colendus summi dei filius
missus apatre incarnatus uir
gine qui moriendo uiuere nos
20   fecit ac resurgendo resurgere
precepit. et te longinqua misit
huc de patria noster ut fautor sis.
et intercessor fidus et iniudicio
dux indistricto cum nil in
25   discussum nec erit absconsum.
Sit uenerandus spiritus iugiter para
clitus cuius iam uigore florent
undique quitecum dira sumpserunt
tormenta trinitatis munere
30   et luce scientie quiineterno beatorum
regno uirginis agnum laudent
ineuum.
Uictor adleta dei diuinam gratiam iugiter
pronobis ora miseris una quo dei-
35   -tas ac ueneranda trinitas in
corde orescat nostro et floreat
et ut ualeamus sub presens
curriculum cernere christum interra
uiuentium.
40 Mundi redemptor spes et protector

nate marie uirginis alme.
Sit tibi summa angelorum gloria qui
patri coeternus uiuus et uerus pneu
mate cum sancto regnas incelo laus secu
lorum nunc et ineuum.   5
Iudex summe mediae rationis et infimae.
Magne rector celi pie redemptor seculi.
Imperatoris heinrici catholici magni
ac pacifici beatifica animam christe.
Qui heu paucis annis rexit summa   10
imperii. ℭmediocris. Imperatoris.
Sciens modum iuris rebus cunctis
Uultu claro monstrauit cordis clementiam.
Clerum populum pro posse semper letificans. Imper.
Summo nisu catholicas auxit ecclesias.   15
Subuenit pupillis clemens et uiduis. Imper.
Gentes suo plurimas sepius imperio
subdit barbaricas.
Hostes ciuiles strenuue animi con
silio uicit nongladio. Imperator.   20
Iuuit domnum summa iuuit et de
missa regni potentia.
Mundi gazas tribuit sic celi diui
tiis uti promeruit. Imperator.
Heu o roma cum italia caput mundi   25
quantum decus perdideras.
Heu o franci heu bauuarii.
uestrum damnum nulli constat in
cognitum.
Mons bauonis nimis felix serua   30
christo regi pignus intrepidum.
Hoc angelica poscit gloria apostolicus
poscit ordo prelucidus.
Hoc eterna uirgo maria finem
mundi poscit beari   35
Dicant omnes precor fideles. regem
regum nunc deprecantes. Imper. ℭthos.
Audi mentis melos utrogamus athana
Sic te uocis nostre conlaudabunt simpho
niae. Impera.   40

7

Aurea personet lira clara modula
Simplex corda sit ⸢mina.
   extensa uoce quindenaria. ⸢ypodorica.
Primum sonum mese reddat lege
5 Philomele demus laudes inuoce
   organica. ⸢musica.
Dulce melos decantantes sicut decet
Sine cuius arte uera nulla ualent
   cantica. ⸢tur cantica.
10 Cum telluris uere noua producun
Nemorosa circum circa frondescunt
   et brachia ⸢gramina.
Flagrat odor quam suauis. florida per
Hilarescit philomela dulcis uocis conscia
15 Et extendens modulando gutturis
   spiramina. ⸢otia.
Reddit uoces adestiui temporis ad
Instat nocti et diei uoce subdulcisona
Soporatis dans quietem cantus per
20 discrimina. ⸢solatia.
Nec non pulchra uiatori laboris
Uocis eius pulchritudo clarior quam
   cithara. ⸢uulas.
Uincit omnes cantitando uolucrum cater
25 Implens siluans atque cunctis modulis
   arbuscula ⸢mina.
Uolitando scandit alta arborum cacu
Gloriosa ualde facta ueris pro
   letitia. ⸢carmina.
30 Ac festiua satis gliscit sibilare
Felix tempus cui resultat talis con
   sonantia.
Utinam perduodena mensium curricula.
Dulcis philomela daret sue uocis
35 Sonos tuos uox nonua ⸢organa
   let imitari lirica. ⸢risona.
Quibus nescit consentire fistula cla
Mira quia modularis melorum tripudia
O tu parua numquam cessa canere
40 auicula.

          -musica.
Tuam decet symphoniam monocordi-
Que tuas
   uoce diatonica.
Nolo nolo ut quiescas temporis adotia.
Sed ut letos det concentus
   tua uolo ligula.
Cuius laudem memoreris
   in regum palatia ⸢umbracula.
Cedit auceps ad frondosa resonans
Cedit cignus et suauis ipsius melodia.
Cedit tibi timpanista et sonora tibia
Quamuis enim uidearis cor-
   pore pre modica.
Tamen te cuncti auscultant
   nemo dat iuuamina. ⸢omnia.
Nisi solus rex celestis qui gubernat
Iam preclara tibi satis dedimus
   obsequia. ⸢uerbis rithmica.
Que inuoce sunt iocunda et in
Ad scolares et ad ludos digne
   congruentia. ⸢uox armonica.
Tempus adest ut soluatur nostra
Nefatigat plectrum lingue cantio
   -num tedia ⸢adcrusmata.
Ne pigrescat auris prompta fidium
Trinus deus in personis unus inessentia.
Nos gubernat et conseruet sua
   sub clementia.
Regnareque nos concedat cum ipso
   ingloria., .,
Magnus cesar otio quem hic modus
   refert innomine otdinc dictus
   quadam nocte somno membra
   dum collocat palatium casu subito
   inflammatur.
Stant ministri regis timent
   dormientem attingere et cordarum pulsu factum excitatum
   saluificant. et domini nomen car
   mini inponebant.

musica

Aurea personet lyra clara modula / Simplex corda sit Ω mina. / excensu uoce quindenaria ʃʃipodorica. / Primum sonum mese reddat lege / Philomele demus laudes in uoce / organica. ✕ musica. / Dulce melos decantantes sicut decet / Sine cuius arte uera nulla ualent / cantica. Ɔ Cur cantica / Cym celsuris uere noua producun / Nemorosa circum uirta frondescunt / & brachia ⌣ gramina. / Flagrat odor quam suauis florida per / hilaresco philomela dulcis uocis ϵ sciᴀ / & extendens modulando gutturis / spiramina. ⌣ oria. / Reddit uoces aestiui temporis ad / Instat nota & dies uoce subdulcisona / Soportus dant quietes cantus per / discrimina. Ω solaria. / Nec non pulchra uictori laboris / Uocis eius pulchritudo clarior qua / cithara. Ω uulas. / Uincit omnis cantando uolucrum ceter / Implens siluans atq; cunctis modulis / arbuscula. Ω mina. / Uolitando scando alta arborum cacu / Gloriosa ualde facta ueris pro / letitia. Ω carmina. / Io festiua siris gliscit sibilare / Felix tempus cui resultat talis con- / sonantia. / Una per duodena mensium curricula / Dulcis philomela claret sue uocis / .... organa / ... imitari linea. Ω sonoria. / Quibus nescit conserrare fistula da / V...q modularis meloχ tripudia / Or parua numquam cessa canere / auicula.

Tua decet symphonia monocordi- / Que tuas uoce diatonica. / Nolo nolo ut quiescas temporis ad otia. / Sed ut letos det concentus / tua uolo ligula. / uius laudem memoreris / in regum palatia Ω ubracula. / Cedit auceps ad frondosa resonans / Cedit cygnus & suauis ipsius melodia. / Cedit & timpanista & sonora tibia. / Quamuis enim uidearis cor- / pore pre modica. / Tamen te cuncti auscultant / nemo dat iuuamina. Ω omnia. / Nisi solus rex celestis qui gubernat / Iam per clara & satis dedimus / obsequia. Ω uerbis rithmica. / Que in uoce sunt iocunda & in / Ad scolares & ad ludos digne / congruentia. Ω uax armonica. / Tempus adest ut soluatur nostra / Hesitatigat plectru lingue cantio- / num tedia. Ɔ aderus mata. / Ne pigrescat auris pempta fidium / Trinus deus in personis unus tessonia. / Nos gubernat & conseruet sua / sub clementia. / Regnareq; nos concedat cum ipso / in gloria. / Magnus cesar otto quem hic modus / refert in uno ordine dictus / quadam nocte somno membra / dum collocat palatium casu subito / inflammatur. / Stant ministri regis timent / dormientem attingere & corda- / rum pulsu factum excitatum / salutificant & dominorum nomen car- / mini imponebant.

Exoneratus spes suus surrexit
timor magnus aduersis max
uenturus nam tunc fama
uolitet unganos signa meu
extulisse.
Iuxta litus sedebant armati
urbes agros uillas uastant
late matres plorant filios &
filii patres undique oculari.
Hec quis ego dixerat ocio uide
or partes diu milites tardus
moneo frustra du ego demoror
crescit clades semp ergo moras
rumpite & parthicis mecum
obuiate.
Dux euonis ad intrepidus quo non
fortior alter miles inquit pete
quem hoc terreat bellum arma
induit armis instant hostes ipse
ego signifer effudero primus
sanguine inimicum.
His incensi bella fremunt arma
poscunt hostes uacant signa se
quuntur cantus tubis clamor
passim oritur & militibus eorum
terrones inmiscentur.
Pauci cedunt plures cadunt
francus instat parthus fugit.
uulgus exangue undis obstat.
litus rubens sanguine danubio
cladem parthicam ostendebat.
Parua manu cesis parthis ante &
post sepe uictor communes cuncas
mouens luctum nomen regnum
optimos hereditans mores filio
obdormiuit.
Adolescens post hunc ocio impauit
multis annis cesar iustus clemens
foras unum modo defuit nam
inclitas raro prolis triumpha
bat.

Eius autem dum plus ocio decus iuuentutis
ut foras felix erat arma quos numquam
militum domuerunt fama nominis satis
Bello foras pace potens utroque uincit
tamen metus uir triumphum bello
pacem semp suos pauperes respexerat
inde petit pauperum fertur.
Eodem modo ne forte notemur ingeniis
culpa tantorum uirtutes ultra quicquam dec
retrices quas denique miro melitus uix
equaret.
Vite dator omni sacrar ds nature for
mator mundi globum sub potentia
claudens uolubilem palmo & in
factura sua splendet magnificus
pauum.
Ipse multos ueritate uetes nec du
sequentes uestigando psophie de
uia uisserat ire improbabilis errori
recta pariter nobis uiam.
Inter quos subalis pacum itas damus
pytagoras metapsicosis que iuxta
famam troie pepta euforbii scito nursus
reddit. obscuras q̃ ueru recta denuo
unius donat intellectus perspicaci pro
scrutari sensu animi.
Ergo uir hic prudens die quadam ferri
fabrica potens pondere non equo
sonoque diuerso pulsare malleolos
senserat itaque tonorum qua in libet in
formem uim late noscens forma
addita parte pulchram primus ad
hanc simphonias artis sub
splendida istas fecit diatesseron
pente diapason infra quatuor unum
que plene armonia sonant que
sententia semis potens solidum ratio
mea in se normula mensura
utilem notitiam & siderum motus
iussit continere materiem traden

Excitatus spes suis surrexit
 timor magnus aduersis mox
 uenturus nam tunc fama
 uolitat ungarios signa ineum
 extulisse.
 Iuxta litus sedebant armati
 urbes agros uillas uastant
 late matres plorant filios et
 filii patres undique exulari.
Hec quis ego dixerat otto uide
 or partis diu milites tardus
 moneo frustra dum ego demoror
 crescit clades semper. ergo moras
 rumpite et parthicis mecum
 obuiate.
 Dux cuonrad intrepidus quo non
 fortior alter miles inquit pereat
 quem hoc terreat bellum. arma
 induit armis instant hostes ipse
 ego signifer effudero primus
 sanguinem inimicum.
 His incensi bella fremunt arma
 poscunt hostes uacant signa se
 quuntur cantus tubis clamor
 passim oritur et milibus centum
 teutones inmiscentur.
 Pauci cedunt plures cadunt
 francus instat parthus fugit.
 uulgus exangue undis obstat.
 litus rubens sanguine danubio
 cladem parthicam ostendebat.
 Parua manu cesis parthis ante et
 post sepe uictor communem cunctis
 mouens luctum nomen regnum
 optimos hereditans. mores filio
 obdormiunt.
 Adolescens post hunc otto imperauit
 multis annis cesar iustis clemens
 fortis unum modo defuit nam
 inclitis raro preliis triumpha
  [bat.

Eius autem clara proles otto decus iuuentutis
 ut fortis felix erat. arma quos numquam
 militum domuerant fama nominis satis
Bello fortis pace potens inutroque [uicit.
 tamen mitis inter triumphum bello
 pacem. semper suos pauperes respexerat.
 inde pater pauperum fertur.
Finem demus modo ne forte notemur ingenii
 culpa tantorum uirtutes ultra quicquam deter
 rere. quas denique miro inclitus uix
 equaret.
Vite dator omni factor deus nature for
 mator. mundi globum sub potenti
 claudens uolubilem palmo in
 factura sua splendet magnificus
 pereuum.
Ipse multos ueritatem ueteres nec dum
 sequentes uestigando per sophie de
 uia iusserat ire improbabilis errori
 rectam pararet nobis uiam.
Inter quos subtilis peracumen mentis claruit
 pitagoras metapsicosis quem iuxta
 famam troie pereptam euforbium seculo rursus
 reddit. obscurosque rerum rite denuo
 uiuum. donat intellectus perspicaci per
 scrutari sensu animi.
Ergo uir hic prudens die quadam ferri
 fabricam pretiens pondere nonequo
 sonoque diuerso pulsare malleolos
 senserat sicque tonorum quamlibet in
 formem uim latere noscens forma
 additi perartem pulchram primus edi
Adhanc simphonias tres sub [dit
 splendam istas fecit diatesseron dia
 pente diapason infra quaternarium
 que pleniter armoniam sonant que
 sententia senis ponens solidum rith
 micam inse normulam mensurarumque
 utilem notitiam et siderum motus
 iussit continere matente traden

traden *et* nomine suo uocauit.
    Y greca idem om*n*is continente*m* sed fissa
    summotenus inramosas binas partes
    uite humane inuenit adsimili
 5 tudine*m* congrua*m*. est na*m* sincera
    et simplex pueritia que *n*on facile
    noscit*ur* utrum uitiis an uirtuti
    animu*m* subicere uelit donec tan
    dem iuuentutis etas illud offerret
10 nobis biuium.
    Hic qui paret uiciis uirtuti nob*is*
    auferat contrariis illam lata*m* ille
    te*r*rit. ipseq*ue* semitamq*ue* postre-
    mo plena poenis graui*bus* se pro
15 sequenti*bus* portas inferi ap*er*it
    seuissimas ubi fremitus dentiu*m*
    et p*er*petui fletus sunt meren
    tiu*m* p*ro*criminis facto cita ubi
    semp*er* mors optatur frustra pro
20 dolor atq*ue* queritur.
    Sed uirtutu*m* gradi*bus* ille nitit*ur* qui
    p*ro*uidus p*er*angustam uadit ille se
    mita*m* que infine locuples letitie
    suis q*ue*q*ue* p*re*ci*bus* pandit et*er*na dulcis
25 uite gaudia ubi bon*orum* anime
    claro iugiter illustrant*ur* lumine
    p*er*petui solis ubi d*e*itatis se conspec
    tu*m* semp*er* cernere se gaudent beati.
    Uite dator om*n*ifactor d*eus* nature
30 formator illum aufer istum con
    fer tuis fideli*bus* callem ut post
    obitu*m* talis uite participes fiant.
    O pat*er* optime
    san*c*to regnans pneumate cunc-
35 tos plectro tibimet laudes dul-
    ce canentes serua semper.
    Qui incruce latrone*m* exaudisti
    pendente*m* atq*ue* spondens luci
    da*m* sedis amoenitatem ut
40 acciperet.

Spolia mundi qui maledicti
    liberasti apoenis at*que* feroce*m* uin
    clo leone*m* colligasti manib*us* ne
    subfraude p*er*deret q*uod* formauit
 5 dext*er*a. adam eua*m*. deniq*ue* plebe*m*
    locasti orto lucido.
Tertia die surrexisti maiesta
    tis tumulo teq*ue* iubente cor
    pora multa surrexere baratro
10 ut tua facta p*ro*derent noncre
    denti pop*u*lo ex hoc signo trepi
    dans ualde miser pilatus se
    planctu cruciat.
Post hec mundu*m* illuxisti
15 duces gentes apposuisti ascen
    disti unde uenisti dextera
    patris orex residens.
Pena mal*is* ecce parata flam*m*a
    picis indeficiens accernentes
20 mala tenentes id sine fine
    post hec retinent.
Uita*m*mundi accipientes prelucen-
    tes inparadiso spe gaudentes
    bona tenenentes semp*er* i*n* euum
25 laudant d*omi*num.
Regnanti gl*oria* ch*ri*sto laus p*er*sec*u*la
    qui cordaru*m* sonitu pangit*ur*
    d*eus* p*er*hennis rector mundi.
Aduertite om*n*es
30 populi ridiculu*m* *et* audite
    quomodo sueuum mulier *et*
    ipse illam defraudarat.
Constantie ciuis sueuulus
    trans equora gazam portans
35 nauib*us* domi coniugem lasciuua*m*
    nimis relinquebat.
Uix remige tristi secat mare
    ecce subito orta te*m*pestate furit
    pelagus certant flamina
40 tolluntur fluctus post mul

tradidit & nomine suo uocauit.
Greca idem omnis continente sed fissa
summotenus in ramosas binas partes
uitae humane inuenit ad similitudinem congruam. est nam sincera
& simplex pueritia que non facile
noscitur utrum uteris an uirata
animum subicere uelit doneo tandem inuenitur etas illud offerre
nobis biuium.

Hic qui paret uicus uirata nos
auferte contrarius illam latam ille
ite. ipseque semitamque postremo plena poenis grauibus se prosequentibus portas inferi aperit
seuissimas ubi frenitus dentium
& perennis fletus sunt merentium
nominis facto orta ubi
semper mors optatur frustra pro
dolor atque queritur.

Sed uiratu gradibus ille intret qui
pudus pangustum uadit ille semitam que in fine locuplos latiore
suis quibusque pedibus pandit eterna dulcis
uite gaudia ubi bonorum animae
claro uigent illustrante lumine
perpetui solis ubi diuitias se conspec-
tu semper cernere se gaudente beatae.

Uite dator omnifactor dominus nature
formator illum aufer istum confer tuis fidelibus callem ut post
obitum talis uite participes fiant.

Opie optime
deo regnans pneumate cane
plectro tibi meo laudes dub-
ce canentes serua semper.

Qui meruce latronem exaudisti
pendentem atque spondens luci-
da sedis amoenitatem ut
acciperet.

Spolia mundi qui maledicta
liberasti apoenis atque feroce un-
do leone colligisti manibus ne
sub fraude perderet q formauit
dextra. adam euam denique plebem
locasti orto lucido.

Tertia die surrexisti maiestatis tumulo atque iubente corpora multa surrexere baratro
uita facta perderent nonere-
denti populo ex hoc signo trepidans ualde miser pilatus se
planctu cruciat.

Post hec mundum illuxisti e-
duces gentes apposuisti ascendisti unde uenisti dextera
patris orex residens.

Pena mater ecce parata flama
pias indeficiens accernentes
mala tenentes id sine fine
post hec retinent.

Uita mundi accipientes plucen-
tes in paradiso spe gaudentes
bona tenentes semper euum
laudant dominum.

Regnante gloria christo laus perfecta
qui cordarum sonitu pangit
dei phennis recor mundi.

Aduertite omnes   A
populi ridiculum & audite
quomodo sueuum mulier &
ipse illam defraudaret.

Consturtae ciuis sueuulus
trans equora gazam portans
nauibus domi coniugem lasciuam
nimis relinquebat.

Uix remige tristi secat mare
ecce subita orta tempestate furit
pelagus certant flamina
tolluntur fluctus post mul-

itaq; equora uagum littore
longinquo nothus exponebat.
Nam interim domi uacant
coniunx mihi aderant iuuenes sequuntur immemor uiri
exulis excepto gaudens atq;
nocte proxima pregnans filium
iniustum fudit isto die.

Duob; uolutis annis exul dicor
reuertatur occurrit in fida est
nux secum trahens puerulum da
tis osculis marito illi dequo
inquit puerum istum habeas
die aut extrema patieris.

At illa marito tantis dolos
uersat in omnia mit tandem
mi ōnyx ait una uice in al
pib; niue sitiens extinxi sitim
de quo ego grauida istum pue
rum damnoso foetu heu
gignebam.

Nam languens amore tuo consur
rexi diluculo prexiq; pedes
nuda pruines & frigora atq;
maria rimabar mesta si forte
uentiuola uela cernerem aut
frontem nauis conspicerem.

Anni post hec quinq; transierunt
aut plus & mercator uagus in
staurauit remos ratim q̄ ssa
reficit uela colligit & nuuis
natum duxit secum.

Transfretato mare producebat
natum & parua bone merca
tori tradens centum libras
accipit atq; uendito infante
diues reuertatur.

Ingressusq; domum adiuxore ait
consolare coniunx consolare
cara natū tuum perdidi quem

non ipsa tu me magis quidem dile
Tempestate orta nos uentosus
furor inuadosas sirtes nimis
fessos eger & nos omnis sol grauitum
torquens at ille tuus natus lique-
Sic perfidus sueuus coniugem deluserat sic fraus fraudem
uicerat nam quem genuit nyx
recte hunc sol liquefecit.

Mendosam quam cantilenam ago
puerilis confectam dabo. quomodo
dulos prindaces nsum auditorib;
ingentem feram liberalis & decora
cuidam regi erat nata.

Quam sublege huiusmodi post ob
ponit querendam.

Siquis insidiendi gnarus usq; ad eo
instet fallendo dum cesans ore
fallax p̄dicetur is ducat filiam.

Quo audito sueuus nil moratus
inquit rapois armis ego q̄ue natu
solus irem lepusculus inter feras
telo tacitus occubebat mox effi
sis intestinis caput auulsum cum
cute cruda.

Cumq; cesum manu leuaretur
caput lesa aure effunduntur
mellis modu centeni sociaq; auris
tacta toni de pisarum fudit q̄b;
intra pelle strictis lepus ipse
dū secatur crepidine summa
aude karta regiam latenter
Que seruiunte firmat ee lepu-
meum. inticur clamat rex
karta & tu.

Sic rege deluso sueuus falsa
gener regius est arte factus.
Rex regum qui
solus in euum regnas incelis
heinricum nobis serua in terrib;
inimicis.

THE CAMBRIDGE SONGS

taque equora uagum littore
longinquo nothus exponebat.
Nam interim domi uacaret
coniunx mimi aderant iuue-
5 nes sequuntur quos et inmemor uiri
exulis excepit gaudens atque
nocte proxima pregnans filium
iniustum. fudit isto die.
Duobus uolutis annis exul dictus
10 reuertitur occurrit infida con
iux secum trahens puerulum da
tis osculis maritus illi dequo
inquit puerum istum habeas
dic aut extrema patieris.
15 Atilla maritum timens dolos
uersat inomnia mitandem
mi coniux ait una uice inal
pibus niue sitiens extinxi sitim
de quo ego grauida istum pue
20 rum damnoso foetu heu
gignebam.
Nam languens amore tuo consur
rexi diluculo perrexique pedes
nuda perniues et frigora atque
25 maria rimabar mesta si forte
uentiuola uela cernerem aut
frontem nauis conspicerem.
Anni post hec quinque transierunt
aut plus et mercator uagus in
30 staurauit remos ratim quassa
reficit uela colligit et niuis
natum duxit secum.
Transfretato mare producebat
natum et proarra bone merca
35 tori tradens centum libras
accipit atque uendito infante
diues reuertitur.
Ingressusque domum aduxorem ait
consolare coniunx consolare
40 cara natum tuum perdidi quem

                  -xisti
nonipsa tu me magis quidem dile-
Tempestate orta nos uentosus
furor inuadosas sirtes nimis
fessos eger et nos omnes sol grauiter
torquens at ille tuus natus lique- 5
Sic perfidus sueuus coniu [-fecit.
gem deluserat sic fraus fraudem
uicerat nam quem genuit nix
recte hunc sol liquefecit.
Mendosam quam cantilenam ago. 10
puerulis commentatam dabo. quomodo
dulos permendaces risum auditoribus
ingentem fera liberalis et decora
cuidam regi erat nata.
Quam sublege huiusmodi procis ob 15
ponit querendam.
Siquis mentiendi gnarus usque adeo
instet fallendo dum cesaris ore
fallax predicitur is ducat filiam.
Quo audito sueuus nil moratus 20
inquit raptis armis ego cum uenatu
solus irem lepusculus inter feras
telo tactus occumbebat. mox effu
sis intestinis caput auulsum cum
cute cruda. 25
Cumque cesum manu leuaretur
caput lesa aure effunduntur
mellis modii centeni sotiaque auris
tacta totidem pisarum fudit quibus
intra pellem strictis lepus ipse 30
dum secatur crepidine summa
caude kartam regiam latentem
Que seruumte firmat esse [cepi
meum. mentitur clamat rex
karta et tu. 35
Sic rege deluso sueuus falsa
gener regius est arte factus.
O rex regum qui
solus ineuum regnas incelis
heinricum nobis serua interris ab 40
                [inimicis.

THE CAMBRIDGE SONGS

Quem uoluisti tibi benedici *et* co
 ronari adaquas graui manu pili
 grimi presulis archi. Or*ex.*
Quem romani at*que* fidi franci cler*us*
5 *et* p*o*p*u*lu*s* ch*ris*t*o* dicatus post cuonradu*m*
 adoptant domnu*m.* Or*ex.*
Dic italia dic pia gallia cum ger
 mania d*e*o deuota uiuat cuon
 radus atq*ue* heinricus. Or*ex.*
10 Agni ut sponsa pace quieta seruare
 suo ualeat sponso d*e*o et*er*no uiuo
 et uero. O rex.
Gaudent om*n*es ch*ris*t*i* fideles senes
 et iuuenes matres infantes reg-
15 nat cuonradus atq*ue* heinricus. or*ex.*
Die qua surrexit qui mundu*m* re
 demit regni monarchiam accepit s*an*c*t*am pius cuonradus gaudeat
 mundus. Or*ex.*
20 Postunius anni recursu*m* acce
 pit s*an*c*t*am regni coronam puer
 heinricus ch*ris*t*o* electus.
Die p*r*edicto a piligrimo archiep*iscop*o
 sibi deuotissimo gaudente clero
25 simul *et* populo. Or*ex.*
Doleat antiquus gentis ini
 micus s*an*c*t*as eccl*es*i*a*s pacificatas
 uiuo cu*u*onrado atq*ue* heinrico. Or*ex.*
Mat*er* ch*ris*t*i* cu*m* ciuib*us* celi. cunctisq*ue*
30 s*an*c*t*is rectores orb*is* iuua cuonradu*m*
 atq*ue* heinricum. Or*ex.*
Ut eccl*es*iarum causas s*an*c*t*orum *et* pu
 pillo*rum* ac uiduarum ualeant
 iusto tractare iudicio. Or*ex.*
35 Laus creatori angelorum regi cui*us*
 imperium manet ineuum p*er*in
 finita s*e*c*u*lorum s*e*c*u*la. Or*ex.*
Lame*n*temur n*os*t*r*a socii
 peccata lamentem*ur* quare tacem*us.*
40 Proiniquitate corru*i*mus late

scimus celi hinc offensu*m*
 regem inmensum.
Heinrico requiem rex ch*ris*t*e* dona
 perhennem.
5 Non fuimus digni munere in
 signi. munus siue donum diue
 heinricum bonum qui exiu
 uentute magne fuit uite. p*ro*creatus
 regum stirpe rexsit *et* ipse. Heinr*ic*o.
10 Orbis erat pignus regno fuit dign*us*
 imp*er*ator romanorum rector
 franco*rum* imp*er*abat sueuis. saxonib*us*
 cunctis. baunaro. truces sola uos
 fecit pacatos. Heinrico.
15 Passumus mirari de d*om*ino tali res
 tractando laicatus. sit litteratus
 prudens insermone. prouidus inop*ere*
 uiduarum. tutor bonus orphanis
 pius. Heinrico.
20 Heinricus s*ecund*us plangat illu*m*
 mundus fines seruans ch*ris*t*i*anos.
 pellit paganos. strauit aduer
 santes pace*m* p*er*sequentes uo
 luntati contradixit sobrie uixit. H*ein*r*ic*o.
25 Quis cesar tam largus fuit pau
 peribus q*ui*s tam loca sublimauit.
 atq*ue* dicauit. atria s*an*c*t*orum. ubere
 bono*rum* exp*ro*priis fecit magnauit
 episcopatu*m.* Heinrico.
30 Ploret hunc europa iam decapita
 ta aduocatum roma ploret. ch*ris*tu*m*
 exoret. ut sibi fidelem prestet
 seniorem se cognoscat graue
 dampnum ecclesiarum. Heinr*ic*o.
35 Dicamus heinrico d*om*ini amico
 utquiescat post obitum semp*er*
 ineuu*m.* dicat om*n*is clerus anime
 illius pace ch*ris*t*i* quiescat gaudia
 noscat. Heinrico.
40 udax es uir iuuenis dum feruet.

Quem uoluisti tibi benedici & coronari adaquas graui manu piligrimi presulis archi. Orex.

Quem romani atq: fidi franci cler?
& ptĩ xp̃o dicatus post cuonradũ
adoptarre domnũ. Orex.

Die italia deo pia gallia cum germania dõ deuota uiuat cuonradus atq: heinricus. Orex.

Agni ut sponsa opare quieta seruari
siue ualeat sponso dõ eterno uiuo
& uero. Orex.

Gaudent omñs xp̃i fideles senes
& iuuenes matres infantes regnat cuonradus atq: heinricus. Oñ.

Die qua surrexit qui mundũ redemit regni monarchiam accepit sctõm pius cuonradus gaudet
mundus. Orex.

Postunctus anima recursus accepit sc̃am regni coronam puer
heinricus xp̃o electus.

Die p̃dicto apiligrimo archiep̃o
sibi deuotissimo gaudente clero
simul & populo. Orex.

Dolete ÷ antiquus gentes inimicus sc̃as ecclas pacificatas
uiuo cuonrado atq: heinrico. Oñ.

M . . . xp̃i cu ciuib: celi cunctisq:
sc̃ĩ rectores orb ĩuua cuonradũ
atq: heinricum. Orex.

V . . . octarum causas sc̃ou & pu-
pillou ac uiduarum ualeant
illo tractare iudicio. Oñ.

. . . gretori angelorum reg̃ cuĩ
. . . perium manet ineuum p̃in-
. . . tra sc̃tou scta. Oñ.

Lucemur nr̃a socii
. . . ata lamentem quare tacem.
. . . iniquitate corrumpis lato

samus celi hinc offensi
regem inmensum.
empuco requiem rex xp̃e dona
per henoem.

Non sumus digni munere insigni. munus siue donum diue
heinricum bonum qui ex ue-
uetate magne fuit uite. p̃ceptus
regum stirpe rex st̃ & ipse Heinr̃.

Orbis erat pignus regno suro digñ
imp̃ator romanorum rector
francou ĩ p̃abat sueuis. saxonib:
cunctis baunariu truces sola uos
fecit pacatos. Heinruco.

Passumus mirari de dñ̃o tali-ter
tractando lucratus st̃ litteratus
prudens in sermone. prouidus inope
uiduaru. actor bonus orphanis
pius. Heinrica.

Heinricus sc̃dr plangat illũ
mundus fines seruans xp̃ianos.
pellit paganos. straut aduer-
santes pace p̃sequentes uo-
luntate contradixit sobrie uixit.

Quis cesar tam largus fuit pau-
perib: qs tãt oca sublimauit.
atq: dicauit atria sc̃ou. ube
bonou ex p̃pris fecit magnu et
episcopatũ. Heinr̃.

Ploret hunc europa uidecaptã
tu aduocatũ roma. ploret xp̃m
exoret. ut sibi fidelem prestet
seniorem se cognoscat graue
dampnum ecclesiarum. heinr̃.

Dicamus heinrico dñi amico
ut quiescat post obitum semp
meũ dicat omñs deni anime
illius pace xp̃i quiescat gaudia
noscat. heinrico.

udax es uir iuuenis dum senex.

A caro mobilis audacter agis p̱p̱era
   tua membra coinquinas.
A tendo homo quia puluis es &
   in puluerem reuerteris.
B reue tempus iuuenis considera q̄
   moneris. ueniet q̄ dies ultimus
   & perdes flores optimos. Adtende.
C arni tue consentiens animam
   tuam decipis dum flectis ad
   libidinem. Adtende.
D entes tui frendidant labia tua
   exasperant lingua mala generat.
   uita tua trepidat. Adt.
E leuas tuos oculos ut uanitatem
   uideas flectitur mens misera.
   membra ad malū erigis. Adt.
F ecisti malum consilium & osten-
   disti nimium quia multum
   securus es amorem libidinis.
G tam queris in populo ⸱ Adt ⸱
   laudem humanam diligis. placere d̄o non curas q̄ de celo
   conspicit. Adtend.
H onorem transitorium presumpsisti. accipe sed magis poena
   sequitur cui maior creditur Adt.
I ntra sep̄ aspicis sep̄ de terra cogitas
   sed hic relinquis om̄ia unde sup-
   -bus ambulas. Adtende.
K aro te xp̄s fouea unde ne male
   moriaris festina te corrigere
   antequam tempus ueniat. Adt.
L uge modo dū tep̄s ne gemas
   in iudicio ubi non ualet gemit9
   nec ulla intercessio. Adtende.
M odo labora fortit̄ dū es isto
   tempore emenda tuum uitiū
   ne gemas in p̱petuum. Adt.
N on te frangat cupiditas nec te
   flectat fragilitas. & noli cum diabolo participare amplius. Adt.
O si corde intellegis que p̄cepta legis sunt
   quod illi qui adulterant lapidibus sub
   iaceant. Adt. ⸫ Adtende.
P er saluatorē q̄ uenit magna redemptio
   ut om̄is q̄ committat penitentiā dormiat.
Q uare om̄is iuuenis reuertat ad d̄n̄m rogans ei de
   mentiam ut donet indulgentiam. Adtende
R umpe iā cordi duriciā iras tue malitia festina te corrigere antequam finis ueniat. Adt.
S uscepit xp̄s ueniā ut donet indulgentiā allu-
   dant uera animā q̄ carnē suā macerant. Dē
T erribilis xp̄s ueniet adiudicandū a s̄c̄m
   tunc reddit ille singulis sec̄m sua
   opa. Adtende. ⸫ Dā patrem.
V ente die iudicii & erit magna districtio
   ut n̄ adiuuat pat̄ filiū nec filius desti-
X po sorius iuuenis adeū oc̄o recurteris
   ut ante eius limina securus sis d̄n̄e
   mine. Adtende. ⸫ V ueniunt
Y des acq̄rit om̄ia peccata delet om̄ia
   humilitas & caritas ad patrem celi
Z elum habet optimum qui d̄n̄m
   amat & p̱mium letabit̄ in s̄c̄m
   & uiuat in p̱petuum. Adt.

D uno almus thero euuigero
   assis thiernun filius benignus Sal-
   tor mihi thaz igie cosan muon
   de quoddā duce themo heron
   hemp̄che qui cum dignita
   thero beiaro piche be manod
   uorant nempe minnius then
   keisar. namoda liephut aur
   in st̄e oddo. then unsan keisar
   quodo. hic adest hempich hy
   hep hepa kuniglich dignun
   fore thim selue more sine
   unc surrexit oddo ther unsan
   keisar quodo. p̄ est ibi obuiā.

THE CAMBRIDGE SONGS

A
caro mobilis audacter agis *perperam*
tua membra coinquinas.
Adtende homo quia puluis es *et*
in puluerem *r*euerteris.
Breue *est* tempus iuuenis considera q*uod*
morieris. uenitq*ue* dies ultimus
et perdes flores optimos. Adtende.
Carni tue consentiens animam
tuam decipis dum flect*er*is ad
libidinem. Adtende.
Dentes tui frendidant labia tua
exasp*er*ant lingua mala generat.
uita tua trepidat. Adt*ende*.
Eleuas tuos oculos ut uanitat*em*
uideas flectitur mens misera
membra ad mal*um* erigis. Adt*ende*.
Fecisti malum consilium *et* offen
disti nimium quia multum
secutus es amorem libidinis.
Glo*ri*am queris inpopulo ⟦Adt*ende*
laudem humanam diligis. pla
cere d*e*o noncuras q*ui*te decelo
conspicit. Adtend*e*.
Honorem transitorium presum
psisti accip*er*e sedmagis poena
sequitur cui maior creditur Adt*ende*
In te*rr*am sem*per* aspicis sem*per* dete*rr*a cogitas
sed hic relinquis om*n*ia unde sup*er*
-bus ambulas. Adtende.
Karo te t*r*axit infoueam uide ne male
moriaris festina te corrigere
antequam tempus ueniat. Adt*ende*
Luge modo du*m* tem*pus est* ne gemas
in iudicio ubi nonualet gemit*us*
nec ulla intercessio. Adtende.
Modo labora fortit*er* du*m* es *in* isto
tempore emenda tuum uitiu*m*
ne gemas inp*er*petuum. Adt*ende*.
Nonte frangat cupiditas necte

flectæt fragilitas *et* noli cum diabolo participare amplius. Adt*ende*.
O si corde intellegis que p*re*cepta legis sunt
quod illi qui adulterant lapidibus sub
iaceant. Adt*ende*. ⟦Adtende.
Per saluatore*m* ig*itur* uenit magna redemptio
ut om*n*is q*ui* comitat*ur* penitentia*m* dormitet.
Quare no*n*uis iuuenis reuerti ad d*omi*n*um* rogans ei*us* cle
mentiam ut donet indulgentiam. Adtende.
Rumpe ia*m* cord*is* duritiam m*en*tis tue malitia*m* festina te corrigere antequ*am* finis ueniat. Adt*ende*.
Suscepit ch*ristus* ueniam ut donet i*n*dulgentiam allu
dant uera*m* anima*m* qui carne*m* suam macerant. Ad*tende*
Terribilis ch*ristus* ueniet adiudicandu*m* *seculum*
tunc reddit ille singulis sec*un*d*um* sua
op*er*a. Adtende. ⟦-dat patrem.
Uenit dies iudicii *et* erit magna districtio
ut no*n*adiuuat pat*er* filiu*m* nec filius defen-
X*risto* seruis iuuenis adeu*m* cito recurreris
ut ante ei*us* limina securus sis decri
mine. Adtende. ⟦ueniunt.
Fides acq*u*irit om*n*ia peccata delet nimia
humilitas *et* caritas adpatrem celi
Zelum habet optimum qui d*e*um
amat *et* p*r*oximum letabit*ur* in sec*u*lum
et uiuat in p*er*petuum. Adt*ende*.
 unc almus thero euuigero
 a∬is thiernun filius benignus fautor mihi thaz igiz cosan muozi
dequoda*m* duce themo heron
heinriche qui cum dignitate
thero beiaro riche beuuarode
Intrans .nempe nuntius then
keisar namoda her thus cur sedes
infit otdo. ther unsar keisar
guodo. hic adest heinrich bri.g
her hera kuniglich dignum tibi
fore thir selue moze sine.
Tunc surrexit otdo ther unsar
keisar guodo. p*err*exi*t* illi obuiam.

THE CAMBRIDGE SONGS

fol. 437 v

inde uilo manig man· *et* excepit
illum mid mihilon eron.
Primitus quo*que* dixit uuillicumo
heinrich ambo uos equiuoci be-
5 thiu goda endi mi. nec non *et*
sotii uuillicumo sidigimi.
Dato responso fane heinriche sosco
ne coniunxere manus her leida
ina inthaz godes hus petier*unt* a*m*bo
10 thero godes genatheno.
Oramine facto intsiegina auer
otdo ducx*it* inconcilium mit michelon eron. *et* amisit illi so uuaz
so her þar hafode *preter* q*uod* regale
15 thes thir heinrih nigerade.
Tunc stetit althiu sprakha sub
firmo heinricho quicquid otdo
fec*it* algeriediz heinrih q*ui*cquid ac
amisit ouch geriediz heinrihc.
20 Hic non fuit ullus thes hafon ig
guoda fulleist nobilis ac libe*ris*. thaz
tid allaz uuar is cui n*on*fecisset
heinrich allero reh to gilich.
Estunus locus homburh
25 dictus i*n*quo pascebat asina*m* alue
rad uiribus fortis atq*ue* fidelis.
Que du*m* in amplum exiret campu*m*
uidit currentem lupu*m* uoracem
caput abscondit. cauda ostendit.
30 Lupus acurrit cauda*m* momordit
asina bina leuauit crura. fec*it*q*ue*
longum cum lupo bellum.
Cum defecisset uires sensisset *pro*tu-
lit magnam plangendo uocem
35 .ocansq*ue* sua*m* moriendo domna*m*.
..diens grande*m* asine uocem aluerad
.currit. sororib*us* dixit cito uenite
me adiuuate.
Asinam caram misi aderba*m* illi*us*
40 magnu*m* audio planctu sp*er*o cu*m* seuo
ut pugnet lupo.

Clamor fororum uenit in
claustrum turbe uiroru*m* ac
mulierum assunt cruentum
ut captent lupum. [hoste*m*.
5 Adela namq*ue* soror aluerade
rikila*m* querit agatham inuenit
ibant ut fortem sternerent
Atille ruptis asine costis sangui
nis undam carne*m*que tota*m* simul
10 uorauit silua*m* intrauit.
Illud uidentes cuncte sorores
crines scindebant pectus tunde
bant flentes insonte*m* asine morte*m*.
Deniq*ue* paruum portabat pullu*m*
15 illum plorabat maxime aluerad sp*er*ans exinde *p*rolem
creuisse.
Adela mitis fritherunq*ue* dulcis
uenerunt ambe ut adaleithe
20 cor c*on*firmarent atq*ue* sanarent.
Delinq*ue* mestas soror querelas
lupus amarum noncurat
fletum d*omi*n*us* alia*m* dabit tibi
asinam.
25 Diapente *et* diatesseron
ſimphonia. *et* intensa *et* re
missa pariter consonantia
diapason modulatione consona
reddunt.
30 Salue festa dies toto uenera
bilis euo qua d*eus* infernum uicit
et astra tenet.
Ecce renascentis testatur grat*i*a
mundi. Om*n*ia cum d*omi*no dona
35 redisse suo. Salue.
Namq*ue* triumphanti post
tristia tartara ch*ris*to. Undiq*ue*
fronde nemus gramina flore
fauent.
40 Legib*us* inferni oppressis sup*er*

inde uido manig man & excepto
illum mid ... mihilon eron.
Primitus quoq; dixit uuillicumo
heinrich ambo uos equiuoci be-
thiu goda endi mi. nec non &
sonu uuillicumo sidrigmi.
Dato responso sane heinriche sosco-
ne coniunxere manus hepi leida-
ma michaz godes bus peaer a bo-
thepio godes gonatheno.
Oramusse facto mi siegina auer-
ordo dugs inconsiliu mito muche-
lon eron. & amisit illi so uuar
so heri hari hasode pe q' regale
thes thir heinrih nigerade.
Tuno stetit althiu sprakha sub
firmo heinricho quicquid ordo
feo algeruedir heinrih decquid ac
amisit ouch geruedir heinrih c.
Hio nonfuit ullus thes haron is
quoda pullest nobilis ac libis dict
to allaz uuap is cui ifecisset
heinrih allepo pon to glich.
Estunus locus homburh
dictus iquo pascebat asinā aluē-
rad uiribus foras atq; fidelis.
Que du inamplum exiret campu
uidit currentem lupū uoracem
caput absondit, cauda ostendit.
Lupus acurrit caudā inmordit
asinā, bina leuauit crura. seq;
lagqum cum lupo bellum.
Cum deferisset uires, sensisset prū
et magnum plangendo modem
suā, morrendo domnā
ns grande asine uoce aluerad
...sororibus dicere otto uenite
...adiuuate
Asirām caram nisi aderit illu
magnū audio plancta spo cum seu on
luc pugne lupo.

Clamor sororum uenit in
claustrum turbe uirorum ac
mulierum assunt cruentum
ut caperent lupum Hoste.
Adela namq; soror aluerade
rikila querit agatham inuento
ibant ut fortem sternerent
Atille rupis asine costas sanguinis undam carnēq; totā simul
uorauit siluā intrauit.
Illud uidentes cunete sorores
crines scindebant pectus tundebant flentes insontē asine morte.
Deniq; paruum portabat pullū
illum plorabat maxime al-
uerad spans geinde glem
creuisse.
Adela mitis fritherunq; dulcis
uenerunt ambe ut adal othe
cor cōfirmarent atq; sanarent.
Deliq; mestas sor' querelas
lupus amarum noncurat
fletum dns alia dabit tibi
asinam.
Diapente & diatesseron
simphonia & intensa & re-
missa pariter consonant
Diapason modulatione consona
reddunt.
Aluesata dies toto uenera-
bilis euo qua dt infernum uicte
& astra tenet.
Ecce renascitur letatur gra
mundi Omis cum dno dona
rediisse suo. Salue.
Nunq; grumphauit post
tristia aurum xpo. Undiq;
fronde nemus gramina flore
siluere.
Legib; inferni oppressis sup

astra meantem. Laudate rex
deum lux poli, aqua freti
Qui crucifixus erit dominus ecce per
omnia regnat. Dantque creatori
cuncta creata precem.

Vestibunt siluae teneras merulis
virgultae suis onerata pomis
canunt de celsis sedibus palumbes
carmina cuncti.

Hic turtur gemit resonat hic
turdus pangit hic priscus melos
sonus passer nec tacens arripiens
garrito alta subulmis.

Hinc laeta canit philomela frondis longis effudit sibilum paruam
sollempne militis tremulaque
uoce aethera pulset.

Et astra uolans aquila maeris
alauda cantu modulis resoluit
desursum uergit dissimili
modo dum tria cangit.

Vdelgo impulte rugit hirundo
pangit cotinus graculus ultra
aues sic cunctis celebrant
estiuum undique carmen.

Nulla istae auis similis est api quae
talem gerit tipum castitatis nisi
maria quae xpm portauit alia
inuiolata.

Hergis urbis magistratu accepit
a rastes quendam uidet ypham
qui ad infernum se dixit raptum.
Inde cumulatas referet causas subiecta trahit eo inferorum
acomitum densis undique siluis.

Hergens ille ridens respondit
subulcum illuc ad pastum nolo
cum macris mittere porcis.

Uirite falcis..........
in templum celi.......

lecum sedentem. & comedentem.
Iohannes baptista erat pincerna, atque
pelari pocula uini porrexit cunctis
uocatis sanctis.

Heriger aut prudentem egit xps iohim
ponens pincernam, quia uinum
non bibit umquam.

Mendax pharis cum petrum dicis illuc
magistrum esse cocorum. est quia
summi ianitor celi.

Honore quali te deus celi habuit
ibi ubi sedisti, uolo ut narres
quid manducasses.

Respondit homo angulo uno parum
pulmonis furabar, cocis hoc man-
ducaui atque recessi.

Heriger illum iussit ad palum loris
ligari scopisque cedi, sermone duro
hunc arguendo.

Sicut adsuum mittet pastum
xps ut secum capias cibum. caue
ne furtum facias.

Sponso sponsa karissimo se ipsam
in coniugio ambosque diu uiuere
post celi culmen cape.

Ne spernas quod sim fragilis. sum
tamen habilis rugosam si me
uideas ut puellam me teneas.

Ueni ueni domine quia fusca sum sed speciosa
dilapsa et latibulis assurgam
tuis uirtutibus. Matrem uenite
Hinc petrus te huc mittit &
charus ut retus ualerius te

Cum maximini principibus se coniungit
agricius orans ut felix uenias
fructu restituas

Ne quidem siresticuis tertiaque redditus
paulini adiutorium habet & nunc
& complures alii ubeirte re-
stituit simeon cuius maxime mandat murii ia
ponere.

astra meantem. Laudant rite
deum lux polus arua fretum
Qui crucifixus erat deus ecce per
   omnia regnat. Dantque creatori
5 cuncta creata precem.
Vestibunt silue tenera merorum
   uirgulta suis onerata pomis
   canunt decelsis sedibus palumbes
   carmina cunctis.
10 Hic turtur gemit resonat hic
   turdus pangit hic priscus melorum
   sonus passer nec tacens arripens
   garrito alta subulmis.
Hinc leta canit philomela fron
15 dis longas effudit sibilum peraura
   sollempne miluus tremulatque
   uoce aethera pulset.
At astra uolans aquila inaeris
   alauda canit modulis resoluit
20 desursum uergit dissimili
   modo dum terram tangit.
Uelox impulit rugitus hirundo
   pangit coturnix. gracellaris ultit
   aues sic cunctis celebrant
25 estiuum undique carmen.
Nulla inter auis similis est api que
   talem gerit tipum castitatis nisi
   maria que christum portauit aluo
   inuiolata.
30 Heriger urbis maguntiacensis
   antistes quendam uidit prophetam
   qui adinfernum se dixit raptum.
Inde cummultas referret cau
   sas. subiunxit totum esse infernum
35 accinctum densis. undique siluis.
Herigers illi ridens respondit meum
   subulcum illuc ad pastum nolo
   cum macris. mittere porcis.
Uir ait falsus. fuit translatus
40 intemplum celi. christumque uidi.

letum sedentem. et comedentem.
Iohannes baptista. erat pincerna. atque
   preclari pocula uini porrexit cunctis
   uocatis sanctis.
Heriger ait prudenter egit christus iohannem
   ponens pincernam. quoniam uinum
   nonbibit umquam.
Mendax probaris cum petrum dicis illuc
   magistrum esse cocorum est quia
   summi ianitor celi.
Honore quali te deus celi habuit
   ibi ubi sedisti. uolo ut narres
   quid manducasses.
Respondit homo angulo uno partem
   pulmonis furabar cocis hoc man
   ducaui atque recessi.
Heriger illum. iussit adpalum. loris
   ligari scopisque cedi. sermone duro
   hunc arguendo.
Site adsuum inuitet pastum
   christus ut secum capias cibum. caue
   ne furtum facias.
Sponso sponsa karissimo se ipsam
   inconiugio ambosque diu uiuere
   post celi culmen capere.
Nec spernas quod sim fragilis. sum
   tamen habilis rugosam si me
   uideas ut puellam me teneas.
Ueni ueni karissime quod fusca sum nondespice
   dilapsa uel lateribus. assurgam
   tuis uiribus. [maternus ueni concutit
Hinc petrus te huc inuitat et eu
   charius uritat ualerius te exig
Cummaximini precibus se coniungit
   agricius orans ut felix uenias et me
   fractam restituas.   [cium
Me quidem si restituis. turritamque reddideris
   paulini adiutorium habebis et nice
Hi et complures alii iubent me
   restitui simeon tuus maxime man
         [dat murum iam
             [ponere.

THE CAMBRIDGE SONGS fol. 438 v

O quam felix tu fueras q*uod* hunc uiru*m*
adduxeras qui me fuscam illumi
nat *et*me fracta*m* resolidat.
Quam libens hic te suscipit qua*m*
5 sanum *esse* p*re*cipit felice*m* om*n*i te*m*pore
q*uod* se*m*p*er* constet stabile.
U*es*t*rum* ambo*rum* meritis ite*rum* ero
treueris tu*rr*ita in late*r*ib*us* *et* firma
cunctis partib*us*. [na sec*u*la ame*n*.
10 Adhoc te de*us* p*re*muniat. *et* s*em*p*er* te custo
diat. cu*m* corpore ac anima i*n*sempit*er*
Emicat o quanta
pietate cecilia s*ancta* int*er* odoriferas c*hristus*
quas p*ro*spicit herbas. [gere i*esum*.
15 Despiciens mundu*m* meruit sibi iun
Gaudia sic thalami co*n*culcans ualeriani.
Hec sibi uirgineas q*u*athra uirtute choreas
Funcit elegit q*u*as hic sapientia co*m*psit.
Luce choru*m* clara docili*s* hu*n*c p*re*nite*t* uuoda.
20 Hancq*ue* meginbergis seq*u*itur ualitudine fortis
Hoc uiret incirco mereHict cu*m* flore decoro.
No*m*ine difficili sophie sed spe iuuenili.
Hinc tenet una locu*m* mitis collega
prio*rum*.,
25 Ia*m* dul s amica   qua*m* sic cor
meu*m* d   ca*m*

Ibi sunt sedilia st   atq*ue* uelis domus
nata flor   herbeq*ue*
30   appos   sis cibis ho
musta ibi claru*m* uinu*m* habundat. *et*
quicquid   cara delectat.
pl   cith   illa
melos cu*m* lira pangit. portantq*ue*
35 ministri pateras   plenas
Ibi sonant dulces simphonie in
flantur *et* altius tibie ibi puer
et docta puella canunt cantica
pulchra.
40 Ego fui sola i*n*silua *et* dilexi loca

                 secreta   is turba*m*
                 a q
           U   ſilen-
                                  mul
                                                      5
           Non   uuiuium
           qu   olloquiu*m*.
                 tas   clara

                                                     10

                        clara pupille
                                                     15
           S   ruo̜nu   fert
                  tempus adest
                  gruonot   gras in
           r̜a
           Quid u s ia*m* s go thu mir   20
           iur̜   hortaris unica*m*
           ma̜   mel
                       coro miner min
           nc   ndes silue nu
           sing..t ela   wualde   25
                   cano philomela kristes
                         a cui me deuoui

           O   a sagic thir
                            sede a me   30

                              ṃinṇo
                              r̜adan
           C   nunna choro miner
                       dabo tibi sup*er* hoc uuerelt   35
           hoc   omne also uuolcan in
           th   umele solu*m* c*hristi* regnu*m*
           th   f̧ęcit   ineuum
           Quod ips   regnat   credo inhumele.   40

O quam felix tu fueras q́ hunc uirū
adduxeras qui me fuscam illumi
nat & me fracta resolidat.
Quam libens hic te suscipit quā
sanum ēē p̄cūpte felicē omi tēpore
q́t sep constet stabile.
Uirm ambon merits tcum ero
tituerit trita in latiōib; & firma
cunctis partib; ffna scīa am
Adhoc te d̄s pmuniat. & sēp te custo
diat cū corpore ac anima i sēmpit
Emicat o quanta
pietate cecilia sc̄a nc̄ odoriferasq́ p̄
quis p̄spicere herbas ss gere ibm.
Despiciens mundū meruit sibi iun
Gaudia sic thalami dulcans ualenani
Hec sibi uirgineas ęthra uirtute choreas
Functe elegit q̄s hic sapientia copsit.
Luce chorū dans docet hc̄ pnitte uuod ai
Hancq́; megistigis secē ualitudine forā
Hocuiret incirco meretli et cū flore d̄cq́ ro
Noīe difficili sophie sed spe iuuenili.
Hinc tenet una locū mc̄is colleg
proxj

[illegible lines]

docta puella caniit conca
tibra
Ego sui sola silua & dilexi loca

[illegible]

H[illegible]ctolle genas desertaq:
lumina uenit. Adhebas argia
tuas age moenib: induc & p̃nos
ostende lares & mutua redde
hospitia heu quid ago? proiectus
cespite nudo hoc p̃re telluris
habes que iurgia certa. Impiũ
ñ fr̃ habet nullasne tuoꝝ. Mo
[illegible] lacrimas. ubi mat̃. ubi īcli
ta fama. Antigone. mihi nẽpe
iaces mihi uictus es uni. Dicebã
quo tendis iter. quid sceptra
[illegible]gata poscis. habes argos.
soceri regnabis in aula. Hic ẽ
longus honor. hic indiuisa
potestas. Quid queror. ipsa dedi
bellũ mestũq: rogaui. Ipsa p̃rẽ
ut talẽ nc̃ te complexa tenerẽ.
Sed bene habet supi. gratum ẽ for
[illegible]una pacta ẽ. spes longinqua
uie. totos inuenimus artus. Ei
mihi sed quanto descendit uuln?
[illegible]natu hoc fr̃ qua parte p̃cor
[illegible]acet ille nefandus. predator
unicã uolucres sit adire potestas
Excludã q: feras an habet fune
stus & ignes. Sed nec te flãmis
inopẽ tua t̃ra uidebit. Ardebẽ lacri
masq: feres q̃s ferre negatũ. Regib:
ẽtnũq: tuo famulata sepulchro.
Durabit deserta fides testisq: doloꝝ
Natus erit paruoq: thorũ polinice
fouebo.

Cante cane cantor care clare ẽ spiritu
cannule compte corde crepent. con
cinnantiam carpe callẽ commoda
conualles construe caput calcem cor
coniunge calles callens corporales
cane corda cane cordis cane can
nulis creatorem.

Quisquis dolosis antiqui circũ uentus
fraudibi inimici. p̃funditatẽ magnoꝝ
incautus incurrerit peccatoꝝ. hoc
sequenti cõmonitus exemplo sit
merens ne desp̃et penitus sed con
fisus in dño liberari posse speret
t̃ mortuũ si penitẽt ẽ inferno.

Cesarie urbis ciuis p̃terius locu
ples ualde nimis unicam habuit
gnatam sacro uelamini destinatã
p̃prius inquã illectus. seruulus inli
citus inflãmat̃ ẽ ardoribꝰ. cuius uin
do coniugii se non posse cernens iungi
auxiliũ agressus est malefici.

A quo praui suscepta scedula nunçu
deferenda demoni iussit cũ nocte
ceca supra gentilẽ recitatẽ tumbã.
iuuenis statim paruit demonum
& ecce sibi agm̃ apparuit. qui
auditis clamorib: infelicis secũ illũ
adduxerat ad principẽ p̃uitatis.

Cui inuisi datis commercii testis ama
lefico missis. tẽ sui causa aduent?
expositis amorisq: furiis. p̃mus
fit discussio de fide xp̃i ac baptis
mi repudio iubetq: de singulis ab
nuntiationis manuscriptũ effici.

Continuo tacta adia- bolo clamat uirgo misere misere- re pat̃ filie moriar nĩ pat̃ modo sĩn iungar tali puero noli pat̃ kare noli tardare ẽũ pater

THE CAMBRIDGE SONGS

   s scono   mis t   dare
    az gil   uuare
   homi   uuemir
                               mi
5   ndig   ne.
    aus   thaz er sibi
    ker   also
   sa ger   sal
  H adtolle genas defectaque
10 lumina uenit Adhebas argia
   tuas age moenibus induc et patrios
   ostende lares et mutua redde
   hospitia heu quid ago? proiectus
   cespite nudo hoc patrie telluris
15 habes que iurgia certe Imperium
   non frater habet nullasne tuorum. Mo
   uisti lacrimas. ubi mater? ubi incli
   ta fama Antigone? mihi nempe
   iaces mihi uictus es uni Dicebam
20 quo tendis iter. quid sceptra
   negata poscis? Habes argos.
   soceri regnabis inaula. Hic tibi
   longus honor. hic indiuisa
   potestas. Quid queror ipsa dedi
25 bellum mestumque rogaui. Ipsa patrem
   ut talem nunc te complexa tenerem
   Sed bene habet superi. gratum est for
   tuna peracta est. spes longinqua
   uie. totos inuenimus artus. Ei
30 mihi sed quanto descendit uulnus
   hiatu hoc frater qua parte precor
   iacet ille nefandus. predator
   uincam uolucres sit adire potestas
   Excludamque feras an habet fune
35 stus et ignes? Sed nec te flammis
   inopem tua terra uidebit. Ardebis lacri
   masque feres quas ferre negatum. Regibus
   eternumque tuo famulata sepulchro.
   Durabit deserta fides testisque dolorum
40 Natus erit paruoque thorum polinice
                fouebo.

Caute cane cantor care clare conspirent
   cannule compte corde crepent. con
   cinnantiam carpe callem commoda
   conualles construe caput calcem cor
   coniunge calles callens corporales
   cane corda cane cordis cane can
   nulis creatorem.
Quisquis dolosos antiqui circum uentus
   fraudibus inimici. profunditatem magnorum
   incautus incurrerit peccatorum hoc
   sequenti commonitus exemplo sit
   merens nedesperet penitus sed con
   fisus in domino liberari posse speret
   uel mortuum si penitet exinferno.
Cesarie urbis ciuis proterius locu
   ples ualde nimis unicam habuit
   gnatam sacro uelamini destinatam
   proprius inquam seruulus inlicitis inli
   citis inflammatus est ardoribus. cuius uin
   clo coniugii se nonposse cernens iungi
   auxilium agressus est malefici.
A quo praui suscepta scedula nuncii
   deferenda demoni iussit eum nocte
   ceca supragentilem recitare tumbam.
   iuuenis statim paruit demonum
   et ecce sibi agmen apparuit qui
   auditis clamoribus infelicis secum illum
   adduxerat adprincipem prauitatis.
Cui inuisi datis commercii literis ama
   lefico missis. item sui causa aduentus
   expositis amorisque furiis. protinus
   fit discussio defide christi ac baptismi repudio iubeturque desingulis abre
   nuntiationis manuscriptum efficere
Continuo tacta adia-   quod effecit.
   -bolo clamat uirgo misere miserere pater filie moriar mi pater
   modo sinon iungar tali puero noli
   pater kare noli tardare dum potes

THE CAMBRIDGE SONGS

me saluare si moraris natam tuam non
habebis. sed indie iudicii quasi properem
tam poenas et tormenta tu subibis
supplicii.
5 Ast flebilis contra pater inquit nata
heu quis te necauit. nata quis te fasci
nauit. ego te christo dedicaui. nonte mecho
destinaui patere mifilia sine me modo
perficere quod uolo si consentis mihi
10 tempus adueniet quando multum
letaberis prauam quod nonuoluntatem
perfeceris male sana quam nunc geris.
   Illa uero abnuente atque pene defici
-ente pater uictus amicorum consiliis consen-
15 sit inuitus accitoque puero substantiam
totam ei suam una cum puella tradidit.
dicens sue filiole uere iam misera
olim multum dolitura patrem quia nones
modo auditura.,   ; nupta
20 Nec multo post; uiri comperta infidelitate
se confestim in lamentis affecerat in
moderate luctusque nullus finis esse
quiuit. donec amarito tandem ex
plorato cuncte sue causa perfidie
25 abeato basilio penitentiam persuasit.
proerrore percipere grauissimo.
   Quem sanctus includens sacro peribulo
incumbens proeo precibus sedulo nunc
proillo orans sepe et ieiunans donec
30 adeo reo impetraret ueniam dari pro
crimine tam graui. dumque sibi peni
tenti ostensus est sanctus prose decertare
atque deantiquo hoste magnifice
uictoriam deportare.
35 Indicta transacta iam penitudine eductus
conciliandus ecclesie ecce repente sancto se
ducente tactus abhoste sacro pellitur
poste donec antistes et populus assis
tens precibus pulsantes deum fugatus est
40 demon clamans ac minitans hoc

basili manu scriptum coram deo restitues
mihi meum.
Nec mora sancto orante manusque cum populo
eleuante cartula desuper lapsa
manibus basilii est ingesta a puero 5
quam cognitam sanctus statim partes
dissipauit inminutas eundemque
uiuificis restitutum sacramentum inces
santer reddidit deo imnizantem.
O mihi deserte 10
natorum dulcis imago.
Arche more orerum et patrie
solamen adempte. 〔sontes.
Seruitiique decus quite mea gaudia
Extinxere dei modo quem 15
digressa reliqui.
Lasciuum et prono uexantem gra
mina cursu. 〔ligatis.
Heu ubi siderei uultus ubi uerba
Imperfecta sonis risusque et murmura 20
soli. 〔lemnon et argos.
Intellecta mihi quoties tibi
Sueta loqui et longa somnum suadere
querelas.
   uc adtolle genas defectaque 25
lumina. uenit   〔induc.
Athebas argia tua eia menibus
Et patrios ostende lares et mutua
Hospicia heu quid agam. 〔redde.
proiectus cespite nudo. 〔certe? 30
Hoc patrie telluris habes. que iurgia
Imperium non frater habet nullusue tuorum.
Mouisti lacrimas ubi mater? ub
inclita fama
Antigone? mihi nempe iaces 35
mihi uictus es uni.
Dicebam quo tendis iter. quid
sceptra negata   〔inaula.
Poscis? habes argos soceri regnabis
Hic tibi longus honos. hic indiuisa 40
      potestas.

me saluare si moraris nata tua non
habebis sed indie iudicii quasi ppetu-
am poenas & tormenta tu subibis
supplicii.
At flebilis contra patrem inquit nata
heu quis te decauit nata qs te fasci-
nauit ego te xpo dedicaui sic mecho
destinaui patre misilia sine me modo
pficero quod uolo si consentis mihi
tempus adueniet quando multū
letaberis praua q̄ nunc uolūtate
pfeceris male sana q̄ nc geris.
Illa uero abnuente atq; pene deficiente patre uictus amicoru̅ cōsilus cōsen-
sit nutus acerbūq; puero substantiā
totā ei suā una cū puella tradidit
dicens sue filiole uere iam misera
olim multū dolitura prem q̄ a nes-
modo audituras., Snupta
Nec multo post; cui̅ cōgta ī fideltatte
se confestim in latinas afferent in
modeste lucusq; nullus finis ce-
quiut. donec amarico tande ex
plorato cuncte sue causa psidiu
a beato basilio penitentiā psuaʃt
peripere pcipe grauissimo.
Quem scs includens sacro pibulo
incumbens peo pcib; sedulo nunc
p illo orans sepe & ieunans donet
a dō reo impetraret uenia̅ dari p
crimine tā graui. dum q; sibi penitentia ostensus è scs ipse decertare
itq; deurt iq; hoste magnifice
uictoriā deportare.
dicta ensacta iā penitudine educt
delandus ecate tr̄ce reperte scs se
ducente tacō ab hoste sacro pelle-
uiste donec antistes & populus assis-
tens pcib; pulsantes dm̄ fugatuus
demon clamans ac minitans hāc

basili manu scrorū cora dō restituet
mihi meii
Nec mora sc̄s angus manu sc̄ti pto
eleuaurū uirtute de sup lapsū
manib; basilius tangitur a puero
quam cognita est statim partes
dissipauto in minutas eundem q;
uiuifices restitutū sacramtū incessi
sant reddidit dō m̄ nizantem.
O mihi deserte
natorum dulcis imago.
Arche more ororum & pirie
solamen adempte. Sortes.
Senum tiq; decus qute mea gaudia
Extinxere dei modo quem
digressa reliqui.
Lasciuū & pno uegante gramina cursu. Ligatos.
heu ubi siderei uultus ubi uerba
imperfecta sonis insusq; & murmura
soli. lemnon & argos.
Intellecta mihi quid es tibi
Sueta loqui & longa sonū suadere
querelas.
uo adtolle genas defectaq;
lumina uento   induc.
A thebas argia tua era menib:
Et prius ostende larrs & miucia
hospicia heu quid agam redde.
pietus cespite nudo. certe.
hoc pire telluris habes que iurgia
impiu non ste habet nullus sue mor-
Amisisti lacrimas ubi mater ubi
melitra fama.
Antigone? mihi nempe iaces
mihi uictus es uni.
Diceba quo tendis ter. quid
sceptra negata iaula.
Poses habes argos soceri regnabis
his tibi long quis honos hic indiuisa
potestas.

Hunc ego te coniunx addebi-
ta regna perfecti.
Ductorē belli generūq; poten
tis adrasti.
Aspicio talisq; tuis occurro
triumphis.
Qui habet uocem serenam
hanc p[rese]nte[m] cantilenā de
anno lamentabili & damno inef
fabili p[er] quo dolet om[n]is homo
forinsecus & in domo suspirat
populus damnū uigilando &
p[er] somnum.
Rex d[eu]s uiuos tuere & defunctis
miserere.

Anno quoq; millessimo nono
atq; tricessimo de x[ri]p[ist]i natiui-
tate nobilitas rure late rure
cesar caput mundi & cum illo
plures su[m]mi occubuere impa-
tor. kuonpadus legu[m] dator. Rex.
Eodē uero tempore occasi[on]i sufuit
g[en]te rure stella matutina
Cunnild regina heu qua[m] cru-
delis annus corri[pui]t erat
herimannus filius [...] in
patrocis dux timidus in inimicis
rure kuono dux franco[rum] &
magna pars ingenuo[rum]. Rex.
I[m]p[er]ato[r]is g[ra]t[i]a sit nob[is] in memo-
na ac frequenti ratione in ratione
uiuat uir indolis bone uiuat
d[omi]nator p[ost] h[unc] & frequenti
carmine nouus e[st] p[er] clara fama
post mortē uitē p[ro]stet hunc
consortem. Rex d[eu]s.

Tempus erat quo p[ri]ma quies
mortalib; egris incipit & donu[m]
diuum gratissima serpit in somnis
est ante oculos mestissimus hector

Visus ade[o] mihi largosq; effundere
fletus. Raptatus bigis ut quonda[m]
alteq; cruento puluere p[er]q; pedes t[umentis]
ictas tumentis si mihi qualis
erat quantu[m] mutatus ab illo hectore
Qui redit exuuias indutus achillis
Vel danaum frigios iaculatus puppib;
ignes. Squalentem barbam & concretos
sanguine crines. Vulneraq; illa
gerens que circum plurima muros
Accepto prios. ultro flens ipse uidebar
Compellare uiru[m] & mestas expromere
uoces. O lux dardanie spes ofidissima
teucru[m] Que tante tenuere more
quib; hector abo[n]s Expectate uenis.
Quib; ludus est animo. & iocularis
cantio. hoc aduertant [r]idiculu[m]
e[st] uero non fictitium.

Sacerdos iam punicola. aetate sub
decrepita. uiuebat amans pecudis.
hic enim mos est rusticis.
Adomus tale studiu[m] om[n]e pate[re]
comodu[m]. nisi foret tam prima
lupo[rum] altrix silvula.
Diminuentes numeru[m] peius sum[m]a
generu[m] dant impares ex paribus
& pares ex imparib;
Qui dolens sui fieri detrimentu[m] peculii
quia diffidit uirib; uindicta querit ab[s]
fossam cauat n[on] modicā intus ponens
agniculam. et ne pate[n]t hostib; sup[er]
ne tegit frondib;
humano dat[u]i comodo nil mauis
est ingenio. lupus du[m] nocte circuit spe prede captus meditat[ur]
Accurrit mane presbyter gaudet
uicisse talem. intus p[re]trepido[...]
lupi mundi oculo.
Iam inquit fera pessima. tibi
rependa[m] debita. aut hic frange[m]

THE CAMBRIDGE SONGS

Nunc ego te coniunx addebi
ta regna perfectum.
Ductorem belli generumque poten
tis adrasti.
Aspicio talisque tuis occurro
triumphis.
Qui habet uocem serenam
hanc proferat cantilenam de
anno lamentabili et damno inef
fabili proquo dolet omnis homo
forinsecus et indomo suspirat
populus damnum uigilando et
persomnum.
Rex deus uiuos tuere et defunctis
miserere.
Anno quoque millessimo nono
atque tricessimo dechristi natiui
tate nobilitas ruit late ruit
cesar caput mundi et cum illo
plures summi occubuit impera
tor kuonradus legum dator. Rex.
Eodem uero tempore occasus fuit
glorie ruit stella matutina
Gunnild regina heu quam cru
delis annus corruerat
herimannus filius im
peratricis dux timendus inimicis
ruit kuono dux francorum et
magna pars ingenuorum. Rex.
Imperatoris gloria sit nobis inmemo-
ria ac frequentione mentione
uiuat uir indolis bone uuat
dominator probus et frequenti
carmine nouus et preclara fama
post mortem uite prestet hunc
consortem. Rex deus.
Tempus erat quo prima quies
mortalibus egris incipit et donum
diuum gratissima serpit insomnis
est ante oculos mestissimus hector.

Uisus adesse mihi largosque effundere
fletus. Raptatus bigis utquondam
alterque cruento. Puluere perque pedes tra
iectus lora tumentes Ei mihi qualis
erat quantum mutatus abillo Hectore
qui redit exuuias indutus achillis.
Uel danaum frigios iaculatus puppibus
ignes. Squalentem barbam et concretos
sanguine crines. Uulneraque illa
gerens que circumplurima muros
Accepit patrios. ultroflens ipse uidebar
Compellare uirum et mestas expromere
uoces. Olux dardanie spes ofidissima
teucrum Que tante tenuere more
quibus hector aboris Expectate uenis.
Quibus ludus est animo. et iocularis
cantio. hoc aduertant ridiculum
exuero nonfictitum.
Sacerdos iam ruricola. aetate sub
decrepita. uiuebat amans pecudis.
hic enim mos est rusticis.
Adcuius tale studium. Omne pateret
commodum. nisi foret tam proxima.
luporum altrix siluula.
Himinuentes numerum pereius summam
generum. dant impares exparibus.
et pares eximparibus.
Qui dolens sui fieri. detrimentum peculii.
quia diffidit uiribus. uindictam querit artibus.
Fossam cauat non modicam. intus ponens
agniculam. Et ne pateret hostibus. Superne tegit frondibus.
Humano datum commodo nil maius
est ingenio. lupus dum nocte circuit. spem prede captus incidit.
Accurrit mane presbiter. gaudet
uicisse taliter. intus protento baculo
lupi minatur oculo.
Iam inquit fera pessima. tibi
rependam debita. aut hic frangetur

baculus. Aut hic crepabit oculus.
  Hoc dicto simul impulit. Uerbo sed
    factom defuit. Nam lupus seruans oculum.
    morsu retentat baculum.
5 Atille miser uetulus. dum sese trahit
    firmius. Ripa cedente corruit. et
    lupo comes incidit.
  Hinc stat lupus hinc presbiter. timent
    sed dispariliter. Nam ut fidenter arbitror
10 lupus stabat securior.
  Sacerdos secum musitat. septemque psal-
    mos ruminat. sed reuoluit frequentius
    miserere mei deus.
  Hoc inquit infortunii. Dant mihi uota
15 populi. Quorum neglexi animas. Quorum
    comedi uictimas.
  Pro defunctorum merito. cantat place-
    -bo domino. et prouotis uiuentium. totum
    cantat psalterium.
20 Post completum psalterium. commune
    prestat commodum. Sacerdotis timidi-
    tas. atque lupi calliditas.
  Namcum accliuis presbiter. perfiniret
    pater noster. Atque clamaret domino. Sed
25 libera nos a malo.
  Hic dorsum eius insilit. et saltu liber
    effugit. et cuius arte captus est.
    illo proscala usus est.
  Ast ille letus nimium. cantat lau
30 -date dominum. et promisit propopulo,
    se oraturum amodo.
  Hinc auicinis queritur. et inuentus
    extrahitur. Sed nonnumquam deuo-
    tius. orauit nec fidelius.
35 Templum christi uirgo casta felix
    mater omaria cuius clausam
    uentris portam noui uite ianua
    patri sanctique spiritus gratia petimus uali
    da prece nos expia abomni
40 macula facinorosa.

Tu regina celi summa castitatis
  tenet sceptra angelorum satis
  digna congaudet frequentia
  quibus nos exoramus socia qui
  uiuis cum patre spirituque sancto pereterna secula. 5
Admensam philosophie sitientes
  currite et saporis tripertiti septem
  riuos bibite uno fonte proceden-
  -tes noneodem tramite.
Hinc fluit gramma prima hinc 10
  poetica ydra lanx hinc satiricorum
  plausus hinc comicorum letificat
  conuiuia mantuana fistula.
Salue uite norma preclare
  flos sinagoge. Aue pie diu 15
  optate tue oliue. Nisibus omni
  genis gratulor modulando
  camenis
  here forma poli serena sol
  atque luna. Uale hora certe 20
  iocunda reddens cristalla.
Presulis eximii ualeat uirtute
  sepulchri.
V   flọ   a
  nna   f   g   et 25
  sic   ad et.
Nosti flores   fert   pulchra
  tex   omi   aḍ
  r
Sic   plic alb   nịdis 30
  u   bus ut
  non
O   mihi
                     tus
  n 35
Post   postquam
                 studium.

Nam   bus
    cum   çor 40

baculus· A· & t· hic crepabit oculus·
Hoc dicto simul impulit. Uerbo sed
facto defuit· Nā lupus seruans oculū
morsu retentat baculū·
Atille insit· uetulus· dū se setrahit
fīmus· & upa cedente corruit· et
lupo comes incidit·
Hinc stat lupus hinc p̄sbiter tunc
sed disparilit̃· Nā ut sīdeōt arbitror
lupus stabat securior·
Sacerdos seuū mussitat septemq; psal-
mos· quuminat· sed reuoluit freqmt̃
miserere meīs·
Hoc incidit infortuniū· Dant in uota
populi· quox̃· neglexi animas· quox̃·
comedi uicarias·
Pro defunctox̃ merito· cantat placebo dn̄o· & p̄uiuis inuertit̃· totum
cantat psalterium.
Post completū psalteriū comune
p̄stat comōdū· Sacerdotis amici-
tia atq; lupi calliditas·
Nā cū acoliuus presbit̃ p̄siniret
pat̃ nr̃. atq; clamaret dn̄o· Sed
libera nos a malo.
Hic dorsū eius insilit· & saltu libr̃
effugit· & cuius arte captus ē
illo psalla usus ē·
Ast ille locus nimiū cantat laudate dn̄m· & p̄misit p populo
se oraturū amodo·
Hic amicius quericō· & inuertius
p̄traitur· Sed nonnumquā deuo-
cius aratur neoc fidelius·
Templū xp̄i uirgo casta solis
uitae omnia cuius clausam
uitalis portā nouiuite ianuā
oens sc̃ïq; sp̄s gr̃a petimus uale-
de prece nos expia ab omni
macula facinorosa·

Uirgina celi fama castitatis
tenet scepta angeloru stas
digna congaudet· Frequentia
quib: nos exorantes socia qui
cuius cū p̄re sp̄ūq; sc̃o p̄tna sc̃ta·
A mensa philosophie fruentes
Accurrat & sapiens tingtū sep-
tinuos bibtae uno fonte p̄ced-
tes neodē tramite·
Hinc fluit grāma prima hinc
poetica petra lanx hinc sat̄ıcox̃
plausus hinc comicorū letifica
conuiuia mattuana fistula·
Salue uite norma pelare
flos sinagoge· Aue pie diu
optate uie oliue· Ñisibus omi
gēnis gr̃atulor modulando
camenis
Here forma poli serena sol
cta· luna· Uale hora certe
iocunda reddens cristalla·
P̄sulis eximii ualet uirtute
sepulchri·

Levis exsurgit zephirus. & sol
 procedit tepidus. iam terra
 sinus aperit. dulcore suo diffluit
Ver purpuratum exuit ornatus
 suos induit. aspergit terra floribus: ligna siluarum frondibus:.
Struunt lustra quadrupe-
 des. & dulces nidos uolucres.
 inter ligna florentia sua de-
 cantando gaudia.
Quod oculis dum uideo. & auribus: dum audio. heu pro tantis gau-
 dijs: tantis inflor suspirijs.
Cum mihi sola sedeo. & hec re-
 uoluens palleo. si forte caput subleuo. nec audio nec
 uideo.
Tu saltim uelis gratia exaudi
 & considera. frondes flores
 & gramina. nam mea
 languet anima.
Gaudet polus ridet tellus
 iocundantur omnia. Angelorum
 sacra canunt in excelsis
 agmina. Quorum psallit
 imitatrix interris ecclesia.
Mundus plaudit & resultat
 letus de te regina.
A caris minus gratulatur
 pulchra uernarum turma.
Que sub tuis alis fulta digna
 tali domina.
Incolomis gubernatrix qua tu
 morbo soluta.
Et uirtutum flore compta
 restauraris maula.
Ne miseris domini iussit solui
 morbi uincula.
Nexus mortis & ligare ne
 fuisset damnosa.

Tu uere optati quam nobis opus seruata
Te reginam nostram mansione facit
 futura. creatura.
Astra celi flores humi te cuncta
 cuncti boni larga culminis es que
 tam apta. in scena.
Mater dulcis & que cuitas secla huius
 blandimentis in terrore sistas puritissima
Monachorum ensis extans clericorum domina
Consolam uiduarum uirginum constantia
Laicorum blandimenta clipeus & galea.
Quare posco quia te crebro te seruet te scla
Dominator qui non nulla semper scandit sup
 sidera.
Ingestis primum uerecum quod a lege ridiculum
 exemplo tam habile quod uobis dicam rethnice.
Obiit abba paruulus. statura non uirtutibus:
 erat maiori socio. qui cum erat iheremo,
 olim dicebat uiuere secure si sic angustius.
 nec ueste nec cibo frui qui laboret ma- tribus:
 maior debebat moneo. ne sis incepti propositi
 fr quod inco et pro modum. sic ne cepisse saucius
Commoneor quando dimicat. ne cadat neque supe-
 ret & nudus heremum interiore penetrat
Septem dies gramineo uix ita durat pabulo.
 octauum fames impatit ut ad sodalem redit
Qui sero clausus ianua tacitus sedet in cellula.
 cum minor uoce debit fratre apellat a pen.
Obijt hospes quidquis notis assistere foribus
 nec spernat tua pietas que redigit necessi-
Respicite ille dei tot. iobis factus angelis mur-
 celi cardines ultra ne currat homines.
Obijt foras excubat. mala qui nocte uole
 & per uoluntariam hanc agit peniten-
 acto mane recipit sacrasque uerbis in-
 sed cepit os ad crustula ferre patienter
Refocillatus dominus grates egit & socio
 hinc rastellum brachijs cepit
Castigat angustia de leuitate ui-
 cum angustis si pocuit uir bonus esse didicit

THE CAMBRIDGE SONGS

Leuis exsurgit zephirus. et sol
　procedit tepidus. iam terra
　sinus aperit. dulcore suo difluit.
Uer purpuratum exuit. ornatus
5　suos induit. aspergit terra flo-
　ribus. ligna siluarum frondibus.
Struunt lustra quadrupe-
　des. et dulces nidos uolucres.
　inter ligna florentia. sua de
10　cantant gaudia.
Quod oculis dum uideo. et au
　ribus dum audio. heu protantis gau
　diis. tantis inflor suspiriis.
Cum mihi sola sedeo. et hec re
15　uoluens palleo. si forte ca-
　pud subleuo. nec audio nec
　uideo.
Tu saltim uelis gratia. exaudi
　et considera. fronde flores
20　et gramina. nam mea
　languet anima.
Gaudet polus ridet tellus
　iocundantur omnia. Angelorum
　sacra canunt inexcelsis
25　agmina. Quorum psallit
　imitatrix interris ecclesia.
Mundus plaudit et resultat
　letus dete regina.
Ac aut minus gratulatur
30　pulchra. uernarum turma.
Que sub tuis alis fulta digna
　tali domina.
Incolomis gubernatrix quod tu
　morbo soluta.
35 Et uirtutum flore compta
　restauraris inaula.
Ne mireris deus iussit solui
　morbi uincula.
Nexus mortis et ligare ne
40　fuisset dampnosa.

Tue uite optatique nobis opus seruata.
Te reginam nostram maris esse fauet
　factura.　　　　[creatura.
Astra celi flores humi te cuncta
Cuncti boni larga culminis es que　　　5
　tam aperta.　　　[inscena.
Mater dulcis et que cunctis secla huius
Blandimentis nonterrore sistis permitissima.
Monachorum ensis extas clericorum domina.
Consolamen uiduarum uirginum constantia.　　10
Laicorum blandimenta clipeus et galea.
Quare posco quo te crebro conseruet te secula.
Deus qui nonnulla semper scandit super
　sidera...,
Ingestis patrum ueterum. quoddam legi ridiculum　15
　exemplo tamen habile quod uobis dicam rithmice.
Iohannes abba paruulus. statura non uirtutibus.
　ita maiori socio. quicum erat inheremo.
Uolo dicebat uiuere. secure sicut angelus.
　nec ueste nec cibo frui qui laboretur ma-[nibus.　20
Maior dicebat moneo. ne sis incepti properus.
　frater quod dico tibi postmodum. sic noncepisse saucius.
At minor qui nondimicat. noncadit neque superat.
　ait et nudus heremum inferiorem penetrat.
Septem dies gramineo. uix ibi durat pabulo.　　25
　octaua fames imperat. ut ad sodalem redeat.
Qui sero clausus ianua. tutus sedet incellula
　cum minor uoce debili. frater apellat aperi.
Iohannes hospes indigus. notis assistit fòribus
　nec spernat tua pietas. quem redigit necessit　30
Respondit ille deintus. iohannes factus angelus miratur
　celi cardines. ultra noncurat homines.
Iohannes foras excubat. malamque noctem tole t
　et preter uoluntariam. hanc agit penitent
Facto mane recipitur. satisque uerbis uritu　　35
　sed contemptus adcrustulam fert patienter o
Refocilatus domino. grates egit et socio de
　hinc rastellum brachiis. temptat mouere[languidis
Castigatus angustia. deleuitate nimia
　cum angelis nonpotuit. uir bonus esse didicit　40

21

THE CAMBRIDGE SONGS

Cordas tange melos pange cum lira
   sonabili. tu magister eam liram fac sonare
   dulciter. et tu cantor insublime uocem
   tuam erige ambo simul adunati canti-
5 lene mistice. O uuillelme decus pulchrum
   aspectu ornabili qui tam clarus permansisti. cum
   tuis assidue. oquis poterit iam esse tam potens inopere
   preter reges quos unxerunt antistites chrismate.
   presules aut plures miror antistitum culmine
10 utriusque sexus namque uiri atque femine tam
   nobili creature se cupibant flectere. omnis
   chorus angelorum. zabulon subtrahite magne
   martir iuliane proillo intercede.

Hec est clara dies clararum clara dierum.
15 hec est sancta dies sanctarum sancta dierum.
   Nobile nobilium rutilans diadema dierum
   Quid est hoc tam dure. quod inuestro manet pectore.
   Amarumque ducitis animum de iesu nobis est dure
   manet innos morseius et ipsa mors est incogni
20 Nostre quedam abiere sepulturam inuisere. celi [ta.
   ciues illum uiuum dicunt iam regnare.
   Salue festa dies. salue resurrectio sancta. salue
   semper aue lux hodierna uale.

Rota modos arte personemus musica. quibus
25 ut his constans gratuletur anima ut afa
   bris clarus didicit pithagoras malleis
   cum quattuor deprendit. consonantias. septem
   planetarum fecit interstitia quarum fit ce
   lestis musica numerorum normula fert
30 ut arithmetica. cunctis dans principia. rex
   mirande panto kraton nos reget persecula.

Miserarum est nec amori dare ludum neque dulci
   mala uino lauere. aut exanimali metuentis patrue uerbera lingue.   [nitar ebri.
35 Tibi squalum cithareae puer ales tibi telas opera seque
   minerue studium aufert. ne obule liparei
   Simul unctos tiberinis humeros lauit inundis
   eques ipse melior belloro fonte neque pugno
   neque seni uictus pede.
40 ptus idem perapertum fugientes agitato grege
   ceruos iaculare. celere alto. latitantem
   frugi. tectum excipere. aprum.

Pulsat astra planctu magno rachel
   plorans pignora queriturque conso
   lari quos necauit improba. dolet. plangit
   crines scindit obsororis crimina uxor
   sine macula casta seruans uiscera.
Felix uirgo deo cara et dilecta femina
   circum circa uolitando filiorum pascua.
   querit lustrat perscrutator perdiuersa
   climata ansit ouis perdita digna
   spondens premia.
Splendor eius splendor solis mane
   dantis lumina sic lunaris candor
   idem foret inter sidera.

O admirabile ueneris idolum. cuius
   materie nihil est friuolum. arcos te
   protegat. qui stellas et polum fecit et
   maria condidit et solum furis in
   genio. nonsentias dolum. cloto te
   diligat. que baiolat colum.
Saluto puerum nonperipotesim. sed
   firmo pectore deprecor lachesim.
   sororis atropos necuret heresim
   neptunum comitem habeas et tetim.
   cum uectus fueris perfluuium tesim. quo
   fugis amabo cum te dilexerim. miser
   quid faciam cumte nonuiderim.
Dura materies exmatris ossibus. creauit
   homines iactis lapidibus. exquibus unus est iste
   puerulus. qui lacrimabiles noncurat
   gemitus cum tristis fuero gaudebit emulus. ut cerua rugio cumfugit
   hinnulus.

Ven   g   am me
   uisere   et a et o   in languore perio
   o et
Ueni   es
   ro
Si cum claue uen   intrare
   et a et o.

Cordas tange melos pange cum lyra
sonabili tu magister ea lyra fac sonare
dulciter & tu cantor in sublime uocem
tuam enge ibo simul adunati carmi-
lone mistice. O uuilhelme dei pulchrum
aspectu ornabilis quam tu clarus permansisti cum
tuis assidue o si poterit iam esse tam potens ope
pontifex reges quos unxerit antistites chrismate.
presules aut plures mitior antistitum culmine
utriusque sexus natiq viri atq femine tam
nobili creature se cupiebant flectere omnis
chorus angelorum zabulon subehrte magne
martir iuliane pillo intercede.

Hec clara dies dararum clara dierum.
hec est sancta dies sanctarum sanctarum dierum.
Nobile nobilium rutilans diadema dierum
Quid hoc tam dure quinto manet pectore.
Amaruque ducitur animum de ibu nobis et dure
manet mors morsuus & ipsa mors est icogni
Nisi quedam abiere sepulta uisere celi
aues illum uiuum dicunt iam regnare.
Salue festa dies salue resurrectio sancta salue
semper aue lux hodierna uale.

Rota modos arte prosonemus musica quibus
ut bis sextans gratuletur anima uti sa-
bris clarus didicit pithagoras malleus
cum quattuor deprendit consonantias septem
planetarum fecit in strata quarum sit celestis musica numerorum normula fert
ut arithmetica. cuncas dans principia reo
mirride partio lunam nos reges psalta.

rerum nec amori dare ludum neque dulci
uino lauere ut gramen ali metuen...
...uerbera lingue. Intrar ebrii
...cithare puerales tela sopa sequ...
...studium aufert ne ebulo liparet...
...tribus humeros laut iundis
...ipse melior bellorum fonte neque pugno
...uictus pede.
...idem paparum fugientes agresto grege

ceruos iaculare celeri alto lanciams
frugi tectum excipe aprum.
Pulsas astra planorum magno rachel
plorans pignora querrturqi consolari quos necauit impia dolore plange
ennes scindit obscoenis crimina uxor
sine macula casta seruans uiscera
elige uirgo deo cara & dilecta femina
circu circa uolitando filios pascua
querunt lustrare perscrutare poluerti-
dum tua ansa ouis perdita digna
spondens premia.

Splendor eius splendor solis mane
dantis lumina sic lunaris candor
ide foret, inter sidera.

Oh admirabile ueneris idolum cuius
materie nichil est friuolum artos te
protegat qui stellas & polum fecit &
maria condidit & soluit furis in
genio inserviens dolum dolorem te
diligat que baiolat eolum.

Salicto puerum non prepotens sed
firmo pectore deprecor lachesim.
sororis atropos ne curret heresim
neptunium comitem habtas ceterum
cum uersus fueris pro fluuium tesim quia
fugis amabo cum te dilexerim miser
quid faciam cum te non uiderim.

Dura mater ex matris ossibus creauit
homines iacus lapidibus exiit unus et iste
puerulus qui lacrimabiles uncinti
gemitus cum tristis fuero gaudebit emulus ut cerua rugio cufugio
hinnulus.

V...

CHAPTER II

A. Description of the Cambridge Manuscript with special Reference to the 'Songs'[1]

THE 'Cambridge Songs,' which are written on ten leaves (folios 432–41) towards the end of the manuscript Gg. 5. 35, form only a small, although perhaps the most important, part of this interesting collection. It is impossible to say if they were written down in England or on the Continent. It seems probable that they were copied, in the monastery of St Augustine at Canterbury (in the library of which the manuscript was preserved for many centuries), from a song book that may have formed the *répertoire* of an early goliard and that was perhaps either acquired or copied by an Englishman who travelled, about the middle of the eleventh century, in the district of the Middle and Lower Rhine. The subject-matter of some of the poems and the portions of the songs that are written in German (North Rheno-Franconian dialect) alike point to the country about Treves and Cologne and Xanten as the district in which the collection was in all probability originally made and used. This song book of a *clericus vagabundus*, of which the ten leaves of our manuscript are apparently a copy[2], is no longer in existence. It may have perished as early as 1168 when a fire destroyed part of the valuable library of the Augustinians at Canterbury. Some of the songs preserved in our Cambridge Manuscript are unique, others exist in only one other codex (see p. 36, note 1 and the notes to the individual numbers, pp. 71 and following), while some of the classical excerpts among them have come down to us in numerous and better manuscripts than the Codex Cantabrigiensis.

The parchment, which has a yellow tint, is on the whole very smooth and in good condition; only in some places are the edges rubbed and worn[3] to such an extent that the

---

[1] See the *Catalogue of Manuscripts preserved in the Library of the University of Cambridge*, Vol. III (1858), 201–5. Here the contents of the whole manuscript are enumerated and fully described. The manuscript is a quarto, written on parchment, and now contains 454 leaves. It is for the most part well preserved, and the handwriting, neat and clear throughout, is not earlier than the time of the Conquest. The portion (No. 42) containing the Songs is thus described (on p. 205): *Lyrics in honour of the Emperors of Germany during the first half of the XIth century*, and it is said to be 'highly probable' that the date of the compilation of the collection was the reign of the Emperor Henry III (1039–55). See also Robert Priebsch, *Deutsche Handschriften in England*, Erlangen, Vol. I (1896), 20–27. In this important publication special attention has been paid to the portion of the manuscript that contains 'the Cambridge Songs,' and several valuable contributions to their study are made. The manuscript seems to have come to Cambridge during the last quarter of the seventeenth century. It was not in the University Library in 1670, but was purchased soon after that date out of Bishop Hacket's bequest. See pages 30 and 105, note 2.

[2] The copy was sometimes made without proper understanding, e.g. fol. 435ra, l. 30 *litus* (for *licus*, i.e. the river Lech); fol. 435rb, l. 10 *miro* (for *maro*); fol. 438va, l. 21 *mereHict* (for *merehilt*?); fol. 437va, l. 11 *intsiegina* (for *intfieg ina*), etc.

[3] Usually the final word or words of the last lines of the second column (recto) are damaged in this way. On fol. 438 the parchment is very brittle at the bottom.

letters on these parts are no longer legible. This is especially to be regretted in the case of fol. 437rb, l. 36. Most of the poems are, however, in perfect preservation and are written in extremely clear and neat characters. Only in the case of some erotic poems (fol. 438^v, fol. 439ra, fol. 440vb, fol. 441vb) has the reading been rendered difficult or impossible by means of erasures or by a very effective blacking of the text. The pages are 21½ cm. high and 15 cm. wide (the text usually 18½ × 13½); the lines were ruled with a sharp instrument, 40 to the page, about 5 mm. apart. On the left side, and also in the middle (leaving a space of some 7 mm.), perpendicular lines divide the writing-space from the margin and separate the two columns. At the head of and between these lines large and small capitals were inserted, the former in red to mark the beginning of a poem. Each manuscript page contains as a rule 80 lines, and thus the whole collection, as we now have it, consists roughly speaking of 1600 lines. It is, however, possible, even probable (see R. Priebsch, *l.c.* page 23), that one leaf is now missing between the present folios 440 and 441. The stanzas of the last poem on fol. 440vb consist of 3 lines each, with the exception of the sixth and last stanza on this page, which has only 2 lines, and consequently it seems probable that the poem (whether the sixth was its last stanza or not) was continued on the now lost folio (*440^a). The present folio 441 begins with a new song, and it is therefore quite conceivable that one or more poems were written on the now lost folio 440^a after the poem that was continued from fol. 440. This would involve the loss of 160 lines. Towards the end of the collection several (though not all) of the love-poems were erased or blacked, and fol. 441 begins with a very charming song of this nature. It therefore seems probable that the lost fol. 440^a contained others of the same kind, to which the monks of St Augustine objected, and on account of which they made away with fol. 440^a, just as they erased and obliterated similar songs on other leaves[1]. Assuming, from the usual length of the poems written on other leaves, that at least three poems have been lost to us in this way, the number of the pieces making up the collection would be raised to no less than half a hundred, of which at present only 47 remain and 43 are legible. The poems are numbered in pencil—up to 49—by a late hand, which has, however, not put a number to every poem. He counts fol. 432ra, ll. 1–13 as two pieces and also counts the doublet-extract twice.

The large coloured initials, by means of which the beginnings of new songs are indicated, were probably not written by the scribe or scribes of the songs, but were added afterwards by some other monk. The initials are written alternately (but not always consistently) in bright and dark red. In many cases (e.g. fol. 435vb, l. 29; 437vb, l. 25 and l. 30; 439rb, l. 1; 440rb, l. 16) a small letter in the margin served to indicate the place where they were to be inserted. See also fol. 441vb. In a few cases even this was forgotten, viz. on fol. 432ra, l. 31 *nclito* for *Inclito*; fol. 436vb, l. 40 *udax* for *Audax*; fol. 437rb, l. 27 *unc* for *Nunc*; fol. 439vb, l. 25 *uc* for *Huc*. On fol. 437ra the first line is erased, with the exception of the initial A. This line was a repetition of the last line of the preceding page (fol. 436vb, l. 40: *Audax es, vir iuuenis*); it was consequently obliterated, and the bright red capital A, which was by mistake omitted on fol. 436vb, l. 40, stands now on fol. 437ra, l. 1 isolated and completely detached. It would have been better if l. 40 on fol. 436vb, which is now underlined in bright red to mark

---

[1] On the inside cover J. M. K(emble) has added a few notes about the manuscript and the Songs. He briefly discusses the date of the manuscript and adds: *The remainder of this volume is filled with scraps of Latin, and there has been some more Ohd. which a barbarian has destroyed by using the infusion of galls....*He calls it *one of the most curious manuscripts in England.*

DESCRIPTION OF THE MANUSCRIPT

that it belongs to the solitary capital A, had been erased and the first line of fol. 437ra had been kept.

The careful handwriting, of the middle of the eleventh century, shows a mixture of continental and Old English (Anglo-Saxon) characters. Priebsch, and before him Jaffé and Pertz, have called attention to the distinctly Anglo-Saxon form of some letters, especially in the case of t, r and g. The Anglo-Saxon letters t and r are especially frequent and are met with on almost every page of the manuscript, the r (ꞃ) occurring with special frequency in the spelling of proper names. But, apart from these, there are found isolated instances of other Anglo-Saxon letters on two consecutive leaves of our songs—and on these leaves (folios 436 and 437) only. These letters are the Anglo-Saxon ᚠ (fol. 437va, l. 14 *hafode*, l. 20 *hafon*, l. 21 *fulleist*, all in the same poem); þ (fol. 437va, l. 14 *þar*, just before *hafode*); and ƿ (fol. 436ra, l. 28 *cƿonrado* = *cuuonrado*). It is also worthy of note that the Anglo-Saxon g's are only frequent on fol. 437 in the song on Henry of Bavaria, in which alone the Anglo-Saxon letters f and þ occur. On some pages no Anglo-Saxon letters at all are used, but only their continental equivalents. Certain differences in the manner of abbreviating words and of indicating or not indicating divisions of words may also be noticed on different folios. All these considerations make it seem likely that, in spite of the general similarity of the writing, the songs were copied by more than one scribe. Some letters of the same value occur in two forms throughout the manuscript and are used indifferently even in the same word. Such are especially d and ð, a and ᴀ, the before-mentioned Anglo-Saxon ꞃ and the continental r, and, to a less extent, the (rarer) Anglo-Saxon ᵹ and the (more frequently used) continental g. See *kuniglich dignum*, fol. 437rb, l. 37. Of capital letters H and ʜ may be mentioned (see on the same fol. 432ra, l. 24 *Hos* and fol. 432rb, l. 31 *Hinc*, but ʜ ll. 4 and 6; again H fol. 436vb, l. 20, ʜ fol. 436vb, l. 3).

In the writing of words, prepositions are usually run together with the following word, and the same is the case with the negation (usually abbreviated n̄). There is no definite principle noticeable in the use of the common abbreviations. The longer forms are often used when there was room for them, while the abbreviated forms occur when there was little room. On some leaves the abbreviations are much more numerous and the lines much more closely packed than on others, which may well be due to the different habits of different copyists. One scribe was obviously anxious to pack his lines as close as possible (e.g. fol. 432va, l. 11), while on other pages nothing of the kind is noticeable and the monk occasionally appears even wasteful of his parchment. Not infrequently some word belonging to the end of one stanza, where there was no room for it, was inserted a few lines before (rarely after) its proper place, wherever there was a blank space available. Such words are usually preceded by some symbol or other (see fol. 434va), for which in the transliteration only one kind of symbol (ᑕ) has been used. See fol. 437rb, l. 18, continued l. 16; *ibid.* l. 23, contin. l. 21; or fol. 432va, l. 12, contin. l. 10; fol. 433va, l. 24, contin. l. 21; *ibid.* l. 34, contin. l. 32, etc. On a few leaves the breaking of a line is marked by an accent ('), e.g. fol. 435va, l. 13 *postre'-mo*; sometimes the break is marked by a hyphen or hyphens, but in the large majority of cases it is not marked at all. The spelling is not always consistent, the same sound being rendered by different symbols, e.g. þ and th (fol. 437va, l. 14 (þ) and l. 15 (th)); ƿ (once) and u in the spelling of the name cƿonrad, cuonrad (fol. 436va, l. 28, and *ibid.* l. 5; cp. also kuonradus fol. 440ra, l. 21)[1]; or h, ch, hc in the spelling of the name heinrih (437va, ll. 15, 18), heinrich

[1] The usual spelling of the name is *cuonrad(us)*. Cp. also *kuono dux francorum* (fol. 440ra, l. 28).

(*ibid.* l. 4), heinrihc (*ibid.* l. 19). Capital letters in the middle of lines occur on fol. 437vb in the song *Salve, festa dies* (fol. 437vb), in part of the tale *Sacerdos et lupus* (fol. 440va), and also in the extracts from Statius and Virgil, when they denote the beginning of a new hexameter verse or of a new sentence; they are not used in the writing of proper names[1].

The conclusion of a poem is sometimes marked by ., ., (fol. 434vb, l. 30), or by ..., (fol. 441rb, l. 14), or merely by ., (fol. 433ra, l. 18 and 438va, l. 24). Otherwise there is no punctuation except full stops, which are usually put to denote the end, or one half, of the metrical line. In some cases full stops are omitted or misplaced. Marks of interrogation occur only in the extracts from Statius (fol. 439ra and 439vb), but not at the end of the extract from Virgil (fol. 440rb, l. 15).

In a very few cases a neumatic notation has been given to stanzas or words, e.g. fol. 439rb, ll. 9 sqq. and 23 sqq.; fol. 441vb, ll. 16 sqq. This has not been indicated in the transcript, but can easily be studied in the photographic reproduction of the manuscript. In the notes to the individual pieces attention is called to the neum-accents.

Specimens of especially well-written pages may be found in fol. 435 and fol. 436^r. The worst page is fol. 438^v. Occasional holes in the parchment (e.g. fol. 440ra) existed before the songs were written down and have in no case spoilt the text.

Obvious misspellings have not been corrected in the transcript. In all cases of doubt the reading of the manuscript (on the opposite page) can easily be ascertained. Only such letters have been transcribed as can be recognised, however faintly, on the leaves of the manuscript, without considering the readings of previous editors. In some cases a few more letters can be dimly recognised in the manuscript than appear in the photographic reproduction[2]. This is especially the case where the other side of the leaf has been blacked by the use of *tinctura gallica*. My transcript must in these cases be taken to represent what can still be read on the folios of the manuscript itself with the help of a good magnifying glass.

B. Tabulated Survey of the 'Cambridge Songs'

The following table affords an easy survey of the 'Cambridge Songs' as they now stand in the manuscript. The exact place of each on the folios is indicated, the poems are counted (including No. 31, the doublet of No. 28), and references are added in parallel columns to the most important books and periodicals in which the songs have already been printed. With regard to the dates and the full titles of the publications of Eccard, Fröhner, du Méril, Jaffé, Piper, and *M.S.D.* = Müllenhoff and Scherer's *Denkmäler*, see Chapters III and VI.

---

[1] Differences of spelling may in some cases also be accounted for by assuming that the Goliard copied his pieces from different manuscripts in which the same words were spelt differently, e.g. *moenibus* (fol. 437ra, l. 11) and *menibus* (fol. 439vb, l. 27) in the corresponding passage. The MS. has nearly always *oe* in the word *poena* (fol. 435va, l. 14; 435vb, l. 2; 437ra, l. 26; 439va, l. 3), but on fol. 435vb, l. 18 it has *pena*. On fol. 436ra, l. 20 we read *foetu*, but fol. 432rb, l. 38 *feta*. The Latin *ae* is usually represented by *e* throughout the manuscript, but in a few cases either *ae* or *ę* are written, e.g. *infimae* (fol. 434rb, l. 6), but *subremę* (fol. 432rb, l. 25); *simphoniae* (fol. 434rb, l. 40), but *uitę* (fol. 433ra, l. 10); *aetate* (fol. 440rb, l. 19), *etatis* (fol. 432ra, l. 31); the Greek y is usually rendered by i, see *lira* (fol. 441vb, l. 1), *rithmica* (fol. 441rb, l. 16), *mistice* (fol. 441va, l. 5), *frigios* (fol. 440rb, l. 7), *pithagoras* (fol. 441va, l. 26), etc., but *symphoniam* (fol. 434rb, l. 1) occurs by the side of *simphonia* (fol. 437vb, l. 26). Initial *c* is often spelt *k*: *karitate* (fol. 433va, l. 30), *karissimo* (fol. 438rb, ll. 23 and 29), *karta* (fol. 436rb, ll. 32 and 35), *karo* (fol. 437ra, l. 31).

[2] For instance, *sedes* and *tibi* (fol. 437rb, ll. 34 and 37) are a little more distinct in the manuscript than in the photographic reproduction, and Dieterich's statement in Haupt's *Zeitschrift* 47, 434-5 should be corrected. On fol. 440rb, l. 40 the abbreviation mark over the *t* can just be recognised in the MS., and on fol. 441rb, l. 38 *languidis* can be read.

DESCRIPTION OF THE MANUSCRIPT

Number	First words as in manuscript	Manuscript Folio	Eccard 1720	Grimm 1838 page	du Méril 1843 page	Fröhner 1859 page	Jaffé 1869 page	Piper 1898 page	Breul 1915 number	M.S.D. MSD¹ 1864	M.S.D. MSD³ 1892
1	Gratuletur omnis caro	432ra, l. 1	sub iv, 55-6	......	287-8	12	461 note	206	7	......	......
2	Melos cuncti	432ra, l. 7	sub iv, 56	......	288-9	12-15	461-2	206-7	15	......	......
3	Grates usie soluimus	432rb, l. 24	......	......	......	......	476-9	207-8	3	xix	xix
4	Inclito celorum	432va, l. 31	......	......	2-5	2-5	474-6	208-9	2	......	......
5	Omnis sonus cantilene	433ra, l. 19	......	......	279-80	6-10	470-1	209-10	24	......	xxiii
6	Qui principium constas	433va, l. 3	sub viii, 59	......	......	......	456-8	210-12	19	......	......
7	Nunc corda pange	433vb, l. 36	......	......	......	......	481-r	212-13	10	......	......
8	Iudex summe	434va, l. 1	sub iii, 55	......	286-7	......	460-1	213	14	......	......
9	Aurea personet lira	434vb, l. 6	......	......	278-9	10-12	490-1 and 560	213-4	31	......	......
10	Magnus cesar otto	434vb, l. 31	sub i, 54	......	273-5	......	a few corr. 451	214-5	12	xxii	xxii
11	Vite dator	435rb, l. 12	......	......	......	......	488-9	215-7	42	......	......
12	O pater optime	435ra, l. 33	......	......	......	......	479-80	217	1	......	......
13	Aduertite omnes	435vb, l. 29	......	......	275-6	5-6	472-4	217-8	22	xxi	xxi
14	Mendosam quam cantilenam	436rb, l. 10	sub vi, 57-8	......	276-8	15-17	471-2	218-9	25	xx	xx
15	O rex regum	436ra, l. 38	sub ii, 54-5	333-5	289-90	......	462-4	219	16	......	......
16	Lamentemur nostra	436rb, l. 38	......	......	285-6	......	458-9	219-20	13	......	......
17	Audax es, uir iuuenis	436rb, l. 40	50	......	[see*]	......	484-87	220-1	39	xviii	xviii
18	Nunc almus thero euuigero	437rb, l. 27	......	337-40	......	......	a few corr. 451	221-2	11	xxiii	xxiv
19	Est unus locus	437va, l. 24	......	......	......	......	some notes 451	222-3	29	......	......
20	Diapente et diatesseron	437vb, l. 25	......	......	......	......	451	223	43	......	......
21	Salue, festa dies	437vb, l. 30	......	......	......	......	......	223	4	......	......
22	Vestibunt silue	438ra, l. 6	sub vii, 58	335-7	......	......	491-2	223	30	......	xxv
23	Heriger	438ra, l. 30	......	......	......	......	455-6	223-4	26	......	......
24	Sponso sponsa karissimo	438rb, l. 23	......	......	......	......	464-5	224	20	......	......
25	Emicat o quanta pietate	438va, l. 12	......	......	......	......	484	225	9	......	......
26	Iam dulcis amica	438vb, l. 25	......	......	......	......	see note 494	225-6	33	......	......
27	S..... ruonu fert	438vb, l. 15	......	......	......	......	494-5	226	35	......	......
28	Huc attolle genas	439ra, l. 9	......	......	......	......	467-9	226-8	46	......	......
29	Caute cane, cantor care	439rb, l. 1	......	......	......	......	......	228	23	......	......
30	O mihi deserte	439vb, l. 10	......	......	......	......	......	228-9	45	......	......
31	Huc attolle genas	439vb, l. 25	sub v, 56-7	......	......	......	see note 452	229	46	......	......
32	Qui habet uocem serenam	440ra, l. 7	......	......	......	......	......	229	17	......	......
33	Tempus erat, quo prima quies	440ra, l. 37	......	340-2	302-9	......	a few corr. 452	229-30	44	xxv	......
34	Quibus ludus est	440rb, l. 16	......	......	......	......	480-1	230-1	28	......	......
35	Templum Christi, uirgo casta	440va, l. 35	......	......	......	......	489-90	231	6	......	......
36	Ad mensam philosophie	440vb, l. 6	......	......	......	......	452-3	231	41	......	......
37	Salue, uite norma	440va, l. 14	......	......	......	......	453	231	47	......	......
38	V....	440vb, l. 24	......	......	......	......	492-3	231-2	37	......	......
39	Leuis exsurgit zephirus	441ra, l. 1	......	......	......	......	465-6	232	32	......	......
40	Gaudet polus, ridet tellus	441ra, l. 22	......	......	......	......	......	232	18	......	......
41	In gestis patrum ueterum	441rb, l. 15	......	......	189-90	......	469-70 and 560	232-3	27	......	......
42	Cordas tange, melos pange	441va, l. 1	......	......	......	......	466-7	233	21	......	......
43	Hec est clara dies	441va, l. 14	......	......	......	......	480	233	5	......	......
44	Rota modos arte	441va, l. 24	......	......	......	......	489	233	40	......	......
45	Miserarum est	441va, l. 32	......	......	......	......	......	233	38	......	......
46	Pulsat astra planctu magno	441vb, l. 3	......	......	......	......	481	233-4	8	......	......
47	O admirabile ueneris idolum	441vb, l. 16	......	......	240-1	......	493-4	234	34	......	......
48	Ven...	441vb, l. 35	......	......	......	......	495	234	36	......	......

As No. 28 and No. 31 are the same piece, there are in fact 47 songs and extracts. Of these 43 are well preserved, and 4 partly erased and obliterated. Of the 43 four are well-known extracts from classical Latin authors (Nos. 28, 30, [31], 33, 45), 39 are medieval poems. Of these 37 are in Latin and 2 are macaronic, a mixture of Latin and German. The numbers of the present edition refer to Chapter v, pages 42 sqq. See also the Alphabetical Index of the songs on pages 112-13.

* This song is reproduced in du Méril's second anthology (1847) on pages 6-7.

C. Survey of Contents and Metrical Forms

No principle of arrangement whatever is discernible in the order of the songs as they follow each other in the manuscript. The songs of the original song book seem to have been written down as they were collected by the goliard, and his song book was apparently copied out without any change being made in the sequence of the pieces which it contained. Paul Piper (in 1897) contented himself with a mere reprint of the poems in the order in which they appear in the manuscript, even reproducing all the marks of abbreviation. He counts two passages as separate items which belong to longer pieces preceding them and thus has 50 numbers.

Philipp Jaffé (who, in 1869, printed 35 of the 47 pieces, omitting only the extracts from the well-known Latin classics and some poems that had been well edited elsewhere, especially in Müllenhoff and Scherer's *Denkmäler*) departed from the order in which the poems appear in the Codex and arranged the collection (see *Zeitschrift für deutsches Alterthum*, XIV. 455) as follows: he assigned the first place to the historical songs, which he arranged chronologically (I–IX); after these he gave those on novelistic (X–XIV), religious (XV–XXII), and didactic subjects (XXIII–XXVI); finally he printed some poems on spring and love (XXVII–XXXIII), the last three of which are almost entirely erased and obliterated in the manuscript. He provided the songs, which in the manuscript are left without any headings, with suitable Latin titles, partly taken by him from previous editions and partly coined by himself.

In the present edition all the 47 pieces are printed. First a transliteration is given of every poem occurring in the manuscript (pp. 3–22). In this the abbreviations are written out in full, the supplied letters being printed in italics. These transliterations face the photographic reproductions of the pages of the manuscript. In Chapter V (pp. 42 sqq.) an attempt has been made to give the goliard's song book with the songs arranged in seven subdivisions and presented, as far as possible, in emended texts. The titles are mostly those given by Jaffé, different or new titles have been provided only in a few cases.

With regard to METRE and STYLE, it is clear that the 'Cambridge Songs' fall into three main groups. There are

(1) Poems composed in the form of Sequences. These had been developed in the monastery of St Gallen in connexion with the services of the Church, but had been subsequently utilized by the *clerici vagabundi* for the effective treatment of historical and even novelistic subjects. The sequences became of the very greatest importance for the elegant secular poetry of the eleventh and following centuries, in Latin and in the vernacular languages[1]. As instances of the various subjects treated in the form of sequences, the following

---

[1] See Paul von Winterfeld, *Die Dichterschule St Gallens und der Reichenau unter den Karolingern und Ottonen* (reprinted in his *Deutsche Dichter des lateinischen Mittelalters*, München, 1913, especially 413–22. See also Hermann Reich in his introduction to Winterfeld's book, pp. 94–96); W. P. Ker, *The Dark Ages*, London and Edinburgh, ²1911, pp. 220–1; Wilhelm Meyer, *Fragmenta Burana*, Berlin, 1901, pp. 171–4; Rudolf Kögel and Wilhelm Bruckner, in Paul's *Grundriss der germanischen Philologie*, ²II. 1 (1901), pp. 133 sqq., and R. Kögel, *Geschichte der deutschen Litteratur bis zum Ausgange des Mittelalters*, I. 2, 244–5, Strassburg, 1897. On the large number of such sequences that have come down to our times see Wilhelm Wilmanns in the *Zeitschrift für deutsches Alterthum*, XV (1872), 267 sqq. The importance of the sequences must, however, not be overestimated. A note of warning has justly been sounded by Philip Schuyler Allen in his article *Mediaeval Latin Lyrics* published in 'Modern Philology,' Vol. V. No. 3 (January 1908), pp. 427–9 and 457–8. Not a few of the Latin poems of the Xth and XIth centuries were not written in the elaborate form of sequences but were composed in light and popular stanzas.

poems may be mentioned: the *Modus qui et Carelmanninc* (religious, No. 2), the *Modus Ottinc* (political, No. 12), the *Modus Liebinc* (novelistic, No. 22), and the *Modus Florum* (novelistic, No. 25)[1]. What a difference between the subject-matter of the first and the last *modus*!

(2) Poems composed in popular metres, mostly rimed, counterparts of which are of frequent occurrence in the later German lyrics written either in Latin or in the vernacular. Instances of this style[2] are the amusing songs of *Herigêr* (No. 26), *Alfrâd* (No. 29), or, in the popular iambic metre of eight syllables, the humorous *Johannes presbiter* (No. 27), *Sacerdos et lupus* (No. 28), or the truly beautiful poem *Verna femine suspiria* (No. 32). There are also poems written in a popular manner in long trochaic lines of 15 syllables (with a break after the eighth), such as the graceful song to the nightingale (No. 31), or the song of joy composed by a lady at court on the recovery of her queen from an illness (No. 18), or again, though slightly modified in every fourth line, the lamentation of Rachel (No. 8).

(3) Poems written in dactylic hexameters (the extracts from Virgil and Statius, Nos. 43–45, and the poem in praise of Sancta Cecilia, No. 9); a processional hymn in distichs (No. 4), and two poems in the form of odes, one an interesting spring-song (No. 30), and the other a bad copy of a well-known Horatian ode (No. 38).

There is throughout the Cambridge collection an astonishing variety of subjects and metrical forms. It fully merits the attention that students of early medieval literature have paid it in an ever-increasing degree, and not merely for the sake of the historical and political songs which first attracted scholars.

CHAPTER III

The Work hitherto done on the 'Cambridge Songs' (1720–1914)

A. Editions and Discussions

For nearly 200 years our Cambridge collection has aroused the interest of scholars, and during the last century its more important songs have been studied with great care. In particular about fifteen poems, mainly historical and novelistic, some of which are only preserved in the Cambridge manuscript, have been investigated with unflagging zeal; and, above all, the oldest, or one of the oldest, of the historical songs, the fascinating and unique macaronic poem of uncertain date on Henry of Bavaria, has received attention. This has been included among the early German poems printed in nearly all the more important selections of Old German texts[3].

[1] On the term 'Modus' see Rudolf Kögel, *Geschichte der deutschen Litteratur bis zum Ausgange des Mittelalters*, I. 2, pp. 244–5, Strassburg, 1897; the same and Wilhelm Bruckner in Paul's *Grundriss d. germ. Phil.* [2]II. 1 (1901–9), p. 133; Wilhelm Hertz, *Spielmannsbuch*, 3rd ed., Stuttgart and Berlin, 1905, pp. 46–47; Philip Schuyler Allen, *l.c.* p. 458. The four Modi are given in Müllenhoff und Scherer's *Denkmäler*, Nos. XIX–XXII, and in this edition as Nos. 2, 12, 22, 25. On the metre and style of part of these poems see the full discussion by Karl Bartsch in his book on *Die lateinischen Sequenzen des Mittelalters*, Rostock, 1868 (before the publication of Jaffé's article), pp. 145–169.

[2] See Jac. Grimm in his *Lateinische Gedichte des x. und xi. Jahrhunderts*. Göttingen, 1838. Introd. pp. xliv sqq.

[3] See Wilhelm Wackernagel, *Altdeutsches Lesebuch*, Basel, [4]1861, pp. 109–12; Oscar Schade, *Altdeutsches Lesebuch*, Halle, 1862, pp. 60–61; Karl Goedeke, *Deutsche Dichtung im Mittelalter*, Dresden, [2]1871, p. 39; Karl Müllenhoff und Wilhelm Scherer, *Denkmäler deutscher Poesie und Prosa aus dem viii.–xii. Jahrhundert*, Berlin, [1]1864, [2]1873, [3]1892 (ed. Elias Steinmeyer), No. XVIII; Paul Piper, *Lesebuch des Althochdeutschen und Altsächsischen*, Paderborn, 1880, p. 189; Wilhelm Braune, *Althochdeutsches Lesebuch*, Halle, [1]1875, [7]1911 (with useful bibliographical

English, American and French scholars have co-operated with the Germans in many fruitful efforts in the way of publishing and elucidating the Cambridge poems, and in this praiseworthy emulation all alike have done excellent work. Among the large number of German scholars thus engaged we meet with the names of nearly all those learned men who during the last century did so much to start and develop a scientific study of the older German language and literature. Among them we find Jacob Grimm, Pertz, Lachmann, Haupt, Wackernagel, Uhland, Schade, Hoffmann von Fallersleben, Fröhner, Müllenhoff, Scherer, Jaffé, Bartsch, and, at a later time, Kögel and von Winterfeld, not to mention the large array of scholars of repute who are still with us. To these must be added the names of Wright, Kemble, and du Méril, whose contributions will be mentioned, each in its proper place, in the following pages.

While the majority of the scholars who edited and discussed certain numbers of the Cambridge collection were mainly interested in the historical and novelistic poems, and in the intricate metrical structure of those of them that were written in the form of Sequences, some paid special attention to certain remarkable erotic songs (viz. *Levis exsurgit Zephirus—Iam, dulcis amica, venito!—O admirabile Veneris idolum*—and the extensively erased macaronic dialogue between a monk and a nun). These are in some cases but imperfectly preserved in our 'Canterbury Book' and the text must be reconstructed, or at least improved, by comparison with some other early manuscripts containing the poem in a less mutilated form.

The first editor, who published nine important historical songs from the Codex Cantabrigiensis, was Johann Georg Eccard. They had been sent to him from Cambridge, but unfortunately he omits to say from whom they were received. Eccard[1], the author of a number of important antiquarian and historical works, who took a special interest in the history of the Salic emperors, published his *Veterum Monumentorum Quaternio* at Leipzig, in 1720. In this book he printed (under Nos. 3 and 4) nine historical songs, most of which related to some old German (Saxon or Franconian) emperors. This early edition, in spite of many imperfections, is nevertheless a work of considerable importance, as by means of it the attention of the learned world was first drawn to the interesting collection of songs that had been sung long ago upon the banks of the Lower and Middle Rhine and the unique copy of which had ultimately found a place of honour on the shelves of the Library of the University of Cambridge.

More than a hundred years, however, elapsed before the study of the 'Cambridge Songs' was taken up in earnest. In 1827 G. H. Pertz came to Cambridge[2] and examined, among

references). See also Hoffmann von Fallersleben's collection of macaronic poems under the title 'In dulci jubilo,' Hannover, ²1861, where it is printed after the text given by O. Schade in 1860. It is given the first place as being the earliest poem of this kind in German literature that has come down to our times. See *In dulci iubilo*, pp. 3 sqq., 27–29, and O. Schade, *Veterum monumentorum theotiscorum decas*, Vimariae [1860], pp. 5–8.

[1] On Eccard see the *Allgemeine deutsche Biographie*, Vol. v. 627–31, especially p. 630; and also Rudolf von Raumer, in his *Geschichte der germanischen Philologie*, München, 1870, pp. 168–73, especially p. 172. Johann Georg Eckhart used to spell his name Eccard before he was ennobled, after which time he printed it Johann Georg von Eckhart (1674–1730). His chief work is his *Commentarii de rebus Franciae orientalis et episcopatus Wirceburgensis*, 2 Vols, 1729. It only goes down to the time of King Konrad I and Bishop Dietho of Würzburg. Eccard died before he was able to complete it. He was specially interested in the poems 11–17.

[2] Pertz's own account of his visit to Cambridge was printed in the *Archiv für ältere deutsche Geschichtskunde*, Vol. vii (1839), pp. 1002–3 and makes interesting reading. In the introductory pages 16–17 Pertz says that he (together with Mr Richard Price) was in Cambridge in 1827 and, on the kind invitation of Mr Thomas Shelford, tutor of Corpus Christi College, stayed at Corpus from June 26 till July 13, during which time he examined the manuscripts of the University Library, Corpus Christi College, Trinity College, Caius College, Jesus College and Clare Hall.

THE WORK DONE UPON THE CAMBRIDGE SONGS

many other manuscripts, the bulky Codex Gg. 5. 35, which contains the songs. He noted down the beginnings of all the songs and also copied a number of them in full, which last he indicated in his list by printing their beginnings in italics. These were intended by him for later use in editing the *Monumenta Germaniae historica*, for which great work Pertz was then engaged in collecting material in many German and foreign libraries. The account of his extensive travels (including his visit to Cambridge) was not published until 1839, and no poems from the Cambridge collection were ever printed by Pertz himself. But he seems to have allowed other scholars to see and make use of the copies of Cambridge poems made by him; at least in 1829 Lachmann[1] printed the 'Modus Liebinc' and the 'Modus Ottinc' in a masterly reconstruction of their original form, for which a copy of the manuscript other than Eccard's had been made use of. In 1830 Wackernagel gave a much improved form of the poem 'De Heinrico[2],' in which, however, the division of the song into stanzas of four and three long lines each still remained unnoticed. This shortcoming of Wackernagel's text was subsequently (in 1833) set right by Lachmann, who also recognised that the song was a *Leich*[3]. Soon afterwards two more poems were published from the Cambridge manuscript, viz. the humorous pieces 'Alfrâd' (No. 29 of the present edition) and 'Sacerdos et Lupus' (No. 28)[4], which raised the number of the pieces that were easily accessible for study in 1838 from nine to eleven.

In the forties of the last century fourteen of the poems were published and annotated by du Méril in two of his valuable anthologies of Early Medieval Latin poetry[5], and in 1859 Fröhner reprinted and fully discussed six of them (all of which had previously been published) in an interesting essay contributed to Haupt's *Zeitschrift für deutsches Alterthum*[6]. Eight, mostly merry tales of a novelistic character, but not a single love-song, were edited, in 1864, in critical texts and with very valuable notes (by Wilhelm Scherer) in the first issue

---

[1] Karl Lachmann, *Über die Leiche der deutschen Dichter des zwölften und dreizehnten Jahrhunderts*, in the 'Rheinisches Museum,' edited by Niebuhr and Brandis, Vol. III (1829), pp. 430-3. Reprinted in Lachmann's *Kleinere Schriften zur deutschen Philologie* (ed. Karl Müllenhoff), Berlin, I (1876), 335-9.

[2] Wilhelm Wackernagel's reconstruction first appeared in Heinrich Hoffmann's *Fundgruben für Geschichte deutscher Sprache und Litteratur*, I (Breslau, 1830), 340-1, and afterwards (1861) in his Old German Reader.

[3] Karl Lachmann, 'Über Singen und Sagen,' a paper read in the Berlin Akademie der Wissenschaften on Nov. 26, 1833. First printed, in the *Abhandlungen der Berliner Akademie für das Jahr* 1833, in 1835. Reprinted in the *Kleinere Schriften*, on pp. 461 sqq. See *ib.* p. 464. Lachmann's reconstruction of the poem was printed in R. A. Köpke's *Jahrbücher des deutschen Reiches unter der Herrschaft König Ottos I*, Berlin, 1838, on p. 97.

[4] In 1836 by Moriz Haupt, in his *Altdeutsche Blätter*, Leipzig, 1836, pp. 390-4, who was able to use a copy of two poems ('Heriger' and 'Alverad') that had been sent to him by Thomas Wright; and in 1838 by Jacob Grimm, in the *Lateinische Gedichte des x. und xi. Jahrhunderts* (edited jointly by Jacob Grimm and Andreas Schmeller, Göttingen, 1838), who had received fresh copies of four of the Cambridge poems from his devoted pupil and friend J. M. Kemble. See p. 343 of Grimm's book, in which the poems are printed on pp. 333-42, with the addition of some notes on pp. 343-5. The poems were: 'In obitum Heinrici II,' 'Heriger,' 'Alveradae asina,' 'Sacerdos et Lupus.' Grimm's introduction to this edition is still worth reading.

[5] Edélestand du Méril, *Poésies populaires latines antérieures au douzième siècle*, Paris, 1843, and, subsequently, *Poésies populaires latines du moyen-âge*, Paris, 1847; in the former du Méril also published, from another source, two poems (our Nos. 27, 31) that are likewise found in the Cambridge collection. See the lists given on p. 27.

[6] Christian W. Fröhner, 'Zur mittellateinischen Hofdichtung,' in Haupt's *Zeitschrift für deutsches Alterthum*, XI (1859), 1-24. The poems given by him are: 'Modus qui et Carelmanninc,' 'Modus Florum,' 'In Heribertum,' 'In obitum Heinrici II,' 'In Conradum Salicum,' 'In coronationem Heinrici III.' See p. 27. Fröhner emended Eccard's text in many cases and called special attention to the frequent use of alliteration in these poems.

of Müllenhoff and Scherer's remarkable collection of all the minor Early German literary documents[1].

The collection was not made known to the learned world in its entirety until the year 1869, when Philipp Jaffé, who had visited Cambridge and had made fresh copies of all the poems, published his most valuable article on 'Die Cambridger Lieder' in Volume XIV of Haupt's *Zeitschrift*[2]. In this article all the poems of the Cambridge manuscript that had so far not been printed were given in critical and mainly trustworthy texts. Many faulty readings of the Codex were corrected by Jaffé (the manuscript readings being in nearly all cases indicated in foot-notes), and as much of the partially erased pieces was printed as he had been able to decipher in September 1868. Jaffé gave 35 numbers, viz. 30 poems entire, two small pieces printed in his preliminary enumeration of the contents of the manuscript, and finally the fragments of the three partially erased poems. He omitted the poems that had already been well edited in the *Denkmäler*, and also the four extracts from the ancient Latin classics, but corrected a few erroneous readings in the former, and these corrections were soon afterwards (in 1873) utilized by Scherer in the second edition of the *Denkmäler*.

When, in the autumn of 1884, I came to reside at Cambridge, my attention was soon given to two treasures of our University Library, the 'Cambridge Songs,' and the equally unique 'Culemann fragments' of the Middle Netherlandish *Reinaert*, which early print was the immediate source of the Middle Low German *Reinke de Vos*[3]. With regard to the Songs I was anxious to learn whether, by prolonged effort, it might not be possible to make out in some cases more than Jaffé had been able to do in 1868, and to suggest any further corrections in the texts as printed by this most careful scholar. It was my wish in this way to make a useful contribution to the third edition of the *Denkmäler*, the earliest preparations for which were then just being made. Thus, in the spring of 1885, the songs were partly collated with Jaffé's text and partly copied afresh. Henry Bradshaw, whose memory will always live in my heart, took the kindliest interest in my work[4], but would not consent to my use of a chemical reagent which I hoped might enable me to read some of the obliterated passages. All the collations, copies and tracings were, in May 1885, sent by me to Wilhelm Scherer, who, finding himself unable to undertake the editing of the new edition of the *Denkmäler*, passed them on to

---

[1] Karl Müllenhoff und Wilhelm Scherer, *Denkmäler deutscher Poesie und Prosa aus dem viii.-xii. Jahrhundert* (abbreviated *M.S.D.* or *Denkm.*), Berlin, 1864, ²1873, ³1892. See p. 27. The eight poems were 'De Heinrico,' 'Modus qui et Carelmanninc,' 'Modus Florum,' 'Modus Liebinc,' 'Modus Ottinc,' 'Alfrâd,' 'Heriger,' and 'Sacerdos et Lupus.' The last of these was omitted from the two later editions, as being a tale probably not of German but of French origin. It was replaced by the poem 'De Lantfrido et Cobbone.' Karl Bartsch, *l.c.*, based his valuable observations on the texts of the first edition of the *Denkmäler* and of Fröhner.

[2] Ph. Jaffé, 'Die Cambridger Lieder,' in Haupt's *Zeitschrift f. d. Alterthum* XIV (1869), 449-95 and 560.

[3] See Friedrich Prien, in Paul and Braune's *Beiträge zur Geschichte der deutschen Sprache und Literatur*, Vol. VIII (1880), 8 sqq., his edition of *Reinke de Vos*, Halle, 1887, Introd. pp. xii-xiii and pp. 267-73, and my article 'Zu den Cambridger Reinaertfragmenten' in Paul and Braune's *Beiträge*, Vol. XIV (1886), 377-8.

[4] Jaffé had already dedicated the offprints of his article to Henry Bradshaw, and I feel a special pleasure in gratefully dedicating this book to the two kind and ever helpful Librarians of our University Library who have invariably and most generously placed their time and knowledge at the disposal of all scholars working at the valuable manuscripts under their charge, and who have taken a special interest in the 'Canterbury Book,' as our Codex Gg. 5. 35 is sometimes called. On Bradshaw see *Englische Studien*, X (1887), 211-14 and XIII (1889), 162-3.

Elias Steinmeyer[1], while the main results of my modest gleanings after Jaffé's rich harvest were published by me in Volume XXX of Haupt's *Zeitschrift*[2].

In 1896 Robert Priebsch gave a fresh account of the manuscript (with special reference to the portion containing the songs) in the first volume of his excellent work on *Deutsche Handschriften in England*[3]. Priebsch had spent some time at Cambridge early in 1894.

The last contribution to the study of the Cambridge collection as a whole was made in the following year (1897), when Paul Piper, in his *Nachträge zur älteren deutschen Literatur*, printed a literal transcript of all the poems without any omission and in the exact order in which they are given on folios 432–41 of the manuscript[4].

Only a very few of the scholars who have written about the Cambridge collection, or about individual songs, or passages from the songs, contained in it, have themselves set eyes on the manuscript. In the case of most of the poems this matters little, and Jaffé's and Piper's reprints are generally sufficient for purposes of ordinary study. With regard, however, to some of the partially erased poems and to certain lines that have become illegible by the effacement of important letters, reference to the manuscript itself, side by side with an absolutely trustworthy transcript, becomes of the very greatest importance. This remark applies with special force to the two macaronic poems of the collection, the oldest of their kind in German literature, both of which have come down to us only in the Codex Cantabrigiensis. Here the correct reading of certain obliterated lines and letters and accurate information about the space once occupied by certain words and letters is most important. In the case of the contested passage in 'De Heinrico[5]' it is a curious fact that the reading *bruother hera kuniglich*, as first printed by Eccard in 1720, was never doubted (either by Pertz, or even by Jaffé) until 1885, when I informed Scherer by letter, enclosing a tracing, that only brı was legible at the end of one line (fol. 437rb, l. 36). This information was passed on by him to Steinmeyer, who was the first to propose the reading *bringit her* instead of *bruother*. See *Denkmäler* II, 106. Nearly all the scholars who since that time have discussed this important passage and suggested emendations of it, have done so without consulting the manuscript.

The only English scholars who have copied songs from this part of the manuscript are the unknown transmitter to Eccard of the nine historical songs[6], and also Wright and Kemble[7]. So far

---

[1] They were fully utilized by Steinmeyer for the third edition of the *Denkmäler* (Berlin, 1892). See his notes to the individual songs in Volume II.

[2] Karl Breul, 'Zu den Cambridger Liedern,' in Haupt's *Zeitschrift für deutsches Alterthum*, Vol. XXX (1886), 186–92. See also my note on l. 7 of 'De Heinrico' in the *Anzeiger für deutsches Alterthum*, XXIV (1898), 59, and the article originally published by me, in March 1898, in *The Modern Quarterly of Language and Literature*, I. 1, which is now reprinted, with various alterations and additions, on pp. 102-11 of this book.

[3] See Chapter II p. 21. To his careful description Priebsch added a few illuminating pages on the contested passage in 'De Heinrico' (see also his note in the *Anzeiger f. d. Alterthum* XX (1894), 207 before the publication of his book). The many speculations and special investigations concerning the poem between 1885 and 1914 cannot be enumerated in this place, but the necessary bibliographical references are given in full in Chapter VII.

[4] Piper's reprints of the 'Cambridge Songs' (in Vol. 162 of Kürschner's *Deutsche National-Literatur*) are not always trustworthy, as unfortunately his very short stay at Cambridge obliged him to do his work in a very limited time (Dec. 25 and 26, 1895). Wherever my transcript differs from his, reference to the photographic facsimile will show the reason of the discrepancy. For Piper's reprint of the Wolfenbüttel MS. see p. 36, note 1.

[5] About this passage see Chapter VII pp. 102 sqq.   [6] See pp. 30 and 105, note 2.

[7] See p. 31, note 4. In the *Altdeutsche Blätter* I (1836), 394 Haupt says: 'Wir verdanken die Mitteilung dieser Lieder der zuvorkommenden Güte des Herrn Thomas Wright in London, der sie aus einer Handschrift

as I know, the only German scholars, who have closely examined the part of the manuscript that contains the songs, are Pertz (in 1827), Jaffé (1868), Breul (1885–), Priebsch (1894), and Piper (1895).

B. Photographic Reproductions

If autopsy of the manuscript is impossible, good photographic reproductions may render the greatest assistance. Only a few poems, or passages from poems, have so far been made generally accessible by means of photographic reproductions, and these are all poems or passages the reading of which presents no difficulty. They are merely specimens of the neat and clear handwriting that is characteristic of the whole collection[1].

C. Translations

Apart from the renderings, in prose, of a few songs or passages from the songs, in critical articles or in histories of literature, and apart from translations of the extracts culled from the ancient Latin classics, only a few verse translations of certain poems have so far been made in spite of the undoubted literary merit of at least a dozen of them. They do not seem to be sufficiently well known outside of the small circle of specialists. Renderings have been made by Symonds, Allen, Heyne, Traube, Müller-Fraureuth, von Winterfeld, Schubiger, Pflüger, Simrock[2]. It is hoped that the present edition of this earliest Latin Song book, made up from various sources by a versatile Rhenish goliard, may tempt some congenial spirit, after the lapse of nearly 900 years, to render *con amore* in one of the modern vernaculars all such of the old Cambridge songs as are of undoubted literary value and of abiding human interest.

der öffentlichen Bibliothek zu Cambridge abgeschrieben hat.' John Mitchell Kemble, 'the recognised exponent of the investigations of Jacob Grimm' (see the *Dictionary of National Biography*, XXX, 371), copied the poems in the University Library and entered a few observations, signed J. M. K., in a clear hand. See p. 24, note 1.

[1] Ludwig Traube reproduced the Cambridge (and the Vatican) manuscript of 'O admirabile Veneris idolum' (No. 34; see the note to this poem on p. 92). Friedrich Vogt (in the illustrated *Geschichte der deutschen Literatur von den ältesten Zeiten bis zur Gegenwart*, written by him and Max Koch, Leipzig) gives on p. 56 of the first volume (^{3}1910) the latter half of 'De Heinrico' (fol. 437va, ll. 1–23, our No. 11), thus omitting the more interesting first portion containing the contested lines. Anselm Salzer, in his *Illustrierte Geschichte der deutschen Literatur von den ältesten Zeiten bis zur Gegenwart*, München, no date [1912], Vol. I. 100–101, gives specimens of two poems (our Nos. 31 and 39), which are all easy reading. Photographic facsimiles of the important beginning of 'De Heinrico,' including the contested passage, were sent by me privately, at the end of 1902, as Christmas cards to a number of *Germanisten*, whom I knew to be interested in the poem. I also sent (in 1895), at his request, several photographs of fol. 437^r to H. Meyer at Göttingen. See *Niederd. Jahrbuch*, XXIII, 74 and *HZ*. 47, 434. Reproductions (with neumes) of two manuscripts of *Invitatio amice* (No. 33) and of the beginning of the *Modus Ottinc* (No. 12) were given by E. de Coussemaker, *Histoire de l'harmonie au moyen-âge*. See p. 92.

[2] John Addington Symonds, *Wine, Women and Song*. Mediæval Latin Students' Songs, now first translated into English verse, with an essay, by J. A. S., London, 1884, ^{2}1907. Reprinted, as No. 35, in the series 'The King's Classics,' London, 1907. Has only one Cambridge poem (No. 33). Mostly translations from the *Carmina Burana*. Philip Schuyler Allen gives a few renderings in his articles in *Modern Philology*, III. V. Moritz Heyne, *Altdeutsch-lateinische Spielmannsgedichte des 10. Jahrhunderts. Für Liebhaber des deutschen Altertums übertragen*, Göttingen, 1900. Ludwig Traube translated 'O admirabile Veneris idolum' in his fine article which bears the title 'O Roma nobilis,' 'Philologische Untersuchungen aus dem Mittelalter.' München, 1891. See p. 92. Carl Müller-Fraureuth, *Die deutschen Lügendichtungen bis auf Münchhausen*, Halle, 1881. Paul von Winterfeld, *Deutsche Dichter des lateinischen Mittelalters in deutschen Versen*, München, 1913. P. Anselm Schubiger, *Die Sängerschule St Gallens vom achten bis zum zwölften Jahrhundert*, Einsiedeln und New York, 1858. W. Pflüger, *Wipo. Das Leben Kaiser Konrad II*, Leipzig, ^{2}1888. Karl Simrock, *Lauda Sion*, Stuttgart, ^{2}1868.

CHAPTER IV

Medieval Latin Lyrics in Germany and the 'Cambridge Songs'

During five centuries of the Middle Ages, Latin poetry claims a place in German literature[1]. From the ninth to the thirteenth century a considerable body of such poetry, epic, lyric, and dramatic, was produced by Germans on German soil; much also was imported by them from France and Italy, and ministered to the enjoyment of courts and monasteries beside works of native growth. Among the examples of this poetry the Collection which is now preserved at Cambridge holds a place of honour.

In the great mass of Latin literature produced in Germany during these centuries four periods may roughly be distinguished, of which the second is best represented by the 'Cambridge Songs'. The earliest is mainly represented by the *Carolingian Court Poetry*, which flourished at the end of the eighth and during part of the ninth century. The Latin productions of the scholars and literary men who grouped themselves round the great Charles are mainly learned in character and, on the whole, of little originality. No real popular lyrics in the German tongue have come down to our times from this period, although there is little doubt that such lyrics must have been in existence. The Latin lyrics, of which a considerable number have been preserved and published[2], are on the whole imitations of ancient classical poetry, the playful productions of learned men who skilfully, but somewhat coldly, made use of the traditional classical forms and whose work was of but little national interest. Certainly the verses of these courtiers and scholars are less important for the development of German literature than the productions of some gifted writers in the next period.

The second period is the time in which the new Medieval Renaissance in Germany reached its climax. It was at its height under the Ottos in the second half of the tenth[3], and extended into the first third of the eleventh, century, when, with the death of the first Salic emperor (Konrad II, † 1039), Latin ceased to be generally understood in good society and at the courts of Germany, and when, at least for a time, the Latin songs of the gifted but often very disorderly members of the *familia Goliae*, the 'Goliards' or *clerici vagabundi*, found more restricted and less favourably disposed audiences[4]. While, during the period of the Saxon

---

[1] The Latin literature of modern times, beginning with the xvith century, the productions of men like Hutten, Hessus, Frischlin, Naogeorg, Balde, and others, does not come within the compass of this discussion. They belong to the modern Renaissance Movement in Germany. The purpose of the present chapter is merely to assign, very briefly, to the 'Cambridge Songs' their proper place within the large number of lyrics that were written in Germany up to the middle of the xiiith century. For a full discussion of medieval Latin literature to 1000 A.D., see Adolf Ebert, *Allgemeine Geschichte der Literatur des Mittelalters im Abendlande*, Leipzig, 3 vols., ²I, 1889; II, 1880; III, 1887.

[2] See *Poetae aevi Carolini*, Vols. I–IV. 1, 1880–1899, edited most ably by Ernst Dümmler, Ludwig Traube, and Paul von Winterfeld. See also A. Ebert, *l.c.* Vol. II (1880). Some poems of this early time have been well translated by Paul von Winterfeld. See also Philip Schuyler Allen in *Modern Philology*, v. 3 (January, 1901), 463 sqq.

[3] See F. A. Specht, *Geschichte des Unterrichtswesens in Deutschland*, Stuttgart, 1885, and W. Wattenbach, *Deutschlands Geschichtsquellen im Mittelalter bis zur Mitte des xiii. Jahrhunderts*, 2 vols., Berlin, ⁶1893–4.

[4] About the goliards and goliardic poetry, see W. Giesebrecht, 'Die Vaganten oder Goliarden und ihre Lieder' (an article published in the *Allgemeine Monatschrift für Wissenschaft und Litteratur*, Braunschweig, 1853). With regard to this fundamental article see Ph. Schuyler Allen, in *Modern Philology*, v (1908), 444 sqq.; also *ibid.* VI (1909), 400 sqq. See also O. Hubatsch, *Die lateinischen Vagantenlieder des Mittelalters*, Görlitz, 1870; Ludwig Laistner, *Golias, Studentenlieder des Mittelalters*, Stuttgart, 1879 (Introduction, and pp. 97–99); Wilhelm Hertz,

Ottos, we do not yet meet upon German soil with any true lyrics written in the vernacular, yet many Latin poems are obviously full of the true German spirit; and in the earliest macaronic poems, which were probably composed in the second half of the tenth century, the vernacular is mixed with the Latin. Instead of the quantitative and rimeless metres of the ancient classical writers of Rome and their Carolingian imitators we now find rhythmical and often rimed lyrics of great beauty, and the Cambridge Collection, which almost alone has preserved these early poems for us, represents the springtime of modern accentual lyric poetry in Germany[1]. The poems, although written in easy and polished Latin, are original, natural, and not infrequently remind the reader of the heartfelt strains of true popular poetry. Several indeed of the 'Cambridge Songs' may be considered as direct forerunners of the early Minnesong[2]. The importance of the new literary type of the sequences for the poetry of this period is very great. The peculiar style of the sequence made for originality of form and expression; it broke away from all recognised patterns of classical antiquity, and before long this form of poetry, that had been invented and studiously developed within the Church and for poetry connected with its services, was successfully adapted by the *clerici vagabundi* for the artistic treatment of every kind of secular subject[3]. This is clearly seen in the 'Cambridge Songs[4].' During this period not only did lyrics written in Latin abound in Germany, but epic poetry also, represented by the *Waltharius*, the *Ruodlieb*, and the *Ecbasis cuiusdam captivi*, flourished by their side, while somewhat earlier the nun Hrotsvith of Gandersheim, a relative of the

Spielmannsbuch, Stuttgart-Berlin, ³1905, pp. 4-5; Anton Schönbach, 'Fahrende Kleriker' (in *Sitzungsberichte der Wiener Akademie*, Philos.-Histor. Kl., XLII. 84-89); Wilhelm Gundlach, *Barbarossa-Lieder*, Innsbruck, 1899, pp. 770 sqq. The goliards should be distinguished from the mimes. On the mimes see Ph. Schuyler Allen in *Modern Philology*, VII (1910), 329-44 and VIII (1910), 1-60. The best explanation of the term 'goliard' is that given by Gaston Paris in the *Bibliothèque de l'École des Chartes*, Vol. L (1889), 258-60; see also John M. Manly, 'Familia Goliae' in *Modern Philology*, V (1907), 201-9. That goliards were found as early as the tenth century is clear from a sentence of condemnation passed on certain French *clerici ribaldi maxime qui vulgo dicuntur de familia Goliae* (Labbe's *Concilia*, IX. 578, quoted in Thomas Wright's Introduction to the *Latin Poems commonly ascribed to Walter Mapes*, London, 1841, p. xiii. note).

[1] The songs are mainly preserved in two manuscripts, one at Wolfenbüttel and the other at Cambridge. The Wolfenbüttel manuscript (W), which may be slightly older than the Codex Cantabrigiensis (C), contains nothing that is not also found in C. It only gives 4 poems, and the names of their interesting melodies, as against the 47 pieces of the Cambridge Collection. Even after the 4 extracts from the ancient classical writers have been deducted, C still contains more than 40 specimens of early medieval Latin poetry. As to their subjects see Chapter V. The poems from the Wolfenbüttel manuscript were first made known by Friedrich Adolf Ebert (in the *Überlieferungen zur Geschichte, Literatur und Kunst der Vor- und Mitwelt*, I. 1, pp. 72-82, Dresden, 1826) under the title 'Alte lateinische Volkslieder der Deutschen.' These were the 'Modus qui et Carelmanninc' (pp. 77-79); 'Modus Florum' (pp. 79-80); 'Modus Liebinc' (pp. 80-81); 'Modus Ottinc' (pp. 81-82). They were printed by Ebert as prose 'in diplomatisch treuer Abschrift und mit der Interpunktion des Originals.' The poems are without any musical notation except the first 3 lines of the 'Modus Ottinc.' The four 'Modi' were reprinted, from a copy taken by himself and another collation by Alfred Holder, by Paul Piper, on pp. 234-7 of his *Nachträge zur älteren deutschen Litteratur*. A few other poems of the Cambridge collection are met with (sometimes in a better state of preservation) in one other early manuscript, while some of the most important are not found anywhere else. See Chapter VI.

[2] See Chapter V pp. 40 and 63-4.

[3] See W. Meyer, *Fragmenta Burana*, p. 174. But Meyer somewhat overstates his case and fails to attach sufficient importance to another kind of lyrics in our Collection, which is altogether free from any influence of the sequence but is simple and popular, obviously inspired by popular poetry in the vernacular which is now lost to us. See also Paul v. Winterfeld, *l.c.* p. 489, and Ph. Schuyler Allen in *Modern Philology*, V, 429 and VI, 403.

[4] See Nos. 2, 12, 22, and 25 of our Collection, in which No. 2 represents the original type of the sequence, and No. 25 shows to what an extent the new form was used for the treatment of amusing secular subjects.

Emperor Otto I, wrote for the edification of her contemporaries her short and effective Latin dramas[1]. These are, however, earlier than most of the Cambridge Songs.

The third period of early Latin lyrics in Germany produced at least one singer of true genius, of whose real name we are ignorant, but who called himself, and was called by his contemporaries, the 'Arch-poet,' *Archipoeta*[2]. He was a *clericus vagabundus* and wrote, among other brilliant pieces, the famous 'Confession of a Goliard,' which he addressed to his jovial and indulgent patron, Reginald of Dassel, Barbarossa's great chancellor, subsequently Archbishop of Cologne. The Archipoeta sang many of his spirited songs on Italian soil in the presence of the Chancellor, and at least one before Frederic the Redbeard[3]. His poems were written about the same time at which there burst forth from every corner of South and Middle Germany the graceful songs of the early Minnesinger (second half of the twelfth century), and it is worthy of note that the great Staufer Frederic not only listened readily to the Latin songs of this goliard, but also lent a willing ear to the German lays composed by a noble singer of the Rhine district, Friderich von Hûsen. Hûsen was not only a Minnesinger of repute, but a gallant knight, and, moreover, a personal friend of the emperor. He took part in the Crusade of 1189 and went with Barbarossa's host to the Holy Land, where he was killed on May 6, 1190, only a few weeks before the aged emperor himself perished in the icy currents of the river Saleph[4].

The fourth and last period represents the rich summer and full bloom of Medieval Latin lyric poetry in Germany, which is illustrated by the important collection of the *Carmina Burana*, compiled in Bavaria about 1225. Parallel with it runs the splendid development of the German Minnesong, the greatest representative of which, Walther von der Vogelweide, probably died at or near Würzburg, about 1228. After the first third of the thirteenth century there is a decline in both kinds of lyric poetry in Germany. Like the 'Cambridge Songs,' the *Carmina*

---

[1] See Paul von Winterfeld, *l.c.* pp. 103 sqq. He also edited her dramas (Berlin, 1902). For a full bibliography see Max Manitius, *Geschichte der lateinischen Literatur des Mittelalters*, Vol. I. § 107, pp. 619-32, München, 1911.

[2] See Jacob Grimm, 'Gedichte des Mittelalters auf König Friedrich I, den Staufer, und aus seiner sowie der nächstfolgenden Zeit' (Address read to the Berlin Academy in 1843, and reprinted, not without many mistakes in the text of the poems, in J. Grimm's *Kleinere Schriften*, Vol. III pp. 13-35, 49-73). See also L. Laistner, *Golias*, Introd. pp. xiii-xiv, and pp. 10 sqq.; 103 sqq., where an excellent rendering of the spirited 'Confessio Goliae' is given, P. v. Winterfeld, *l.c.* pp. 29, 120, 124 sqq., the literary references given by Ph. Schuyler Allen in *Modern Philology*, V (1908), p. 446, n. 3, and now especially B. Schmeidler's article 'Zum Archipoeta' in *Historische Vierteljahrschrift*, XIV (1911), 367-95, in which the latest literature on the subject is given and where mistakes of previous writers are corrected. See also B. Schmeidler, *Die Gedichte des Archipoeta übersetzt und erläutert*. Leipzig, 1911; capital renderings of the nine principal poems (written between 1161-64), with good introduction and notes. The excellent article by W. Meyer on the somewhat older famous French goliard 'Die Oxforder Gedichte des Primas (des Magister Hugo von Orleans)' in the *Nachrichten von der Kgl. Ges. d. Wiss. zu Göttingen*, 1907, pp. 75-175, also contains good notes on the German Archipoeta (on pp. 88, 170-2). See also W. Gundlach, *l.c.* pp. 773-89. At this same time the poetry of the Troubadours flourished in the valleys of Provence. The authorship of the lyrics ascribed to Walter Map (a born Welshman) is exceedingly doubtful. See Th. Wright, *Latin Poems commonly ascribed to Walter Mapes*, London, 1841, and Sir John Sandys, in the *Cambridge History of English Literature*, I (1907), 189 and 191. The famous lines 'Meum est propositum in taberna mori,' sometimes ascribed to Map, belong to the 'Archipoeta,' who wrote the 'Confessio Goliae' at Pavia, of which remarkable poem they form part.

[3] See J. Grimm, *Kl. Schriften*, III. 66-70; P. v. Winterfeld, *l.c.* pp. 126-8; and Schmeidler's transl. pp. 38 sqq.

[4] See the references given in Karl Lachmann and Moriz Haupt, *Des Minnesangs Frühling* (*M.F.*) (last edition, largely re-written, 1911, by Friedrich Vogt), No. IX pp. 42-58; 322-32. In *M.F.* all the poetry of Hûsen that has come down to our times is printed in critically edited texts. A few of his poems have been translated by Frank Nicholson, *Old German Love Songs*, London, 1907, pp. 17-21; and by J. Bithell, *The Minnesingers*, London, 1909, pp. 27-30.

Burana[1] are an international collection in which are contained Latin songs composed by French and Italian goliards as well as a considerable number evidently written in Germany by German vagrant clerks. It is by far the largest and most varied collection of Medieval Latin lyrics made on German soil[2]. Many of the poems contained in it go back to the twelfth century or to even earlier times[3]. One piece is in part found among the 'Cambridge Songs[4].' In this interesting manuscript, the contents of which are written by more than six different scribes, many early German lyrics stand side by side on the same folio with Latin songs; and, as in the Cambridge Codex, there are several macaronic songs, usually of a loose and erotic character. In wit and elegance of diction these gifted, learned and light-hearted goliards are worthy rivals of the knightly Troubadours and Minnesingers, and many of their spirited songs, so full of the exuberant joy of life, are to-day as fresh and as irresistibly charming as they were when they were first sung, seven hundred years ago, on the high-roads and in green meadows, at banquets in the monasteries and before large gatherings at the courts of bishops and princes.

The large Beuern Collection is a systematic compilation, drawn from many sources, like the great Minnesinger manuscripts that were compiled in South Germany or Switzerland at a somewhat later date. After the compilation of the manuscript of the *Carmina Burana* there was an end to the general vogue of this kind of poetry, although Latin songs and macaronic ditties were never quite absent from German literature, even in its later periods.

CHAPTER V

The Goliard's Song Book

In the following pages an attempt is made to group the pieces of the Codex Cantabrigiensis in a systematic way and thus to make of the older and shorter Cambridge collection a similarly well-arranged song book to that so carefully made by the compilers of the *Carmina Burana*. In order to represent the whole of the *répertoire* of our goliard[5], the few short and well-known extracts from Horace, Virgil and Statius which figure in it have not been rejected (as they were by Jaffé), but will be found inserted in their proper places among the later pieces. The poems are printed in this chapter in improved texts for which, first and foremost,

---

[1] They were first edited (at Jacob Grimm's suggestion) by J. A. Schmeller (from the celebrated manuscript that was originally the property of the Benedictine Monastery of Beuern (Benediktbeuern) in the Bavarian highlands, now preserved in the Royal Library at Munich) under the title *Carmina Burana*, Breslau, 1847, ²1883, ⁴1904. Some lost portions of this collection, on 7 scattered and mutilated leaves, were subsequently discovered and published by Wilhelm Meyer as *Fragmenta Burana*, Berlin, 1901 (with 15 plates). Meyer added to this important publication a valuable introduction, partly reprinted in his *Gesammelte Abhandlungen zur mittellateinischen Rythmik*, I (1905), 1–58. Many poems from the *Carmina Burana* were well translated into English by John Addington Symonds in *Wine, Women and Song*, 1884 (see p. 34, note 2), and into German by Ludwig Laistner in his *Golias*, Stuttgart, 1879. See also Bernhard Lundius, 'Deutsche Vagantenlieder in den C. B.' in *Zs. f. d. Phil.*, Vol. 39 (1907), 330–493.

[2] The Zürich MS. (ed. by Jakob Werner, *Beiträge zur lateinischen Literatur des Mittelalters.* Aarau, ²1905) cannot be called a German collection as it was compiled in France, and the Herdringen MS. (published by A. Bömer in Haupt's *Zs. f. d. A.*, Vol. 49 (1908), 161–238), written at Liège, is also largely drawn from French sources.

[3] See Wilhelm Meyer, *Fragmenta Burana*, p. 17.

[4] See the note to No. 41 ('De mensa Philosophie') of the 'Cambridge Songs,' p. 97.

[5] It cannot be proved beyond doubt, but it seems very probable that the collection really was a song book and a commonplace book compiled by a *clericus vagabundus*.

THE GOLIARD'S SONG BOOK

Jaffé's excellent article in Haupt's *Zeitschrift* has been used throughout. The third edition of Müllenhoff and Scherer's *Denkmäler*, and various publications by du Méril, Meyer, Traube, v. Winterfeld, Schröder, Dreves, and others, have also been laid under contribution. The actual readings of the manuscript can in all cases be ascertained by referring to pages 3-22. Fuller information will be found in each case in the bibliographical references of the next chapter.

The principle according to which the pieces have been grouped in the present chapter is as follows. The 47 pieces fall into seven sub-divisions containing (*a*) religious (10); (*b*) historical and personal (11); (*c*) novelistic and humorous poems (8); (*d*) poems on spring and love (9, four of which are partly erased); (*e*) didactic (5); (*f*) classical (3, and one put under 'love'); (*g*) some unconnected lines that appear to be nothing but metrical experiments.

It is clear that in the ten folios of the Codex Cantabrigiensis we possess a unique collection of early medieval poems, nearly all written in Latin, which language at that time was equally well known at the courts and in the monasteries. It comprises many different specimens of the smaller literary *genres*, whether of German or foreign origin, that would be of interest whether to laity or clergy living on the banks of the middle and lower Rhine in the first half of the eleventh century. Men and women, old and young, scholars and politicians, soldiers and hunters, the grave and the frivolous—all were sure to find in this collection some pieces to interest them, and the versatile goliard would at all times know how to select from his rich and varied stock just the songs that would appeal most to the tastes of his very heterogeneous audiences. These he would find at the courts of the Emperors and of the princes and prelates of the Rhineland, in large and in humble religious foundations, at banquets and social gatherings where the wandering minstrel, the bringer of interesting news and the singer of stirring and of facetious songs, was always sure of a welcome.

The collection includes songs on *religious* subjects, such as praises of Christ and Mary, praises of patron saints and pious inmates of religious houses, and songs hailing the approach of some great festival day of the Church. There are not a few *historical* and *personal* poems referring to memorable events that had occurred during the second half of the tenth and the first half of the eleventh century, the principal figures being Saxon and Franconian Emperors and several Rhenish Archbishops; there is also a simple and heartfelt poem of rejoicing at the recovery of a beloved queen, probably composed by a lettered lady at court. These are all poems of genuine German growth, and the date or place of their original composition is in most cases clearly traceable; in one case (No. 17) we even know the name of the author[1]. There is a considerable number of poems in which *novelistic* and *humorous* themes are treated, the subjects of some of which were foreign in origin and of greater antiquity than the songs of the previous class. Several well-known novelistic subjects are met with for the first time in German literature among the Latin songs of our Cambridge collection, although some of them may claim either Italy or France as the land of their origin. The story of the snow-child, the tale of the two devoted friends, the legend of the luckless youth who made a compact with the devil in order to win the hand of the girl he loved, and who nevertheless was ultimately saved from the clutches of the evil one, the amusing account of good Bishop Heriger's close examination of an impudent braggart who asserted that he had visited heaven and hell, the jesting tale of a cunning Swabian arch-liar, some amusing anecdotes of priests, hermits and nuns, the humorous story of a parish priest and a wolf—such songs were at all times certain to delight large audiences, and were, moreover, probably set to attractive

[1] We also know the names of the authors of the poems No. 4, 7, 27 and 31.

melodies[1]. Some *contemplative* and *didactic* poems for the older and more sedate are not wanting in the collection. These include poems on music and philosophy. Some very *pathetic* extracts from the epics of Virgil and Statius show what kinds of passages from the ancient classical writers of Rome appealed most to the taste of the courtiers and noble ladies during the height of the new Medieval Renaissance movement in Germany. Finally, there are not wanting songs dealing with the charms of spring, the sweet voice of the nightingale, the love-longing of a lonely maiden, the tempting invitation of a lover to his mistress to come to a feast at his well-appointed house, and other erotic songs, some of which, however, were subsequently blacked with an infusion of galls and partly erased by the austere brotherhood who owned the manuscript and evidently felt strong objections to such wanton and frivolous songs.

These Latin love-poems, in rhythmical and rimed stanzas of simple and musical structure, are a clear proof that in the early eleventh century poems existed and were sung along the banks of the Rhine which in style and spirit are the forerunners of those which about 200 years later are met with in the *Carmina Burana*, and to some extent also in the German songs of *Minnesangs Frühling*[2]. In two cases the text is provided with neum-accents. Two poems are written in macaronic style—half Latin and half German, these being the oldest specimens of this remarkable style in German literature[3]. Along with them must be grouped the much-discussed short love-greeting from *Ruodlieb*[4]. One of the two macaronic poems of our collection is a political ballad in the form of a 'leich'; the other, almost entirely erased and most effectively blacked, is nothing less than a dialogue between a cleric and a nun who, however, apparently rejected the amorous pleadings of the monk. Of the poems written in Latin only, some have the conventional and polished form of the ancient classical metres (hexameters, elegiacs, Horatian odes); others, the subject-matter of which varies very considerably, exhibit the elaborate metrical system of sequences; while others again are composed in popular accentual metres with the modern embellishment of rime. See pages 28–9.

Our *clericus vagabundus*, during his wanderings from place to place in the pleasant country round the Rhine and the Moselle, may have drawn on his storehouse of songs and poems somewhat in the following way:

[1] See the interesting account given by the satiric poet Sextus Amarcius who wrote about 1046, probably at Speier on the Rhine. Amarcius mentions the subjects of four poems that were sung by a mime before a Rhenish audience, and no less than three of these songs (Nos. 22, 31, 41) are actually found among the songs of the Cambridge Collection. Cp. *Sexti Amarcii Galli Piosistrati Sermonum libri IV*, ed. Max. Manitius, Leipzig, 1888. The interesting description of the arrival of the mime (*mimus*, l. 428; *iocator*, l. 424) and the delivery of his songs is given in Book I especially in ll. 424-43; Wilhelm Scherer, *Geschichte der deutschen Dichtung im xi. und xii. Jahrhundert*, Strassburg, 1875, p. 16; Paul v. Winterfeld, *Deutsche Dichter des lateinischen Mittelalters*, München, 1913, pp. 490-1; Ludwig Traube in the *Anzeiger für deutsches Alterthum*, XV (1889), 200.

[2] See p. 36 and the able articles of Ph. Schuyler Allen in Vols. III and V of *Modern Philology*.

[3] On the macaronic poetry in German literature see Hoffmann von Fallersleben, *In dulci jubilo*, Hannover, ²1861, the valuable supplementary article by Johannes Bolte, also called 'In dulci jubilo,' and contributed by him to the *Festgabe an Karl Weinhold*, Leipzig, 1896, pp. 91 sqq., and Emil Henrici, *Sprachmischung in älterer Dichtung Deutschlands*, Berlin, 1913. See also the general remarks made on this kind of poetry by Edélestand du Méril, *Poésies populaires latines antérieures au douzième siècle*, Paris, 1843, pp. 100-2.

[4] The love-greeting of a noble lady is given in Müllenhoff and Scherer's *Denkmäler* as No. XXVIII. Cp. the notes in Vol. II of the third edition (1892). See also the discussion of it in H. Paul's *Grundriss der germanischen Philologie*, ²II. 1, 138 (by R. Kögel); R. Kögel, *Altdeutsche Literatur*, I. 2, 139 and 398. K. Liersch, in Haupt's *Zeitschrift für deutsches Alterthum*, Vol. 36 (1892), 154 sqq.; see the well-considered remarks, directed against him, of Ph. Schuyler Allen in *Modern Philology*, V. 3 (Jan. 1908), 435-6. A photographic facsimile of the love-greeting may be found in E. Petzet and O. Glauning, *Deutsche Schrifttafeln des ix. bis xvi. Jahrhunderts*, II Abteilung, München, 1911, Tafel 16, a.

Arriving at the court of a great prince the goliard would either judiciously select, according to circumstances, some joyous song such as the one on the coronation of a new emperor (No. 15): *Melos cuncti concinnantes*; or would impart or repeat the sad news of the premature death of the same well-beloved emperor by reciting some stanzas of Wipo's doleful nenia (No. 17): *Qui habet vocem serenam*; or, finding himself among friends and adherents of the late Duke Henry of Bavaria, he would extol his merits and the great honour shown him by the emperor himself by reciting the old macaronic ballad on the meeting of Henry and the emperor (No. 11): *Nunc almus assis filius thero euuigero thiernun!* At a certain religious foundation of nuns, the patron-saint of which was Saint Cecilia, he would sing (No. 9): *Emicat o quanta pietate Cecilia sancta!* while, before a bishop, he might choose the fine sequence on the life of our Lord which was set to the popular melody called the 'Modus qui et Carelmanninc' (No. 2): *Inclito celorum laus sit digna deo!* Among the jovial brotherhood of a monastery he would in a spirited manner recite after dinner some amusing tale such as the story of the snow-child, the famous 'Modus Liebinc' (No. 22): *Advertite, omnes populi, ridiculum!* or the humorous tale of the silly young monk who wished to become an angel (No. 27): *In vitis patrum veterum*, or of the priest and the wolf (No. 28): *Quibus ludus est in animo*, or of Sister Alfrad and her she-ass (No. 29): *Est unus locus Hôinburh dictus*. Leaving the monastery and proceeding once more to a great court, the goliard would entertain a large audience of lords and ladies with the marvellous story of the two staunch friends, Lantfrid and Cobbo (No. 24): *Omnis sonus cantilene*, or of the love-sick youth who in despair promised his soul to the foul fiend in order to win the fair daughter of Proterius (No. 23): *Caute cane, cantor care*. He would make a party of hunters[1] roar over the excellent 'Modus Florum' (No. 25): *Mendosam quam cantilenam ago*, while some of the grave scholars who heard him would be entertained by his praise of Dame Musica (No. 40): *Rota modos arte personemus musica*, or of the generous hostess, Philosophy (No. 41): *Ad mensam Philosophie sitientes currite!* or would nod approval to his alphabetical song of admonition to the light-hearted and careless youth (No. 39): *Audax es, vir juvenis*. Finding himself surrounded by a crowd of miscellaneous listeners, he would select the generally acceptable story of good Bishop Heriger of Mayence and the tramp who said that he had visited heaven and hell (No. 26): *Herigêr, urbis Maguntiensis antistes*. At the approach of spring he was sure to delight his youthful audiences with songs on the charms of re-awakening nature, such as (No. 30): *Vestiunt silve tenera merorem*, or on the sweet note of the nightingale (No. 31): *Aurea personet lira clara modulamina*. He would thrill the maidens' hearts with the recital of the song of passionate vernal longing (No. 32): *Levis exsurgit Zephirus*, in which some inmates of nunneries might well find their own feelings forcibly expressed; and he would please young men and women alike by the graceful delivery of the tempting invitation to a dinner *à deux* sent by a wealthy youth to his beloved mistress (No. 33): *Iam, dulcis amica, venito!* These and many other songs would be sung by the versatile goliard, each at the proper time and in the proper place; and that he did not forget to make the necessary appeal to the generosity of his noble listeners is shown by the conclusion of the 'Modus Ottinc' (No. 12): *Magnus cesar Otto quem hic modus refert in nomine* (lines 61–62).

What a wealth of themes and what a variety of metrical and musical forms are contained in this unique Song book of an early goliard which stands so full of promise at the threshold of Medieval German lyric poetry!

[1] Probably originally composed for the amusement of the youthful pupils of a monastery school. See page 85.

CARMINA IN CODICE CANTABRIGIENSI SCRIPTA

1. CARMEN CHRISTO DICTUM

1 O pater optime, sancto regnans pneumate, cunctos plectro tibimet laudes dulce canentes serva semper.
2 Qui in cruce latronem exaudisti pendentem atque spondens, lucide sedis amenitatem ut acciperet.
3 Spolia mundi qui maledicti liberasti a penis; atque ferocem vinclo leonem colligasti manibus, ne sub fraude perderet quod formavit dextera, Adam Evam, denique plebem locasti orto lucido.
4 Tertia die resurrexisti maiestate tumulo, teque iubente corpora multa surrexere baratro, ut tua facta proderent non credenti populo; ex hoc signo trepidans valde miser Pilatus se planctu cruciat.
5 Post hec mundum illuxisti, duces genti apposuisti; ascendisti, unde venisti, dextera patris, o rex, residens.
6 Pena malis ecce parata, flamma picis indeficiens; ac cernentes, mala tenentes, id sine fine post hec retinent.
7 Vitam mundi accipientes, prelucentes in paradiso, spe gaudentes, bona tenentes, semper in evum laudant dominum.
8 Regnanti gloria Christo, laus per secula, qui chordarum sonitu pangitur, deus perhennis, rector mundi.

2. MODUS QUI ET CARELMANNINC

Inclito celorum   laus sit digna deo.

Qui, celo scandens, soli regna
visitavit; redempturus hominem,
maligni seductum   suasione vermis.
Quem, quis qualis quantus quid sit,   5
ratione gestiens rimari
inmensum quem scias,   benignum, potentem.
Patris verbum caro factum,
mundi lumen tenebras superans,
puellam regalem   matrem fecit Mariam.   10
Castam intrans, carnem sumpsit,
qui peccati maculam non novit;
ut unus regnaret,   factus homo, deus.

Joseph iustus quem accepit,
angelico doctus verbo,   15
regem regum   agnovit maximum.
angelus pastorum   monstrat gregi deum.
Celum torquens, astra regens,
involutus pannis, plorans
rusticorum   tecmina pannorum   20
pertulit, qui cuncta   potestate protulit.

Quem Herodes, regno timens,
instrumentis bellorum quesivit
perdendum, hunc magi   munere querebant.
Stella duxit quos fidelis,   25
donec puer erat ubi contulit.
intrantes dederunt   munera supplices.

Monstrant auro regem esse,
presulem designant thure,
mirram signum tumuli   tribuere domino.   30
Hunc Iohannes baptizavit
unda pulchri Iordanis,
et vox patris natum iussit   exaudiri populis.

Hic clara   natus matri dedit signa,
celorum   demonstrat se fore deum.   35
aqua suam   gaudens mutat naturam,
et convivis unda mitis   versa vinum placuit.
Lazarum   terre tenebris conclusum
amissum   sumere precepit flatum,
ut qui seva   committat piacula,   40
dum laborat emendando,   mortis surgat tumulo.
Iuvenem,   quem reliquit vite flamen,
dum turba   urbe portat luctuosa,
surgere   iubet, mortis victa lege;
quo loquele det iniuste   hoc exemplum venie.   45
Puellam   vite lumine privatam
in domo   vite restauravit verbo:
cogitando   qui peccavit animo,
discat deo confiteri   tecta mente crimina.

Hic in cruce pendens,   50
quos creavit princeps regum, redemit.
inferni confregit vectem,   alligando principem.
Rex resurgens morte
victor fulget ascendendo, thronum
tenet, quo coronas sanctis   coronandis imponit.   55

Spiritum tunc sacrum,   sibi coeternum
nuncios transmisit   consolari bis senos,
quo linguis loquendo   gentibus non timidi
verba vite predicarent,   que Iudea sperneret.
Agmina celorum   gaudeant, quod incola,   60
quem gignebat virgo,   presidet in celo,
tincta veste de Bosra,   gentium redemptio,
terram polum ignem pontum   rex in pace componens,

Regnum cuius finem nescit,   sceptrum splendet nobile,
celo sedens, mundum implens,   factor facta continens.   65

3. LAUDES CHRISTO ACTE

Grates usie
solvimus supreme,
cui nihil accedit
neque recedit,
omnia continenti 5
non contento
invisibili domino.

Cuncta qui initio
creavit ex nihilo,
suam et hominem 10
formavit ad imaginem
vice dampnatorum
angelorum
sui ordinis decimi.

Hinc stimulatus, 15
serpens antiquus
suasit amarum
mandere pomum,
quo nos omnes
heu mortales 20
subiacemus dire mortis imperio.

Factor sed sue
condolens facture,
misit huc filium
sibi coeternum 25
tectum forma sub servili.

Virgo Maria
maris stella,
feta de celo
pneumate sancto, 30
edidit salo
tempestuoso
lucem sempiternam,
salvatorem Christum,
dominum sanctissimum. 35

Postquam innumera
fecit signa,
tolerat sputa,
alapas, flagella,
crucis inhonestam 40
patitur mortem,
ponitur in sepulchrum,
adit infernum,
frangit mortis imperium.

Tertia die 45
surgit a morte,
trahens microcosmum
ad semet ipsum,
scandit omnes
super celos. 50
nunc a dextris
sedet patris
altithroni.

Inde venturus,
potens est deus, 55
oves salvare,
hedos dampnare,
has in celis
gavisuras,
hos in penis 60
luituros
pro meritis.

Non longo post cum discipulis,
in conclavi congregatis,
spiritus etherea 65
imbuit aula
pectora beatorum
individue trinitatis fidelium.

Qui pergentes predicabant:
pater, natus, 70
sanctus spiritus,
simplex usia
personis distincta
est unus
hic deus, 75
temporis expers,
non sumens
matre principium.

Unum baptisma,
fides et una, 80
deus et hominum
pater cunctorum,
qui super omnes
est potentes
exaltatus 85
et benedictus
in secula.

Hinc vos omnes
precor fideles:
mecum eternum 90
psallite deum,
sono tantum
non chordarum,
sed canoro
iubilo. 95

Quo nos omnes
se laudantes
semper salvet
et conservet
ad honorem sui 100
nominis incliti
hic et in eterna
maiestatis triumphali potentia.

Nunc o summi
cives celi 105
nec non sancti
vos prophete et bis seni
principales apostoli,
martires, confessores,
virgines omnes, 110
adiuvate nos precibus.

Sit prepotenti
laus creatori,
patri, filio,
pneumati sancto 115
nunc et in eternum,
sempiterna
creature letitia.

4. HYMNUS PASCHALIS

1 Salve, festa dies, toto venerabilis evo,
   Qua Deus infernum vicit et astra tenet.
     Salve, festa dies, toto venerabilis evo.
2 Ecce, renascentis testatur gratia mundi
   Omnia cum domino dona redisse suo.
     Qua Deus infernum vicit et astra tenet.
3 Namque triumphanti post tristia tartara Christo
   Undique fronde nemus, gramina flore favent.
     Salve, festa dies, toto venerabilis evo.
4 Legibus inferni oppressis super astra meantem
   Laudant rite Deum lux, polus, arva, fretum.
     Qua Deus infernum vicit et astra tenet.
5 Qui crucifixus erat, Deus, ecce, per omnia regnat
   Dantque creatori cuncta creata precem.
     Salve, festa dies, toto venerabilis evo.

5. RESURRECTIO

Hec est clara dies, clararum clara dierum;
hec est sancta dies, sanctarum sancta dierum;
nobile nobilium rutilans diadema dierum.
Quid est hoc tam dure, quod in vestro manet pectore, amarumque ducitis animum?
'De Iesu nobis est dure, manet in nos mors eius, et ipsa mors est incognita.
Nostre quedam abiere sepulturam invisere. celi cives illum vivum dicunt iam regnare.'
   Salve, festa dies, salve resurrectio sancta,
   Salve semper, ave; lux hodierna vale!

6. AD MARIAM

1 Templum Christi, virgo casta, felix mater o Maria,   cuius clausa ventris porta nove vite ianua;
    patris sanctique spiritus gratia   petimus, valida prece nos expia ab omni macula facinorosa.
2 Tu regina celi summa, castitatis tenes sceptra;   angelorum satis digna congaudet frequentia.
    quibus nos, exoramus, socia,   qui vivis cum patre spirituque sancto per eterna secula.

7. DE EPIPHANIA

Gratuletur omnis caro
Christo nato domino,
Qui pro culpa protoplasti
Carnem nostram induit,
Ut salvaret, quod plasmavit
Dei sapientia.

8. RACHEL

1 Pulsat astra planctu magno Rachel, plorans pignora,
queriturque consolari, quos necavit improba;
dolet, plangit, crines scindit ob sororis crimina.
    uxor sine macula,   casta servans viscera.
2 Felix virgo, deo cara et dilecta femina,
circumcirca volitando filiorum pascua
querit, lustrat, perscrutatur per diversa climata,
    an sit ovis perdita   digna spondens premia.
3 Splendor eius splendor solis mane dantis lumina,
sic lunaris candor idem foret inter sidera
....
....

9. DE DOMO S. CECILIE COLONIENSI

Emicat o quanta pietate Cecilia sancta
inter odoriferas, Christus quas prospicit, herbas.
despiciens mundum, meruit sibi iungere Iesum,
gaudia sic thalami conculcans Valeriani.
hec sibi virgineas quathra virtute choreas   5
fultas elegit, quas hic sapientia compsit.
luce chorum clara docilis hunc prenitet Uuoda;
hanc Meginbergis sequitur, valitudine fortis;
hoc viret in circo Merehilt cum flore decoro,
nomine difficili, sophie sed spe iuvenili   10
hinc tenet Una locum mitis collega priorum.

10. DE S. VICTORE CARMEN XANTENSE

Nunc chorda pange
melos devote
filio sancte
virginis Marie.
honor et vita, 5
salus et letitia,
pax inremota,
altitudo inclita,
lux permansura,
laus indeficua 10
sancto sit cuncta
Victori per secula.

Ave, recolende
Victor et amande,
semper in evum 15
honor Sanctensium.

Tibi nunc canoris
modulemur chordis,
certior quo tua
nobis sit gratia, 20
sis et intercessor
fortis et adiutor,
tutela fidelis.

Sit benedictus
pater eternus, 25
qui te in sortem
sublimavit propriam,
militibus adhibitis
triginta trecentis,
teque ductorem 30
mitem ac principem
misericordem
fecit atque humilem,
preces ut tuorum
audias servorum, 35
quoties tuam
implorent clementiam,
hic et ubique
Victor invictissime.

Sitque colendus 40
summi dei filius,
missus a patre
incarnatus virgine;
qui moriendo
vivere nos fecit 45
ac resurgendo
resurgere precepit,
et te longinqua
misit huc de patria,
noster ut fautor 50
sis et intercessor,
fidus et in iudicio
dux in districto,
cum nil indiscussum
nec erit absconsum. 55

Sit venerandus spiritus
iugiter paraclitus,
cuius iam vigore
florent undique,
qui tecum dira 60
sumpserunt tormenta
trinitatis munere
et luce scientie;
qui in eterno
beatorum regno 65
virginis agnum
laudent in evum.

Victor, athleta
dei, divinam
iugiter gratiam 70
pro nobis ora
miseris, una quo deitas
ac veneranda trinitas
in corde crescat
nostro et floreat 75
et ut valeamus
sub presens curriculum
cernere Christum
in terra viventium.

Mundi redemptor, 80
spes et protector,
nate Marie
virginis alme!

Sit tibi summa
angelorum gloria, 85

qui patri coeternus
vivus et verus
pneumate cum sancto
regnas in celo,
laus seculorum 90
nunc et in evum.

11. DE HEINRICO

1 Nunc almus assis filius   thero êuuigero thiernun
   benignus fautor mihi,   thaz ig iz côsan muozi
   de quodam duce,   themo hêron Heinrîche,
   qui cum dignitate   thero Beiaro rîche beuuarode.

2 Intrans nempe nuntius,   then keisar manoda her thus: 5
   'cur sedes,' infit, 'Otdo,   ther unsar keisar guodo?
   hic adest Heinrîch,   bringit her hera kuniglîch,
   dignum tibi .....   fore thir selvemo ze sîne.'

3 Tunc surrexit Otdo,   ther unsar keisar guodo,
   perrexit illi obviam   inde vilo manig man   10
   et excepit illum   mid mihilon êron.

4 Primitus quoque dixit: 'uuillicumo Heinrîch,
   ambo vos equivoci,   bêthiu goda endi mî:
   nec non et sotii,   uuillicumo sîd gî mî.'

5 Dato responso   fane Heinrîche sô scôno   15
   coniunxere manus.   her leida ina in thaz godes hûs:
   petierunt ambo   thero godes genâtheno.

6 Oramine facto   intfieg ina aver Otdo,
   duxit in concilium   mit michelon êron
   et commisit illi   sô uuaz sô her thâr hafode,   20
   preter quod regale,   thes thir Heinrîh ni gerade.

7 Tunc stetit al thiu sprakha   sub firmo Heinrîche:
   quicquid Otdo fecit,   al geried iz Heinrîh:
   quicquid ac omisit,   ouch geried iz Heinrîhc.

8 Hic non fuit ullus   (thes hafon ig guoda fulleist   25
   nobilibus ac liberis,   thaz thid allaz uuâr is);
   cui non fecisset Heinrîch   allero rehto gilîch.

12. MODUS OTTINC

1 Magnus cesar Otto,
quem hic modus refert in nomine,
Ottinc dictus, quadam nocte
membra sua dum collocat,
palatium casu subito inflammatur. 5
Stant ministri, tremunt,
timent dormientem attingere,
et chordarum pulsu facto
excitatum salvificant,
et domini nomen carmini inponebant. 10

2 Excitatus spes suis surrexit,
timor magnus adversis mox venturus:
nam tum fama volitat
Ungarios signa in eum extulisse.
    Iuxta litus sedebant armati, 15
urbes agros villas vastant late:
matres plorant filios
et filii matres undique exulari.

3 'Ecquis ego,' dixerat
Otto, 'videor Parthis? 20
diu diu milites
tardos moneo frustra.
dum ego demoror, crescit clades semper:
ergo moras rumpite
et Parthicis mecum hostibus obviate.' 25
Dux Cuonrât intrepidus,
quo non fortior alter,
'miles,' inquit, 'pereat
quem hoc terreat bellum.
arma induite: armis instant hostes. 30
ipse ego signifer
effudero primus sanguinem inimicum.'

4 His incensi bella fremunt,
arma poscunt, hostes vocant,
signa secuntur, tubis canunt: 35
clamor passim oritur,
et milibus centum Teutones inmiscentur.
Pauci cedunt, plures cadunt:
Francus instat, Parthus fugit:
vulgus exangue undis obstat: 40
Licus rubens sanguine
Danubio cladem Parthicam ostendebat.

5 Parva manu cesis Parthis,
ante et post sepe victor,
conmunem cunctis movens luctum, 45
nomen, regnum, optimos
hereditans mores filio obdormivit.
    Adolescens post hunc Otto
imperabat annis multis,
Cesar iustus clemens fortis. 50
unum modo defuit:
nam inclitis raro preliis triumphabat.
    Eius autem clara proles,
Otto decus iuventutis
ut fortis ita felix erat: 55
arma quos nunquam militum
domuerant, fama nominis satis vicit.
    Bello fortis, pace potens,
in utroque tamen mitis,
inter triumphos, bella, pacem 60
semper suos pauperes
respexerat: inde pauperum pater fertur.

6 Finem modo demus,
ne forte notemur
ingenii culpa 65
tantorum virtutes
ultra quicquam deterere,
quas denique Maro inclitus vix equaret.

13. NENIA DE MORTUO HEINRICO II IMPERATORE

1 Lamentemur nostra, socii, peccata;
  lamentemur et ploremus; quare tacemus?
  Pro iniquitate corruimus late;
  scimus celi hinc offensum regem inmensum.
  Heinrico requiem, rex Christe, dona perhennem!   5

2 Non fuimus digni munere insigni.
  Munus dico sive donum Heinricum bonum,
  qui ex iuventute magne fuit vite.
  Procreatus regum stirpe rexit et ipse.
  Heinrico......

3 Orbis erat pignus, regno fuit dignus;   10
  imperator Romanorum, rector Francorum,
  imperabat Suevis, Saxonibus cunctis,
  Bauvaro truces Sclavos fecit pacatos.
  Heinrico......

4 Possumus mirari de domino tali:
  res tractando laicatus fit litteratus,   15
  prudens in sermone, providus opere,
  viduarum tutor bonus, orphanis pius.
  Heinrico......

5 Heinricus secundus— plangat illum mundus—
  fines servans christianos pellit paganos;
  stravit adversantes pacem persequentes;   20
  voluptati contradixit, sobrie vixit.
  Heinrico......

6 Quis cesar tam largus fuit pauperibus?
  quis tam laute sublimavit atque ditavit
  atria sanctorum ubere bonorum?
  Ex propriis fecit magnum episcopatum.   25
  Heinrico......

7 Ploret hunc Europa iam decapitata.
  Advocatum Roma ploret; Christum exoret,
  ut sibi fidelem prestet seniorem;
  recognoscat grave dampnum ecclesiarum.
  Heinrico......

8 Dicamus Heinrico, domini amico: 30
  ut quiescat post obitum semper in evum.
  Dicat omnis clerus anime illius:
  'In pace Christi quiescat; gaudia noscat.'
  Heinrico requiem, rex Christe, dona perhennem!

14. NENIA IN FUNEBREM POMPAM HEINRICI II IMPERATORIS

1. Iudex summe, medie rationis et infime,
magne rector celi, pie redemptor seculi!
   Imperatoris Heinrici catholici magni ac pacifici
beatifica animam, Christe!

2. Qui, heu, paucis annis rexit summa imperii,
sciens modum iuris rebus cunctis mediocris;
   Imperatoris......

3. Vultu claro monstravit cordis clementiam,
clerum, populum pro posse semper letificans;
   Imperatoris......

4. Summo nisu catholicas auxit ecclesias,
subvenit pupillis clemens et viduis.
   Imperatoris......

5. Gentes suo plurimas sepius imperio subdit barbaricas;
hostes civiles strennue animi consilio vicit, non gladio.
   Imperatoris......

6. Iuvit domnum summa, iuvit et demissa regni potentia.
mundi gazas tribuit; sic celi divitiis uti promeruit.
   Imperatoris......

7. Heu o Roma cum Italia, caput mundi, quantum decus perdideras;
Heu o Franci, heu Bauuarii, vestrum damnum nulli constat incognitum!
Mons Bavonis nimis felix, serva Christo regi pignus intrepidum.
Hoc angelica poscit gloria, apostolicus poscit ordo prelucidus,
hoc eterna virgo Maria ad finem mundi poscit beari.
Dicant omnes, precor, fideles, regem regum nunc deprecantes:
   Imperatoris......

8. Audi mentis melos, ut rogamus, Athanatos;
sic te vocis nostre conlaudabunt simphonie.
   Imperatoris......

15. CANTILENA IN CONRADUM II FACTUM IMPERATOREM

1. Melos cuncti concinentes, gratiarum actiones solvimus illi, aciem qui nostre mentis roboravit ad cernendum summi patris coeternum verbum; per quod cuncta restaurantur et reguntur elementa, mira cuius bonitate atque dono salutem haurimus.

2. Voces laudis humane, curis carneis rauce, non divine maiestati tantum sufficiunt;

3. Que angelicam sibi militiam in excelsis psallere sanctam iussit simphoniam;

4. Nec non variam mundi discordiam semovendo concordare fecit armoniam;

5. Que imperium confirmando Romanum suos agnos fonte lotos a luporum morsibus pia pace custodivit.

6 Hos Cuonradus pius, unctus domini, iam defendit imperando;

7 Quem providentia dei preclara predestinavit et elegit regere gentes strennue Davidis exemplo Messieque triumpho.

8 Ortus avorum stemmate regum per iunioris gradus etatis proficiebat regiis moribus et factis, ut probavit eventus.

9 Tiro fortis et fidelis, passus plures mundi labores, propinquorum causas et amicorum haud secus quam suas desideravit cunctis viribus iuvare pro possibilitate.

10 Pater ut suum nutrit natum, nunc adolando nunc flagellando, tempestates mundi per varias Christus hunc probavit, ut didicisset prona pietatis scala condescendere reis.

11 Post Heinrici mortem omni deflendam gregi catholicorum
Hunc rex regum fidum ecclesiarum iussit fore patronum.

12 Hunc Romani principatus cuncti mox elegere sibi defensorem et propugnatorem fortem orthodoxorum.

13 Gaudent omnes circumquaque gentes, gratias Christo dantes, qui viduarum atque pupillorum audit voces suorum.

14 Age, gaude Roma, urbium domna, cum consensu cleri devoto te Cuonradi precepto subdi; qui non tantum suas sed affective omnium subditorum querit utilitates.

15 Ad haec publicarum principes rerum et private dediti vite, iure tenti familiari, vitam et salutem imperatori nostro poscite Cuonrado, christo dei electo.

16 Laus sit regi seculorum, patri, nato, pneumati sancto, cui soli manet imperium, honor et potestas, quem angelorum laudes hominum et voces laudant rite per evum.

16. CANTILENA IN HEINRICUM III ANNO 1028 REGEM CORONATUM

1 O rex regum, qui solus in evum
regnas in celis, Heinricum nobis
serva in terris ab inimicis,

2 quem voluisti tibi benedici
et coronari ad Aquasgrani 5
manu Piligrimi presulis archi;
O rex......

3 quem Romani atque fidi Franci,
clerus et populus Christo dicatus
post Cuonradum adoptant domnum.
O rex......

4 Dic Italia, dic pia Gallia 10
cum Germania deo devota:
"Vivat Cuonradus atque Heinricus!"
O rex......

5 agni ut sponsa pace quieta
servari suo valeat sponso,
Deo eterno vivo et vero. 15
O rex......

6 Gaudent omnes Christi fideles,
senes et iuvenes, matres, infantes:
regnat Cuonradus atque Heinricus.
O rex......

7 Die, qua surrexit, qui mundum redemit,
regni monarchiam accepit sanctam 20
pius Cuonradus; gaudeat mundus.
O rex......

8 Post unius anni recursus
accepit sanctam regni coronam
puer Heinricus Christo electus.
O rex......

9 Die predicto   a Piligrimo   25
    archiepiscopo   sibi devotissimo,
    gaudente clero   simul et populo.
       O rex......

10 Doleat antiquus   gentis inimicus
    sanctas ecclesias   pacificatas
    vivo Cuonrado   atque Heinrico.   30
       O rex......

11 Mater Christi   cum civibus celi
    cunctisque sanctis   rectores orbis
    iuva Cuonradum   atque Heinricum,
       O rex......

12 ut ecclesiarum   causas sanctarum
    et pupillorum   ac viduarum   35
    valeant iusto   tractare iudicio.
       O rex......

13 Laus creatori,   angelorum regi,
    cuius imperium   manet in evum
    per infinita   seculorum secula.
       O rex......

17. NENIA DE MORTUO CONRADO II IMPERATORE

1 Qui habet vocem serenam   hanc proferat cantilenam
    de anno lamentabili   et damno ineffabili,
    pro quo dolet omnis homo   forinsecus et in domo,
    suspirat populus domnum   vigilando et per somnum:
    Rex deus, vivos tuere   et defunctis miserere!   5

2 Anno quoque millesimo   nono atque trigesimo
    de Christi nativitate   nobilitas ruit late,
    ruit Cesar caput mundi,   et cum illo plures summi,
    occubuit imperator   Kuonradus legum dator.
       Rex deus......

3 Eodem vero tempore   occasus fuit glorie,   10
    ruit stella matutina   Gunnild regina,
    [Heu quam crudelis annus   corruerat Herimannus]
    ⟨et⟩ filius imperatricis   dux timendus inimicis,
    ruit Kuono dux Francorum,   et pars magna ingenuorum.
       Rex deus......

4 Imperatoris gloria   sit nobis in memoria,
    ac frequenti mentione   vivat vir indolis bone,   15
    vivat dominator probus   et frequenti carmine novus,
    et preclara fama post mortem   vite prestet hunc consortem.
       Rex deus......

18. GRATULATIO REGINE A MORBO RECREATE

Gaudet polus, ridet tellus, iocundantur omnia;
angelorum sacra canunt in excelsis agmina,
quorum psallit imitatrix in terris ecclesia;
mundus plaudit et resultat letus de te, regina.
Ac haut minus gratulatur pulchra vernarum turma,   5
que, sub tuis alis fulta, digna tali domina:
incolumis gubernatrix quod tu, morbo soluta
et virtutum flore compta, restauraris in aula.
Ne mireris; deus iussit solvi morbi vincula
nexus mortis et ligare, ne fuisset dampnosa   10
tue vite optate, que nobis opus servata.
Te reginam nostram maris esse favet factura,
astra celi, flores humi, te cuncta creatura,
cuncti boni larga culminis es que tam aperta
mater dulcis, et que cunctis secli huius in scena   15
blandimentis non terrore sistis permitissima.
Monachorum ensis extas, clericorum domina,
consolamen viduarum, virginum constantia,
laicorum blandimenta clipeus et galea.
Quare posco, quo te crebra conservet per secula   20
deus, qui nonnulla semper scandit super sidera.

19. CANTILENA IN HERIBERTUM ARCHIEPISCOPUM COLONIENSEM

1 Qui principium constas rerum, fave nostris piis ceptis atque mentis plectrum rege, precamur, rex regum.
Pater, nate, spiritus sancte, te laudamus ore corde in huius vite siti fragilitate.

2 Inmortales celi cives, pia prece nos mortales, iam concives vestros, conmendate redemptori.
Pater......

3 Fidis chordis caute tentis, melos concinamus; partim tristes partim letas causas proclamantes de pastore pio ac patrono Heriberto.   Pater......

4 Quem etate iuvenili deus preelegit sibi, servum valde fidum bona super pauca, supra multa tandem ministrum constituendum.   Pater......

5 Mane etatis puer bone indolis sarculo verbi vinea Christi libens studuit; sciens sibi tandem denarii premia dari. scolis sublatus, fit cancellarius tertii Ottonis imperatoris. omnium morum speculum bonorum, placuit clero simul et populo, mitis atque pius, omni egenti largus census sui, tiro fortis Christi, pollens omni karitate, scandit dextram note viam Pithagorice.   Pater......

6 Post non magnum temporis curriculum, summo pontifice largiente, miles domini sublimari meruit in sedem pontificalem. tunc sibi subditus clerus et populus vivere patronum optant pium. cui Christus talem auxit honorem, ovis ut ovilis sibi conmissi—belli tempore longo—non pateretur pene damna rerum nec ullum excidium; sed summi pastoris, sub quiete congaudentes, vocem sanctam audierunt. Pater......

7 Circumquaque ministravit ecclesiis magno sumptu, tempestate bellicosa tunc temporis devastatis. severitatem facie tristem monstrans, letum toto corde sprevit mundum. pectore pio iugem compassionem gerit omni mala mundi patienti. Pater.....

8 Adventantes longe plures consolatur peregrinos, incessanter alimenta pauperibus erogavit, fovit infirmos atque vestivit nudos. munia divina complens rite cuncta, tantum vacans vite contemplative, sanxit cunctis se virtutum ornamentis. Pater......

9 Augens demum cumulum bonorum summa sanctitatis, erexit templum sancte dei genitrici speciosum, Rehni littore situm. in quo defunctam carnis sue sanctam iussit condere glebam, ut resurrectionis diem magnum ac tremendum hic secure expectaret. Pater......

10 Postquam mundus fuerat indignus tantum cernere domnum, Christus plura loco sue sepulture fecit signa, sui ad honorem nominis sancti, et ut magis sanctam confirmaret fidem: premia daturum se in celis propter eum hic in terris laboranti. Pater......

11 O cunctipotens mundum regens, finis rerum creatarum, omnem finem nostrum fac finiri in te solum! Pater......

20. ECCLESIE TREVIRENSIS NOMINE SCRIPTI AD POPPONEM ARCHIEPISCOPUM VERSUS

Sponso sponsa karissimo   se ipsam in coniugio,
ambosque diu vivere,   post celi culmen capere.
  Ne spernas, quod sim fragilis;   sum tamen satis habilis:
rugosam si me videas,   ut puellam me teneas.
Veni, veni, karissime!   Quod fusca sum, non despice,   5
dilapsa vel lateribus;   assurgam tuis viribus.
Hinc Petrus te huc invitat   et Eucharius uritat,
Valerius te exigit,   Maternus 'veni' concutit.
Cum Maximini precibus   se coniungit Agricius
orans, ut felix venias   et me fractam restituas.   10
Me quidem si restituis   turritamque reddideris,
Paulini adiutorium   habebis et Nicecium.
Hi et complures alii   nunc iubent me restitui;
Simeon tuus maxime   mandat murum iam ponere. —
O quam felix tu fueras,   quod hunc virum adduxeras,   15
qui me fuscam illuminat   et me fractam resolidat.
Quam libens hic te suscipit,   quam sanum esse precipit,
felicem omni tempore;   quod semper constet stabile. —
Vestrum amborum meritis   iterum ero Treveris
turrita in lateribus   et firma cunctis partibus.   20
Ad hoc te Deus muniat   et semper te custodiat
cum corpore ac anima   in sempiterna secula.   Amen.

21. DE WILLELMO

Chordas tange, melos pange cum lira sonabili;
tu magister eam liram fac sonare dulciter,
et tu cantor in sublime vocem tuam erige,
ambo simul adunati cantilene mistice.
O Uuillelme, decus pulchrum aspectu ornabili, 5
qui tam clarus permansisti cum tuis assidue.
O quis poterit iam esse tam potens in opere
preter reges, quos unxerunt antistites chrismate.
....
presules aut plures miror antistitum culmine.
Utriusque sexus namque viri atque femine 10
tam nobili creature se cupibant flectere.
Omnis chorus angelorum, zabulon subtrahite;
magne martir Iuliane, pro illo intercede!

22. MODUS LIEBINC

I a Advertite, omnes populi, ridiculum
et audite, quomodo
Suevum mulier et ipse illam defraudaret:

b Constantie civis Suevulus trans equora
gazam portans navibus 5
domi coniugem lascivam nimis relinquebat.

II a Vix remige triste secat mare,
ecce subito orta tempestate
furit pelagus, certant flamina, tolluntur fluctus:
post multaque exulem 10
vagum litore longinquo Nothus exponebat.

b Nec interim domi vacat coniux.
mimi aderant, iuvenes secuntur:
quos et inmemor viri exulis excepit gaudens,
atque nocte proxima 15
pregnans filium iniustum fudit iusto die.

III a Duobus volutis annis
exul dictus revertitur.
occurrit infida coniux
secum trahens puerulum. 20
datis osculis maritus illi:
'de quo,' inquit, 'puerum
istum habeas, dic, aut extrema patieris.'

b At illa maritum timens
dolos versat in omnia. 25
'mi,' tandem, 'mi coniux,' inquit,
'una vice in alpibus
nive sitiens extinxi sitim:
unde ego gravida
istum puerum damnoso fetu, heu, gignebam.' 30

c ['Nam languens amore tuo,
consurrexi diluculo
perrexique pedes nuda
per nives et ⟨per⟩ frigora,
atque maria rimabar mesta,
si forte ventivola
vela cernerem aut frontem navis conspicerem.']

IV a Anni post hec quinque   transierunt aut plus,
et mercator vagus   instauravit remos,
ratim quassam reficit:
vela alligat et nivis natum duxit secum.

b Transfretato mare   producebat natum, 35
et pro arrabone   mercatori tradens
centum libras accipit,
atque vendito infanti dives revertitur.

c Ingressusque domum   ad uxorem ait:
'consolare coniux,   consolare cara: 40
natum tuum perdidi,
quem non ipsa tu me magis quidem dilexisti.

d Tempestate orta   nos ventosus furor
in vadosas sirtes   nimis fessos egit
et nos omnes graviter 45
sol torret: at ille nivis natus liquescebat.'

Sic perfidam Suevus coniugem deluserat.
sic fraus fraudem vicerat:
nam quem genuit nix, recte hunc sol liquefecit.

23. DE PROTERII FILIA

1. Caute cane, cantor care, clare conspirent cannule, compte chorde crepent concinentiam. carpe callem commodam, convalles construe. caput calcem cor coniunge, calles callens corporales. cane chorda, cane chordis, cane cannulis creatorem!

2. Quisquis dolosis antiqui circumventus fraudibus inimici, profunditatem magnorum incautus incurrerit peccatorum, hoc sequenti conmonitus exemplo sit, merens ne desperet penitus; sed confisus in domino, liberari posse speret vel mortuum, si penitet, ex inferno.

3. Cesarie urbis civis Proterius, locuples valde nimis, unicam habuit gnatam, sacro velamini destinatam, proprius in quam servulus inlicitis inflammatus est ardoribus. cuius vinclo coniugii se non posse cernens iungi, auxilium agressus est malefici.

4. A quo pravi suscepta scedula nuncii, deferenda demoni, iussit eum nocte ceca supra gentilem recitare tumbam. iuvenis statim paruit; demonum et ecce sibi agmen apparuit. qui, auditis clamoribus infelicis, secum illum adduxerunt ad principem pravitatis.

5. Cui invisi datis commercii literis a malefico missis, item sui causa adventus expositis amorisque furiis, protinus fit discussio de fidei Christi ac baptismi repudio. iubeturque de singulis abrenuntiationis manu scriptum efficere. quod effecit.

6. Continuo tacta a diabolo, clamat virgo misere: 'miserere pater filie; moriar, mi pater; modo si non iungar tali puero. noli, pater kare, noli tardare, dum potes me salvare. si moraris, natam tuam non habebis. sed in die iudicii quasi pro perempta poenas et tormenta tu subibis supplicii.'

7. Ast flebilis contra pater inquit: 'nata, heu, quis te cecavit? nata, quis te fascinavit? ego te Christo dedicavi, non te mecho destinavi. patere, mi filia, sine me modo perficere quod volo. si consentis mihi, tempus adveniet, quando multum letaberis, pravam quod non voluntatem perfeceris, male sana quam nunc geris.'

8. Illa vero abnuente atque pene deficiente, pater, victus amicorum consiliis, consensit invitus. accitoque puero substantiam totam ei suam una cum puella tradidit; dicens sue filiole: 'vere iam misera, olim multum dolitura, patrem quia non es modo auditura.'

9. Nec multo post nupta, viri comperta infidelitate, se confestim in lamentis affecerat inmoderate. luctusque nullus finis esse quivit, donec a marito tandem explorata cuncte sue causa perfidie, a beato Basilio penitentiam persuasit pro errore percipere gravissimo.

10. Quem sanctus includens sacro peribulo, incumbit pro eo precibus sedulo, nunc pro illo orans, sepe et ieiunans; donec a deo reo impetraret veniam dari pro crimine tam gravi, dumque sibi penitenti ostensus est sanctus pro se decertare atque de antiquo hoste magnifice victoriam reportare.

11. Indicta transacta iam penitudine, eductus conciliandus ecclesie; ecce repente, sancto se ducente, tactus ab hoste, sacro pellitur poste; donec antistite et populo assistente precibus pulsantibus deum, fugatus est demon, clamans ac minitans: 'hoc, Basili, manu scriptum coram deo restitues mihi meum.'

12. Nec mora, sancto orante manusque cum populo elevante, cartula, desuper lapsa, manibus Basilii est ingesta. a puero quam cognitam sanctus statim partes dissipavit in minutas; eundemque, vivificis restitutum sacramentis, incessanter reddidit deo imnizantem.

24. DE LANTFRIDO ET COBBONE

1 Omnis sonus cantilene trifariam fit.   nam aut fidium concentu sonus constat: pulsu, plectro manuque;   ut sunt discrepantia vocum variis   chordarum generibus.

2 Aut tibiarum canorus redditur flatus,   fistularum ut sunt discrimina queque   folle ventris orisque   tumidi flatu perstrepentia pulchre   mentem mulcisonant.

3 Aut multimodis   gutture canoro   idem sonus redditur plurimarum faucium,   hominum volucrum   animantiumque.   sicque inpulsu   guttureque agitur.

4 His modis canamus   carorum sotiorumque actus,   quorum in honorem   pretitulatur prohemium hocce pulchre   Lantfridi Cobbonisque   pernobili stemmate.

    5 Quamvis amicitiarum
      genera plura legantur,
      non sunt adeo preclara
      ut istorum sodalium.
      qui conmunes extiterunt   5
      in tantum, ut neuter horum
      suapte quid possideret
      gazarum nec servorum
      nec alicuius suppellectilis.
      alter horum quicquid vellet,   10
      ab altero ratum foret.
      more ambo coequales,
      in nullo umquam dissides;
      quasi duo unus essent,
      in omnibus similes.   15

    6 Porro prior orsus Cobbo
      dixit fratri sotio:
      'diu mihi hic regale
      incumbit servitium,
      quod fratres affinesque   20
      visendo non adeam,
      inmemor meorum.
      ideo ultra mare revertar,
      unde huc adveni.
      illorum affectui,   25
      veniendo ad illos,
      ibi satisfaciam.'

    7 'Tedet me,' Lantfridus inquit,
      'vite proprie tam dire,
      ut absque te tescis hic degam.   30
      iam arripiens coniugem mecum,
      pergam exul tecum,
      ut tu diu, factus mecum,
      vicem rependas amori.'
      sicque pergentes litora maris   35
      applicarunt pariter.

      tum infit Cobbo sodali:
      'hortor, frater, redeas;
      redeam, visendo te,
      en vita comite.   40
      unum memoriale,
      frater, fratri facias.

    8 Uxorem, quam tibi solam
      vendicasti, propriam
      mihi dedas, ut licenter   45
      fruar eius amplexu.'
      nihil hesitando, manum
      manui eius tribuens hilare:
      'fruere ut libet, frater, ea;
      ne dicatur, quod semotim   50
      fisus sim quid possidere.'
      classe tunc apparata
      ducit secum in equor.

    9 Stans Lantfridus super litus,
      cantibus chordarum ait: 55
      'Cobbo frater, fidem tene,
      hactenus ut feceras;
      nam indecens est, affectum
      sequendo voti, honorem perdere;
      dedecus frater fratri ne fiat.'   60
      sicque diu canendo
      post illum intuitus,
      longius eum non cernens
      fregit rupe timpanum.

    10 At Cobbo, collisum   65
      fratrem non ferens,
      mox vertendo, mulcet:
      'en habes, perdulcis amor,
      quod dedisti, intactum
      ante amoris experimentum.   70
      iam non est, quod experiatur ultra.
      ceptum iter relinquam.'

25. MODUS FLORUM

1 Mendosam quam cantilenam ago
puerulis commentatam dabo,
quo modulos per mendaces risum
auditoribus ingentem ferant.

2 Liberalis et decora 5
cuidam regi erat nata,
quam sub lege huius modi
procis obponit querendam:

3 'Si quis mentiendi gnarus
usque adeo instet fallendo, 10
dum cesaris ore fallax
predicitur, is ducat filiam.'

4 Quo audito Suevus
nil moratus inquit:
'raptis armis ego 15
cum venatum solus irem,
lepusculus inter feras
telo tactus occumbebat.
mox, effusis intestinis,
caput avulsum cum cute cedo. 20

5 Cumque cesum manu
levaretur caput
aure leva effunduntur
mellis modii centeni,
sotiaque auris tacta 25
totidem pisarum fudit.
quibus intra pellem strictis,
lepus ipse dum secatur,
crepidine summe caude
kartam regiam latentem cepi, 30

6 Que servum te firmat esse meum.'
'Mentitur,' rex clamat, 'karta et tu!'

7 Sic rege deluso Suevus
arte regius est gener factus.

26. HERIGÊR

1 Herigêr, urbis
Maguntiensis
antistes, quendam
vidit prophetam
qui ad infernum 5
se dixit raptum.

2 Inde cum multas
referret causas,
subiunxit totum
esse infernum 10
accinctum densis
undique silvis.

3 Herigêr illi
ridens respondit:
'meum subulcum 15
illuc ad pastum
volo cum macris
mittere porcis.'

4 Vir ait falsus:
'fui translatus 20
in templum celi
Christumque vidi
letum sedentem
et comedentem.

5 Ioannes baptista 25
erat pincerna
atque preclari
pocula vini
porrexit cunctis
vocatis sanctis. 30

6 * * *

7 Herigêr ait:
'prudenter egit
Christus Iohannem
ponens pincernam,
quoniam vinum 35
non bibit umquam.

8 Mendax probaris
 cum Petrum dicis
 illic magistrum
 esse cocorum, 40
 est quia summi
 ianitor celi.

9 Honore quali
 te deus celi
 habuit ibi? 45
 ubi sedisti?
 volo ut narres
 quid manducasses.'

10 Respondit homo:
 'angulo uno 50
 partem pulmonis
 furabar cocis:
 hoc manducavi
 atque recessi.'

11 Herigêr illum 55
 iussit ad palum
 loris ligari
 scopisque cedi,
 sermone duro
 hunc arguendo: 60

12 'Si te ad suum
 invitet pastum
 Christus, ut secum
 capias cibum,
 cave ne furtum 65
 facias (spurcum).'

27. DE IOHANNE ABBATE

1 In vitis patrum veterum
 quiddam legi ridiculum,
 exemplo tamen habile;
 quod vobis dico rithmice.

2 Iohannes abba, parvulus 5
 statura, non virtutibus,
 ita maiori socio,
 quicum erat in heremo:

3 'Volo,' dicebat, 'vivere
 secure sicut angelus, 10
 nec veste nec cibo frui,
 qui laboretur manibus.'

4 Respondit frater: 'Moneo,
 ne sis incepti properus,
 frater, quod tibi postmodum 15
 sit non cepisse satius.'

5 At ille: 'Qui non dimicat,
 non cadit neque superat.'
 ait, et nudus heremum
 inferiorem penetrat. 20

6 Septem dies gramineo
 vix ibi durat pabulo;
 octava fames imperat,
 ut ad sodalem redeat.

7 Qui sero, clausa ianua, 25
 tutus sedet·in cellula,
 cum minor voce debili
 appellat: 'Frater, aperi:

8 Iohannes opis indigus
 notis assistit foribus; 30
 nec spernat tua pietas,
 quem redigit necessitas.'

9 Respondit ille deintus:
 'Iohannes, factus angelus,
 miratur celi cardines; 35
 ultra non curat homines.'

10 Foris Iohannes excubat
 malamque noctem tolerat,
 et preter voluntariam
 hanc agit penitentiam. 40

11 Facto mane recipitur
 satisque verbis uritur;
 sed intentus ad crustula
 fert patienter omnia.

12 Refocillatus domino 45
 grates agit et socio;
 Dehinc rastellum brachiis
 temptat movere languidis.

13 Castigatus angustia
 de levitate nimia, 50
 cum angelus non potuit,
 vir bonus esse didicit.

28. SACERDOS ET LUPUS

1 Quibus ludus est animo
et iocularis cantio,
hoc advertant ridiculum;
narrabo non ficticium.

2 Sacerdos iam ruricola 5
etate sub decrepita
vivebat amans pecudis;
hic enim mos est rusticis.

3 Ad cuius tale studium
omne pateret commodum, 10
nisi foret tam proxima
luporum altrix silvula.

4 Hi minuentes numerum
per eius summam generum
dant impares ex paribus 15
et pares ex imparibus.

5 Qui dolens sibi fieri
detrimentum peculii,
quia diffidit viribus,
vindictam querit artibus. 20

6 Fossam cavat non modicam
intus ponens agniculam
et, ne pateret hostibus,
superne tegit frondibus.

7 Humano datum commodo 25
nil maius est ingenio:
lupus dum nocte circuit,
spe prede captus incidit.

8 Accurrit mane presbiter,
gaudet vicisse taliter. 30
intus protento baculo
lupi minatur oculo.

9 'Iam,' inquit, 'fera pessima,
tibi rependam debita:
aut hic frangetur baculus 35
aut hic crepabit oculus.'

10 Hoc dicto simul impulit,
verbo sed factum defuit;
nam lupus servans oculum
morsu retentat baculum. 40

11 At ille miser vetulus,
dum sese trahit firmius,
ripa cedente corruit
et lupo comes incidit.

12 Hinc stat lupus, hinc presbiter, 45
timent sed dispariliter;
nam ut fidenter arbitror
lupus stabat securior.

13 Sacerdos secum mussitat
et septem psalmos ruminat, 50
sed revolvit frequentius
'miserere mei, deus.'

14 'Hoc,' inquit, 'infortunii
dant mihi vota populi,
quorum neglexi animas, 55
quorum comedi victimas.'

15 Pro defunctorum merito
cantat 'placebo domino,'
et pro votis viventium
totum cantat psalterium. 60

16 Post completum psalterium
commune prestat commodum
sacerdotis timiditas
atque lupi calliditas.

17 Nam cum acclivis presbiter 65
perfiniret 'pater noster'
atque clamaret domino
'sed libera nos a malo!'

18 Hic dorsum eius insilit
et saltu liber effugit; 70
et cuius arte captus est,
illo pro scala usus est.

19 At ille letus nimium
cantat 'laudate dominum'
et promisit pro populo 75
se oraturum a modo.

20 Hinc a vicinis queritur
et inventus extrahitur,
sed non unquam devotius
oravit nec fidelius. 80

29. ALFRÂD

1 Est unus locus,
Hôinburh dictus,
in quo pascebat
asinam Alfrâd
viribus fortem 5
atque fidelem.

2 Que dum in amplum
exiret campum,
vidit currentem
lupum voracem, 10
caput abscondit,
caudam ostendit.

3 Lupus accurrit:
caudam momordit,
asina bina 15
levavit crura
fecitque longum
cum lupo bellum.

4 Cum defecisse
vires sensisset, 20
protulit magnam
plangendo vocem
vocansque suam
moritur domnam.

5 Audiens grandem 25
asine vocem
Alfrâd cucurrit,
'sorores,' dixit,
'cito venite,
me adiuvate! 30

6 Asinam caram
misi ad erbam.
illius magnum
audio planctum,
spero cum sevo 35
ut pugnet lupo.'

7 Clamor sororum
venit in claustrum,
turbe virorum
ac mulierum 40
assunt, cruentum
ut captent lupum.

8 Adela namque
soror Alfrâde,
Rîkilam querit, 45
Agatham invenit,
ibant ut fortem
sternerent hostem.

9 At ille ruptis
asine costis 50
sanguinis undam
carnemque totam
simul voravit,
silvam intravit.

10 Illud videntes 55
cuncte sorores
crines scindebant,
pectus tundebant,
flentes insontem
asine mortem. 60

11 Denique parvum
portabat pullum;
illum plorabat
maxime Alfrâd,
sperans exinde 65
prolem crevisse.

12 Adela mitis
Fritherûnque dulcis
venerunt ambe,
ut Alverâde 70
cor confirmarent
atque sanarent.

13 'Delinque mestas,
soror, querelas!
lupus amarum 75
non curat fletum:
dominus aliam
dabit tibi asinam.'

30. CARMEN ESTIVUM

1 Vestiunt silve tenera merorem
virgulta, suis onerata pomis;
canunt de celsis sedibus palumbes
carmina cunctis.

2 Hic turtur gemit, resonat hic turdus, 5
pangit hic priscos merula sonores;
passer nec tacet, arridens garritu
alta sub ulmo.

3 Hic leta canit philomela frondis,
longas effundit sibilum per auras 10
sollempne; milvus tremulaque voce
ethera pulsat.

4 Ad astra volat aquila; in auris
alauda canit, modulos resolvit,
de sursum vergit dissimili modo, 15
dum terram tangit.

5 Velox impellit rugitus hirundo,
clangit coturnix, graculus fringultit;
aves sic cuncte celebrant estivum
undique carmen. 20

6 Nulla inter aves similis est api,
que talem tipum gerit castitatis
nisi que Christum baiulavit alvo
inviolata.

31. DE LUSCINIA

Aurea personet lira clara modulamina!
simplex chorda sit extensa voce quindenaria;
primum sonum mese reddat lege ipodorica.
philomele demus laudes in voce organica,
dulce melos decantantes, sicut docet musica, 5
sine cuius arte vera nulla valent cantica.

Cum telluris vere nova producuntur germina
nemorosa circumcirca frondescunt et brachia,
flagrat odor quam suavis florida per gramina,
hilarescit philomela, dulcis vocis conscia; 10
et extendens modulando gutturis spiramina,
reddit voces. ac estivi temporis ad otia
instat nocti et diei voce sub dulcisona;
soporatis dans quietem cantus per discrimina,
nec non pulchra viatori laboris solatia. 15
vocis eius pulchritudo, clarior quam cithara,
vincit omnes cantitando volucrum catervulas,
implens silvas atque cunctis modulis arbustula.
volitando scandit alta arborum cacumina,
gloriosa valde facta—veris pro letitia— 20
ac festiva satis gliscit sibilare carmina.

Felix tempus, cui resultat talis consonantia!
utinam per duodena mensium curricula
dulcis philomela daret sue vocis organa!

Sonos tuos vox non valet imitari lirica, 25
quibus nescit consentire fistula clarisona:
mira quia modularis melorum tripudia.
o tu parva, numquam cessa canere, avicula!
tuam decet simphoniam monocordi musica,
que tuas remittit voces voce diatonica. 30

Nolo, nolo, ut quiescas temporis ad otia,
sed ut letos det concentus tua volo ligula,
cuius laudem memoreris in regum palatia.

Cedit auceps ad frondosa resonans umbracula,
cedit cignus et suavis ipsius melodia, 35
cedit tibi timpanista et sonora tibia.
quamvis enim videaris corpore premodica,
tamen cuncti te auscultant. nemo dat iuvamina
nisi solus rex celestis, qui gubernat omnia.

Iam preclara tibi satis dedimus obsequia, 40
que in voce sunt iucunda et in verbis rithmica,
ad scolares et ad ludos digne congruentia.

Tempus adest, ut solvatur nostra vox armonica,
ne fatigent plectrum lingue cantionum tedia,
ne pigrescat auris prompta fidium ad crusmata. 45

Trinus deus in personis, unus in essentia,
nos gubernet et conservet sua sub clementia
regnareque nos concedat cum ipso in gloria.

32. VERNA FEMINE SUSPIRIA

1. Levis exsurgit Zephirus
   et sol procedit tepidus;
   iam terra sinus aperit,
   dulcore suo diffluit.

2. Ver purpuratum exiit, 5
   ornatus suos induit;
   aspergit terram floribus,
   ligna silvarum frondibus.

3. Struunt lustra quadrupedes
   et dulces nidos volucres; 10
   inter ligna florentia
   sua decantant gaudia.

4. Quod oculis dum video
   et auribus dum audio,
   heü, pro tantis gaudiis 15
   tantis inflor suspiriis.

5. Cum mihi sola sedeo
   et hec revolvens palleo,
   sic forte caput sublevo,
   nec audio nec video. 20

6. Tu saltim, Veris gratia,
   exaudi et considera
   frondes, flores et gramina;
   nam mea languet anima.

33. INVITATIO AMICE

1. Iam, dulcis amica, venito,
   quam sicut cor meum diligo;
   Intra in cubiculum meum,
   ornamentis cunctis onustum.

2. Ibi sunt sedilia strata 5
   et domus velis ornata,
   Floresque in domo sparguntur
   herbeque fragrantes miscentur.

3. Est ibi mensa apposita
   universis cibis onusta; 10
   Ibi clarum vinum abundat
   et quidquid te, cara, delectat.

4. Ibi sonant dulces simphonie,
   inflantur et altius tibie;
   Ibi puer et docta puella 15
   pangunt tibi carmina bella:

5. Hic cum plectro citharam tangit,
   illa melos cum lira pangit;
   Portantque ministri pateras
   pigmentatis poculis plenas. 20

6. Non me iuvat tantum convivium
   quantum post dulce colloquium,
   Nec rerum tantarum ubertas
   ut dilecta familiaritas.

7. Jam nunc veni, soror electa 25
   et pre cunctis mihi dilecta,
   Lux mee clara pupille
   parsque maior anime mee.

8. Ego fui sola in silva
   et dilexi loca secreta; 30
   Frequenter effugi tumultum
   et vitavi populum multum.

9. ⟨Karissima, noli tardare;
   studeamus nos nunc amare,
   Sine te non potero vivere: 35
   iam decet amorem perficere.

10. Quid iuvat deferre, electa,
    que sunt tamen post facienda?
    Fac cita quod eris factura,
    in me non est aliqua mora.⟩ 40

THE CAMBRIDGE SONGS

34. MAGISTER PUERO

1 O admirabile Veneris idolum,
cuius materie nihil est frivolum:
Archos te protegat, qui stellas et polum
fecit et maria condidit et solum.
Furis ingenio non sentias dolum: 5
Cloto te diligat, que baiulat colum.

2 Saluto puerum non per ipotesim,
sed firmo pectore deprecor Lachesim,
sororem Atropos, ne curet heresim.
Neptunum comitem habeas et Thetim, 10
cum vectus fueris per fluvium Tesim.
quo fugis, amabo, cum te dilexerim?
miser quid faciam, cum te non viderim?

3 Dura materies ex matris ossibus
creavit homines iactis lapidibus. 15
Ex quibus unus est iste puerulus,
qui lacrimabiles non curat gemitus.
cum tristis fuero, gaudebit emulus:
ut cerva rugio, cum fugit hinnulus.

35. CLERICUS ET NONNA
S..................

36. 'IN LANGUORE PERIO'
Ven..................

37.
V..................

38. LAMENTATIO NEOBULE

1 Miserarum est neque amori dare ludum neque dulci
mala vino lavere aut exanimari metuentis
patrue verbera lingue.

2 Tibi qualum Citheree puer ales, tibi telas
operoseque Minerve studium aufert, Neobule, 5
Liparei nitor Ebri,

3 Simul unctos Tiberinis humeros lavit in undis,
eques ipso melior Bellerofonte, neque pugno
neque segni pede victus,

4 Catus idem per apertum fugientis agitato
grege cervos iaculari et celer arto latitantem
fruticeto excipere aprum.

39. ADMONITIO IUVENUM

1. Audax es, vir iuvenis,
   dum fervet caro mobilis;
   audenter agis perperam,
   tua membra coinquinas.
   Attende homo, quod pulvis es
   et in pulverem reverteris.

2. Breve est tempus, iuvenis, 5
   perpende, quod morieris,
   venietque dies ultimus
   et perdes flores optimos. *Attende...*

3. Carni tue consenties,
   animam tuam decipis, 10
   libidine dum flecteris
   male deceptus permanes. *Attende...*

4. Dentes tui fremidant,
   labia tua exasperant,
   lingua mala generat, 15
   vita tua trepidat. *Attende...*

5. Eleves tuos oculos,
   ut vanitatem videas;
   flectetur mens misera,
   ad malum erigis membra. *Attende...* 20

6. Fecisti malum consilium
   et offendisti nimium,
   quia multum secutus es
   amorem et libidines. *Attende...*

7. Gloriam populi queris, 25
   laudem humanam diligis,
   non cupis placere deo,
   qui conspicit te de celo. *Attende...*

8. Honorem transitorie
   presumpsisti accipere; 30
   sed maior pena sequitur
   cui maior honor creditur. *Attende...*

9. In terram semper aspicis,
   semper de terra cogitas,
   sed omnia hic reliquis, 35
   unde superbus ambulas? *Attende...*

10. Karo te traxit in foveam,
    vide, ne malus moriaris;
    festina te corrigere,
    antequam finis veniet. *Attende...* 40

11. Luge modo, dum est tempus,
    ne gemas in iudicio,
    ubi non valet gemitus,
    nec ulla intercessio. *Attende...*

12. Modo labora fortiter, 45
    dum es in isto corpore,
    emenda tuum vitium,
    ne gemas in perpetuum. *Attende...*

13. Non te frangat cupiditas,
    nec te flectat fragilitas, 50
    et noli cum diabulo
    participare amplius. *Attende...*

14. O si corde intellegis,
    que sunt precepta legis,
    sed illi, qui adulterant, 55
    lapidibus subiaceant. *Attende...*

15. Per salvatorem denuo
    venit magna redemptio,
    qua cuncta, que committuntur,
    penitendo remittuntur. *Attende...* 60

16. Quare recurrere non vis
    ad dominum, vir iuvenis?
    roga eius clementiam,
    ut donet indulgentiam. *Attende...*

17. Rumpe cordis duritiam, 65
    mentis tue malitiam,
    te corrigere festina,
    antequam tempus pereat. *Attende...*

18. Suscipit Christus veniam,
    ut donet indulgentiam 70
    ad illam veram animam
    que macerat carnem suam. *Attende...*

19 Terribilis Christus veniet
    ad iudicanda secula,
    tunc ille singulis reddet 75
    secundum sua opera. *Attende...*
20 Veniet Christus iudicio,
    erit fortis districtio,
    ut pater filium non iuvet
    nec filius patrem defendat. *Attende...* 80
21 Xristo servias, iuvenis,
    ad eum mox recurreris,
    ut ante eius limina
    securus sis de crimine. *Attende...*
22 Y, dei quere gratiam, 85
    delet peccati maculam
    humilitas, et caritas
    ducit ad celi patriam. *Attende...*
23 Zelum habet optimum,
    qui deum amat et proximum, 90
    letabitur in seculum
    et vivet in perpetuum. *Attende...*

40. DE MUSICA

Rota modos arte personemus musica,
quibus uti constans gratuletur anima;
ut a fabris clarus didicit Pithagoras,
malleis cum quattuor deprendit consonantias.
Septem planetarum fecit interstitia, 5
quarum fit celestis numerorum normula.
fert ut arithmetica, cunctis dans principia.
rex pantokrator nos reget per secula.

41. DE MENSA PHILOSOPHIE

Ad mensam Philosophie sitientes currite
et saporis tripertiti septem rivos bibite,
uno fonte procedentes, non eodem tramite.
    Hinc fluit gramma prima, hinc poetica ydra,
lanx hinc satiricorum, plausus hinc comicorum, 5
letificat convivia Mantuana fistula.

42. DE SIMPHONIIS ET DE LITTERA PITHAGORE

1 Vite dator, omnifactor deus, nature formator, mundi globum sub potenti claudens volubilem palmo, in factura sua splendet magnificus per evum.

2 Ipse multos Veritatem veteres necdum sequentes vestigando per sophie devia iusserat ire, improbabili errore parare nobis viam.

3 Inter quos subtilis per acumen mentis claruit Pitagoras; metapsicosis quem iuxta famam Troie peremptum Euforbium seculo rursus reddit, obscurosque rerum rite denuo vivum donat intellectus perspicaci perscrutari sensu animi.

4. Ergo vir hic prudens, die quodam ferri fabricam preteriens, pondere non equo sonoque diverso pulsare malleolos senserat, sicque tonorum quamlibet informem vim latere noscens, formam addidit, per artem pulchram primus edidit.

5 Ad hanc simphonias tres subplendam istas fecit: diatesseron diapente diapason, infra quaternarium, que pleniter armoniam sonant; que sententia senis ponens solidum, rithmicam in se normulam mensurarumque utilem notitiam et siderum motus iussit continere, ma ten tetraden et nomine suo vocavit.

6 Y grecam, I de imis continentem sed fissam summotenus in ramosas binas partes, vite humane invenit ad similitudinem congruam. est nam sincera et simplex pueritia, que non facile noscitur, utrum vitiis an virtuti animum subicere velit, donec tandem iuventutis etas illud offerret nobis bivium.

7 Hic qui paret viciis, virtuti—nobis auferat—contrariis, illam latam ille terit ipseque semitam, que postremo, plena penis gravibus, se prosequentibus portas inferi aperit sevissimas, ubi fremitus dentium et perpetui fletus sunt merentium pro criminis facto; cita ubi semper mors optatur, frustra pro dolor atque queritur.

8 Sed virtutum gradibus ille nititur, qui providus per angustam vadit illam semitam, que in fine locuples letitie suis queque precibus pandit eterna dulcis vite gaudia; ubi bonorum anime claro iugiter illustrantur lumine perpetui solis, ubi deitatis se conspectum semper cernere se gaudent beati.

9 Vite dator, omnifactor deus, nature formator, illum aufer, istum confer tuis fidelibus callem, ut post obitum talis vite participes fiant.

43. DIAPENTE ET DIATESSERON

Diapente et diatesseron simphonia et intensa et remissa pariter consonantia diapason modulatione consona reddunt.

44. UMBRAM HECTORIS VIDET ENEAS

Tempus erat, quo prima quies mortalibus egris
incipit, et dono divum gratissima serpit.
in somnis, ecce, ante oculos mestissimus Hector
visus adesse mihi, largosque effundere fletus,
raptatus bigis, ut quondam, aterque cruento 5
pulvere, perque pedes traiectus lora tumentes.
Ei mihi, qualis erat! quantum mutatus ab illo
Hectore, qui redit exuvias indutus Achilli,
vel Danaum Frigios iaculatus puppibus ignes!
squalentem barbam, et concretos sanguine crines, 10
vulneraque illa gerens, que circum plurima muros
accepit patrios. Ultro flens ipse videbar
compellare virum, et mestas expromere voces:
'O lux Dardanie, spes o fidissima Teucrum,
que tante tenuere more? quibus Hector ab oris 15
exspectate venis?'

45. HIPSIPILE ARCHEMORUM PUERUM A SERPENTE NECATUM PLORAT

O mihi deserte natorum dulcis imago,
Archemore, o rerum et patrie solamen adempte
servitiique decus, qui te, mea gaudia, sontes
extinxere dei, modo quem digressa reliqui
lascivum et prono vexantem gramina cursu? 5
heu ubi siderei vultus? ubi verba ligatis
imperfecta sonis risusque et murmura soli
intellecta mihi? quotiens tibi Lemnon et Argo
sueta loqui et longa somnum suadere querella!

46. ARGIE LAMENTATIO MARITUM POLINICEM A FRATRE INTERFECTUM INVENIENTIS

'Hunc ego te, coniunx, ad debita regna profectum
ductorem belli generumque potentis Adrasti
aspicio, talisque tuis occurro triumphis?
huc adtolle genas defectaque lumina: venit
ad Thebas Argia tua: age, menibus induc 5
et patrios ostende lares et mutua redde
hospitia. heu quid ago? proiectus cespite nudo
hoc patrie telluris habes? que iurgia? certe
imperium non frater habet! nullasne tuorum
movisti lacrimas? ubi mater? ubi inclita fama 10
Antigone? mihi nempe iaces, mihi victus es uni!
dicebam: 'Quo tendis iter? quid sceptra negata
poscis? habes Argos, soceri regnabis in aula;
hic tibi longus honos, hic indivisa potestas.'
quid queror? ipsa dedi bellum mestumque rogavi 15
ipsa patrem, ut talem nunc te complexa tenerem.
sed bene habet, superi; gratum est, Fortuna; peracta
spes longinqua vie: totos invenimus artus.
ei mihi, sed quanto descendit vulnus hiatu!
hoc frater? qua parte, precor, iacet ille nefandus 20
predator? vincam volucres (sit adire potestas)
excludamque feras; an habet funestus et ignes?
sed nec te flammis inopem tua terra videbit:
ardebis lacrimasque feres, quas ferre negatum
regibus eternumque tuo famulata sepulchro 25
durabit deserta fides, testisque dolorum
natus erit, parvoque torum Polinice fovebo.'

47. NISUS OMNIGENI

Salve, vite norma, preclare flos sinagoge.
Ave pie diu optate tue olive.
Nisibus omnigenis gratulor modulando Camenis.
    here forma poli serena, sol atque luna.
Vale, hora certe iocunda, reddens cristalla. 5
Presulis eximii valeat virtute sepulchri.

CHAPTER VI

NOTES

THE following abbreviations will be used:

ALLEN, *Mod. Phil.* = Philip Schuyler Allen, in various volumes of *Modern Philology*. Especially Vol. III, 4 (April, 1906); Vol. V, 3 (Jan. 1908); Vol. VI, 1–3 (July, 1908—Jan. 1909). University of Chicago Press.

BARTSCH, *Lat. Seq.* = Karl Bartsch, *Die lateinischen Sequenzen des Mittelalters in musikalischer und rhythmischer Beziehung dargestellt*. Rostock. 1868.

BREUL, *H.Z.* = Karl Breul, *Zu den Cambridger Liedern* in 'Haupt's Zeitschrift für deutsches Alterthum.' Vol. XXX (1886) 186–92. Berlin.

DU MÉRIL 1 and 2 = Edélestand du Méril, (1) *Poésies populaires latines antérieures au douzième siècle*. Paris. 1843. (2) *Poésies latines du moyen-âge*. Paris. 1847.

ECCARD = Johann Georg Eccard, *Veterum monumentorum Quaternio*. Leipzig. 1720.

FRÖHNER, *H.Z.* = Christian W. Fröhner, *Zur mittellateinischen Hofdichtung*, in 'Haupt's Zeitschrift für deutsches Alterthum.' Vol. XI (1859) 1–24. Berlin.

GRIMM = Jacob Grimm und Andreas Schmeller, *Lateinische Gedichte des x. und xi. Jahrhunderts*. Göttingen. 1838.

HAUPT 1 and 2 = Moriz Haupt, (1) *Altdeutsche Blätter*. Leipzig. 1836. (2) *Exempla poesis latinae medii aevi*. Vindobonae. 1834. (pp. 29–30 'Invitatio amicae.')

HEYNE = Moritz Heyne, *Altdeutsch-lateinische Spielmannsgedichte des x. Jahrhunderts. Für Liebhaber des deutschen Altertums übertragen*. Göttingen. 1900.

JAFFÉ, *H.Z.* = Philipp Jaffé, *Die Cambridger Lieder*, in 'Haupt's Zeitschrift für deutsches Alterthum.' Vol. XIV (1869), 449–95 and 560. Berlin.

KELLE = Johann Kelle, *Geschichte der deutschen Litteratur von der ältesten Zeit bis zur Mitte des elften Jahrhunderts*. Vol. I. Berlin. 1892.

KÖGEL 1 and 2 = Rudolf Kögel, (1) *Geschichte der deutschen Litteratur bis zum Ausgange des Mittelalters*. Vol. I, 2: Strassburg. 1897. (2) in Paul's 'Grundriss der germanischen Philologie,' II, 1 (second edition. Strassburg, 1901. The Old High German and Old Low German Literature was revised after Kögel's death by Wilhelm Bruckner).

MEYER, *F.B.* = Wilhelm Meyer, *Fragmenta Burana*. Berlin. 1901. (Pages 145–86 of the valuable Introduction, containing the observations on the 'Cambridge Songs,' were reprinted in Meyer's 'Gesammelte Abhandlungen zur mittellateinischen Rythmik.' Berlin. 1905. I, 1–58.)

MS. = the Manuscript (Codex Cantabrigiensis Gg. 5. 35) containing the 'Cambridge Songs' and the transliteration of folios 432–41 given on pages 3–22 of the present book.

M.S.D. = Karl Müllenhoff und Wilhelm Scherer, *Denkmäler deutscher Poesie und Prosa aus dem viii.–xii. Jahrhundert*. Berlin. 1864. ²1873. ³1892 (edited by Elias Steinmeyer, in 2 vols. Vol. I: Texts. Vol. II: Notes). Only the third edition is referred to unless otherwise stated.

PIPER = Paul Piper, *Nachträge zur älteren deutschen Literatur*, in Kürschner's 'Deutsche National-Literatur.' Vol. 162. Stuttgart. No Year. [1897.]

SCHMELLER, *C.B.* = J. A. Schmeller, *Carmina Burana. Lateinische und deutsche Lieder und Gedichte einer Handschrift des xiii. Jahrhunderts aus Benedictbeuern*. Breslau. 1847. ²1883. ⁴1904.

NOTES

TRAUBE = Ludwig Traube, *O Roma nobilis. Philologische Untersuchungen aus dem Mittelalter*, in 'Abhandlungen der Philosophisch-Philologischen Klasse der Kgl. Akademie der Wissenschaften zu München.' Vol. XIX, Part II. 1891, especially pp. 304 sqq.

W = The Wolfenbüttel Manuscript, as printed by Piper in his 'Nachträge zur älteren deutschen Litteratur,' pages 234–7. See p. 36, note 1.

WINTERFELD = Paul von Winterfeld, *Deutsche Dichter des lateinischen Mittelalters in deutschen Versen* [edited, with an introduction, by Hermann Reich]. München. 1913.

1. Carmen Christo Dictum.

MS. fol. 435va l. 33–435vb l. 28.—pp. 27 (sub 12) and 42.—Jaffé 479–80. The first five portions of this sequence are also found in two manuscripts of Benevento the oldest of which goes back to the eleventh century. See Clemens Blume, *Analecta Hymnica Medii Aevi*. Vol. LIII: *Die Sequenzen des Thesaurus Hymnologicus H. A. Daniels und anderer Sequenzenausgaben*. Part I. Leipzig. 1911. Pages 105–6. Blume says: 'In MS. B ist die liturgische Bestimmung für Dominica II post Octavas Paschae.' 'Diese bisher unedierten Sequenzen aus Benevent bieten einen poetisch minderwertigen, aber historisch sehr bedeutungsvollen Beitrag zur Sequenzendichtung.' Stanza 3 of the Cambridge Manuscript (*Spolia mundi...*) follows in the Benevento Manuscripts after Stanza 4 (*Tertia die...*).

The text of the present edition follows on the whole the Cambridge Manuscript which is fuller and at least as good as the Italian texts from which, however, two readings have been adopted, viz. in Stanza 2: *lucidae* for *lucidam*, and in Stanza 4 *resurrexisti maiestate* for *surrexisti maiestatis*. Perhaps it will be better to transpose the last words of Stanza 5 and to read with the Italian manuscripts: *dextra patris residens, o rex*.

In Stanza 3 *orto* (*lucido*) stands for *horto* (*lucido*). An initial *h* is frequently omitted in the Songs, e.g. *erbam* (29, 6, 2), *imnizantem* (23, 12), *armoniam* (15, 4), *armonica* (31, 43), *ipodorica* (31, 3), *Ebri* (38, 2, 3). On the other hand we find *perhennem* (13, 5), *prohemium* (24, 4), *honusta* (33, 10), *habundat* (33, 11).

2. Modus Qui et Carelmanninc.

MS. fol. 432va l. 31–433ra l. 18.—pp. 27 (sub 4) and 42–43. Preserved in two Manuscripts, C and W. For W see Piper pp. 234–5. The text given on pp. 42–43 follows on the whole the critical text given in *M.S.D.* I, 40 sqq. which is largely based on W. The readings of C can easily be ascertained from pp. 2–3 of the present edition. The very meagre punctuation of *M.S.D.* has, however, not been adopted.

The sequence was obviously intended for use at the service in church and will hardly have been sung outside of religious houses. It is the only one among the poems in this form preserved in C which is still purely religious. 'Modus qui et Carelmanninc' means 'the tune to which also the song on Karlmann is being sung.' This was perhaps a German song.

See *M.S.D.* I, 40–42 (critical text and various readings) and II, 107–112 (notes and discussion where the older literature is mentioned). See also Bartsch, *Lat. Seq.* pp. 157 sqq., and compare the critical remarks of W. Wilmanns in his review of *M.S.D.* in *Göttinger Gelehrte Anzeigen*, 1893, pages 534–5.

After l. 30 there follows another stanza of 3 lines in C which has been omitted in the present edition. See the note in *M.S.D.*³

3. Laudes Christo acte.

MS. fol. 432rb l. 24–432va l. 30.—pp. 27 (sub 3) and 44–45.—Jaffé, pp. 476–9 (on which the text here given is based).

For lines 79 and following compare St Paul's Epistle to the Ephesians iv. 5–6. With regard to the metre, see the notes to Poems 10 and 26.

4. *Hymnus Paschalis.*

MS. fol. 437vb l. 30–438ra l. 5.—pp. 27 (sub 21) and 45.—These lines are part (ll. 31–40) of a much longer elegiac poem of 110 lines by Venantius Fortunatus (530–609), Bishop of Poitiers, called *De Resurrectione Domini.* See Guido Maria Dreves *Hymnographi Latini. Lateinische Hymnendichter des Mittelalters. Zweite Folge.* Leipzig. 1907 (in *Analecta Hymnica Medii Aevi*, herausgegeben von Clemens Blume und Guido M. Dreves. Vol. L, pages 76 sqq.). On p. 79 Dreves says 'Zahllos ist die Zahl der Handschriften, die Bruchstücke des Ganzen als österlichen Prozessionshymnus bieten, und unübersehbar bunt die Auswahl, die getroffen wird. Viel häufiger ist eine andre Auswahl, die nach dem Rundreime mit V. 31 einsetzt. Diese Auswahl hat aus dem durchaus nicht liturgischen Original einen liturgischen Hymnus weitester Verbreitung herausgeschält.' In H. A. Daniel's *Thesaurus hymnologicus* I (Halle, 1841) pp. 169–70 the five stanzas of the Cambridge MS. are found which are followed by nine additional stanzas, enclosed in brackets. On pp. 171–2 Daniel adds an interesting note. He quotes from Mon. Salisb.: 'zw österleicher czeit das frewden gesangk "Salve, festa dies" daz wirt gesungen all suntag so man vmb dy kirchen mit der proces get....' German beginnings are given as 'Grüest seyst heyliger tag' and 'Sey gegrüst du heiliger tag.' See also K. S. Meister, *Das katholische deutsche Kirchenlied in seinen Singweisen*, Vol. 1 (Freiburg, 1862), pp. 364–8: 'Sey gegrüst, du hoher Festag!'; and Philipp Wackernagel, *Das deutsche Kirchenlied von der ältesten Zeit bis zum Anfang des xvii. Jahrhunderts*, Vol. 1 (Leipzig, 1864), pp. 66–7. The refrain 'Salve festa dies...astra tenet' is really ll. 39–40 of the versus 'De Resurrectione Domini' the beginning of which is: *Tempora florigero.* Stanzas 2 to 5 of the present 'Hymnus Paschalis' represent ll. 31–38 of the poem on the Resurrection. From the same poem processional hymns were extracted for Ascension Day and for Whitsuntide. The opening line is very similar to Sedulius: *Haec est alma dies, sanctarum sancta dierum*, but the rest is different. The text of the present edition is based on Dreves.

The hymn is printed, with refrain, in the Rev. R. M. Moorsom's *Historical Companion to Hymns Ancient and Modern*, London, ²1903, pp. 63–64; also in *Hymnarium, Blüthen lateinischer Kirchenpoesie*, Halle, ²1868, p. 96, No. 59, under the title: *In festo Paschali.* The hymn was translated into English by the Rev. John Ellerton (*Hymns*, No. 497) beginning: 'Welcome, happy morning!' age to age shall say. It was translated into German, in the metre of the original, by Karl Simrock in his *Lauda Sion*, Stuttgart, ²1868. This translation begins:

Heil dir, festlicher Tag, ehrwürdig den kommenden Zeiten,
Wo die Hölle bezwang Gott und zum Himmel sich hob!

5. *Resurrectio.*

MS. fol. 441va l. 14–23.—pp. 27 (sub 43) and 45.—Jaffé, p. 480 (on whom the present edition is based).

6. *Ad Mariam.*

MS. fol. 440va l. 35–440vb l. 5.—pp. 27 (sub 35) and 46.—Jaffé, pp. 480–1 (on whom the text of the present edition is based).

7. *De Epiphania.*

MS. fol. 432ra ll. 1–6.—pp. 27 (sub 1) and 46.

This is only the opening stanza of a much longer poem that was first printed by P. Gall Morel in his *Lateinische Hymnen des Mittelalters, größtenteils aus Handschriften schweizerischer Klöster*, Einsiedeln, New York and Cincinnati, 1868, p. 12, No. 21. In Dreves und Blume's *Analecta Hymnica medii aevi*, Vol. L (Leipzig, 1907), 195–6, the poem has 14 stanzas and is given under the title 'De Nativitate Domini.' Its author is the famous prelate Magnentius Hrabanus Maurus, Abbot of Fulda (822–42) and Archbishop of Mayence (847–56). On him see E. Dümmler's article in the *Allgemeine Deutsche Biographie*, Vol. XXVII (1888), 66–74.

NOTES

In l. 5: *Ut salvaret quod plasmavit* the *Analecta Hymnica* print *quos plasmavit*, adding, however, a note to the effect (p. 196) that many manuscripts have *quod*. Consequently *quod* has been retained. The refrain: *caute cane* etc. of the Cambridge Manuscript does not belong to this poem and has for this reason been omitted on p. 46. See also Jaffé, p. 461, note. The words *conspira karole* do not make any sense and should be emended from the beginning of No. 23 (p. 57): *(clare) conspirent cannule*.

8. Rachel.

MS. fol. 441vb ll. 3–14.—pp. 27 (sub 46) and 46.—Jaffé, p. 481.

A fragment of only 2½ stanzas. It breaks off abruptly in the MS. without any indication of anything being omitted, and is immediately followed by *O admirabile Veneris idolum*.

The complaint of Rachel is based on the well-known passage in Matthew ii. 16–18: 'tunc Herodes...mittens occidit omnes pueros...tunc impletum fuit quod ait Dominus per Ieremiam prophetam dicentem: "Vox in Rhama audita est, lamentatio, et fletus, et ejulatus multus: Rachel plorans filios suos, et noluit consolationem admittere, de eo quod non sint."' Similarly in other Latin texts. See Jaffé, p. 481 n. The passage from Jeremiah (xxxi. 15) runs thus in the text of the Vulgate: 'Haec dicit Dominus: Vox in excelso audita est lamentationis, luctus et fletus Rachel plorantis filios suos et nolentis consolari super eis quia non sunt.'

The metrical form of the poem is interesting. The first three lines of each stanza are the well-known long trochaic lines of 15 syllables, with a break after the eighth, as they occur in poems No. 18, 21, and 31. The fourth line, the concluding line of each stanza, shows a slight reduction of the first three in so far as each half has only seven syllables, and the caesura rimes with the end. The effect is very pleasant, but I have not come across this particular stanza in any other religious poem. The reduced line stands in a relation to the longer ones similar to that in which the pentameter stands to the hexameter. With regard to the pleasant effect of the long lines see also R. Atkinson's remarks on the Hymns of S. Colman MacMurchon and Cuchuimne in the *Irish Liber Hymnorum* (Henry Bradshaw Society Publications), Vol. xiv, London, 1898, pp. xiv–xvi.

A similar beginning is found in several hymns of different metrical structure, e.g. *Pulset astra vox sublimis, sublimari digna nimis*, or *Pulset coelum laus amoena, laus cunctorum fidelium*. See U. Chevalier, *Repertorium Hymnologicum*, ii (Louvain, 1897), 371.

The Goliard's collection includes complaints of various kinds; see also Nos. 32, 38, 45, 46.

As the ten lines are only a fragment, perhaps only a small fragment, and possibly not even the opening lines of the poem, a satisfactory interpretation of them is hardly possible. The 'soror' is probably Leah, and Rachel and Leah seem to stand here for the Gospel (the Church) and the Law (Synagogue). Once Rachel was taken as representing the Gospel as distinguished from Law, as the Church in contrast with the Synagogue, she would naturally be represented as 'virgo' and 'sine macula,' the bride of Christ (see Ephesians v. 27–29); 'pignora,' 'dear children,' would be a natural expression for the martyrs, and the Church would be taken as the 'mother' of the faithful ones. The evil sister, 'improba,' seems to refer to the Synagogue, although it never had the power of putting Christians to death except by stirring up the heathen authorities against them. As the festivals of the Church brought back the memory of the deaths of the martyrs, the hymn-writer wished to give voice to the compassion of the Church to their sufferings. If 'improba' is not taken to refer to Leah (the Jews), one might be inclined to assume that it refers to Babylon (the heathen world). A short Latin *Lamentatio Rachel* (9 lines), followed by some consoling lines ('Noli, Rachel, deflere pignora!') spoken by an Angel, with the refrain 'Ergo gaude!,' seems to belong to an old Mystery-play on the massacre of the Innocents. See E. de Coussemaker, *Histoire de l'harmonie au moyen-âge*, Paris, 1852, p. 128.

9. *De Domo S. Cecilie Coloniensi.*

MS. fol. 438va ll. 12–24.—pp. 27 (sub 25) and 46.—Jaffé, p. 484 (on whom the text is mainly based), and Edward Schröder, in the *Anzeiger für deutsches Alterthum*, 23 (1897), 202–3 and 401, whose valuable emendations have been utilised.

The poem, in leonine hexameters, refers to a religious foundation the patron-saint of which was Saint Cecilia. In the 8th, 9th and 10th century there existed in the town of Cologne a 'conventus Sanctae Caeciliae.' A church of St Caecilia, dating from 930–41, stood near the Neumarkt, in the centre of Cologne.

Uuoda (l. 7) probably stands for *Uoda* just as on fol. 438vb l. 25 *uuualde* is written for *uualde*. On the name see E. Förstemann, *Altdeutsches Namenbuch*, ²I (1900), p. 1629 (Wuoda) and p. 1176 (Uoda). On Oda = Uote as a typical name for mothers of great kings and warriors, see Jacob Grimm, Haupt's *Zeitschrift für deutsches Alterthum*, Vol. I, 21 (reprinted in Grimm's *Kleinere Schriften*, VII, 68 sqq.).

Mere Hict was obviously another mistake (see p. 23, note 2) of the Anglo-Saxon scribe of the 'Canterbury Book' who did not understand the name. Several instances of the name *Merihilt, Merehild* are found in E. Förstemann's *Altdeutsches Namenbuch*, ²I (1900), p. 1104. On *Una* as a name see *Anzeiger f.d.A.* 23, 401.

The beginning of the poem is typical in Medieval Latin Church poetry, see: *Emicat virtutibus | confessor Eligius* in U. Chevalier, *Repertorium Hymnologicum*, Vol. IV (Louvain, 1912), p. 119, No. 37048; or *Emicat hic pater haelisio | sanctus Eparchius astrigero*, ibid. III, 194, No. 26070. *Emicat* is used especially frequently with regard to festival days, e.g. *emicat alma dies, emicat ecce dies lucida*, etc., ibid. I, 321; III, 194.

10. *De S. Victore Carmen Xantense.*

MS. fol. 433vb l. 36—fol. 434rb l. 5.—pp. 27 (sub 7) and 47–48.—Jaffé, pp. 481–4 (on whom the text of the present edition is mainly based).

On Saint Victor in Xanten see the *Annales Xantenses*, 864, *Monumenta Germaniae*, SS. II, 231; also Rettberg, *Kirchengeschichte Deutschlands*, I, 102 sqq.; Rektor Möders in his *Führer durch Xanten* (Xanten, ³1912), says: *Der heilige Victor wurde nach der Legende i.J. 286 nach Christo mit 330 Soldaten der thebäischen Legion auf Befehl des Kaisers Maximian bei Xanten (= ad sanctos martyres) ermordet. Die heilige Helena, Mutter Konstantins des Großen, ließ die Gebeine der Märtyrer sammeln, in Steinsärge legen, vor dem Südtore der Colonia Trajana begraben, und über dem großen Grabe eine Kirche bauen (327). 451 zerstörte ein Schwarm Hunnen auf dem Wege nach Gallien die Kirche. Den zweiten Dom vernichteten 864 die Normannen, wie die 'Annales Xantenses' erzählen. Ein drittes Gotteshaus wurde 1109 durch Feuer zerstört. Ein vierter (romanischer) Dom wurde 1213 eingeweiht. Der jetzige prächtige gotische Dom wurde 1263 begonnen (der Grundstein zum Kölner Dom wurde 1248 gelegt) und 1525 vollendet.* In the Nibelungenlied 'the far-famed town *ze Santen*' is the birthplace of valiant Siegfried and the residence of his father Siegmund, king of the district of the Lower Rhine.

For the metre of this poem see the notes to *Heriger* (No. 26) and to poem No. 16.

In lines 68–69 St Victor is called *athleta dei*. Adam of St Victor, who in the 'prose' beginning 'Ecce dies triumphalis' (see Léon Gautier, *Oeuvres poétiques d'Adam de S. Victor*, Paris, 1859, II, 88) calls St Victor *Christi miles indefessus*, actually addresses him as *athleta* in another prose, ibid. p. 95. The designation *athleta* is most frequently given to Saint George, e.g. *O athleta, victor, laeta | Georgi fulgens laurea*, in Guido Maria Dreves, *Analecta Hymnica medii aevi*, Vol. XIX (Leipzig, 1895), p. 143, No. 239. In Chevalier, *Repertorium Hymnologicum*, Vol. II (1897), pp. 175–6, several hymns to saints are quoted which begin *O athleta (gloriose)*.

NOTES

11. *De Heinrico.*

MS. fol. 437rb l. 27–437va l. 23.—pp. 27 (sub 18) and 48. See also Chapter VII, pp. 102–11.

This poem is possibly the oldest of the political poems (Nos. 11–17) contained in the Goliard's Song Book. It seems to refer to events of the year 948, although it may have been written at a considerably later date. But see the note to *De Willelmo* (No. 21) which probably falls before 968. The last political poem (No. 17) of the Cambridge Collection laments the death of Emperor Conrad II (June 4, 1039).

The only other macaronic poem of our Collection, *Clericus et Nonna*, is half erased and very badly blacked. See fol. 438vb l. 16–439ra l. 8. There are many specimens of 'mixed prose,' i.e. prose half Latin and half German, among the Old High German writings of Notker and Williram.

The text of the present edition follows mainly W. Braune's *Althochdeutsches Lesebuch*. In l. 7 it admits the reading *bringit* (see pp. 33 and 104 sqq.), but in l. 5 it adheres to the old emendation *manoda* for *namoda*.

12. *Modus Ottinc.*

MS. fol. 434vb l. 31–435rb l. 11.—pp. 27 (sub 10) and 49.

Like the other *modi* (Nos. 2, 22, and 25) the *Modus Ottinc* has come down to us in the two manuscripts, C and W. The text given on p. 49 of the present edition follows on the whole the critical text of *M.S.D.* ³I, 46–48, which was mainly made by K. Lachmann. A photographic reproduction of the neumes of W. is contained in E. de Coussemaker's *Histoire de l'harmonie au moyen-âge*, Paris, 1852, planche viii.

The older literature, up to 1892, has been partly mentioned and utilized in *M.S.D.* ³II, 117–21. See also Ludwig Uhland, *Schriften zur Geschichte der Dichtung und Sage*, I, 475–7 (Stuttgart, 1865); Wilhelm Wattenbach, *Deutschlands Geschichtsquellen im Mittelalter bis zur Mitte des xiii. Jahrhunderts*, ⁶I (Berlin, 1893), 327, note 2; Meyer, *F. B.*, pp. 176–7; and especially the valuable observations of Joseph Seemüller, *Studien zu den Ursprüngen der altdeutschen Historiographie*, Halle, 1898, pp. 72–74.

'Modus Ottinc' (see ll. 2–3) means 'the Otto melody,' i.e. the tune which the court minstrels were playing when they desired to rouse by means of their music the Emperor from his sleep and thus to save him from the fire that had broken out in his palace (ll. 3–16). The tune probably was the melody of a popular German song. See Uhland, *l.c.* p. 476. The present poem was to be sung to the melody of this well-known song.

The 'Modus,' which deals with the Saxon Emperors, Otto I (936–73), Otto II (973–83), and Otto III (983–1002), is really a poem in praise of the last-mentioned Emperor, who is celebrated for his own sake as well as for the sake of his illustrious ancestors. It was probably written between the years 992 and 996. It shows the double influence of the German popular historical songs, which are as such (in their German form) lost to us, and of the Renaissance poetry of the learned clerics. It is not only written in the very skilfully composed metrical form of a sequence (one of the most artistic specimens of this kind) but it abounds with reminiscences from the ancient classical writers, of whom Virgil is even mentioned in l. 68 immediately after a quotation from Horace (ll. 65–67 are clearly reminiscences from Horace, 'Carmina,' I, 6, 11–12, *laudes egregii Caesaris et tuas culpa deterere ingeni*). There are frequent reminiscences of Virgil. With *moras rumpite* (l. 24) cp. Virgil, *Georg.* III, 43; *Aen.* IV, 569 and IX, 13. With *sanguinem inimicum* (l. 32) cp. *Aen.* XI, 720. With *bella fremunt* (l. 33) cp. *arma fremunt* in *Aen.* VII, 460 and XI, 453. The expression *fremere bellum* actually occurs in a fragment of an early Latin dramatist; but the author of the 'Modus' could of course hardly have met with it then (Dr Reid). For l. 55 cp. Cicero 'Pro Murena,' § 38: *cum fortis...tum etiam felix*.

The earlier portion of the 'Modus' (ll. 11–42) gives the description of the famous battle of the plains around the Lech (*licus*, l. 41) in which Otto I routed the Hungarian raiders. Wattenbach, *l.c.* ⁶I, 327, speaks of this poem as 'den Ereignissen schon so fern stehend, daß wir hinter ihm uns eine Fülle deutscher Lieder zu denken haben, von jenen *Mimi* gesungen, deren Widukind gedenkt.' *Dux Cuonrât intrepidus* (l. 26) is Duke Cuonrât

of Franconia, whose bravery in this battle was also praised by the contemporaneous historians. He was killed during the battle by an arrow when he lifted his helmet to get some fresh air.

The poem has been well translated into modern German verse by Winterfeld, on pp. 202-4, under the heading 'Die Ottonen.' He made some useful remarks on the poem on pp. 442-3 and 489, as did H. Reich, in editing Winterfeld's book, on pp. 84-85. The opening lines of Winterfeld's translation runs thus:

> Otto war's der Große,
> Dessen diese Weise
> Den Namen trägt 'Otten Weise.'
> Nächtens hatt' er ermüdet sich hingestreckt,
> Da lichterloh
> Stund die Königsburg jäh in Flammen.

13. *Nenia de Mortuo Heinrico II Imperatore.*

MS. fol. 436va l. 38–436vb l. 39.—pp. 27 (sub 16) and 50.—Grimm, pp. 333-5, 343, Introd. xliv.—Jaffé, pp. 458-9 (who utilized many emendations proposed by Grimm and on whom the text of the present edition is based). Du Méril, pp. 285-6, has some useful notes.

This song of lamentation, which expresses the universal mourning of the clergy at the death of Henry II, the last emperor of the Saxon family, was composed in the summer of 1024, between the death of Henry (July 13) and, as is shown by Stanza 7, l. 3, the election of his successor Conrad II (September 8). This poem and the next (No. 14), both of which have been preserved only in the Cambridge Manuscript, refer to the same event and may have been composed by Wipo. See the note to No. 17.

The structure of the stanzas is simple and popular, the rhythm regular, the caesurae riming with the end of each line. The refrain at the end of each stanza of this song is a leonine hexameter.

Line 25: *magnum episcopatum* refers to the see of Bamberg (*Mons Bavonis*, Poem No. 14, l. 17) which Henry founded, munificently endowed, and where he was buried. From his many pious benefactions and his deep interest in the welfare of the Church he was given the surname 'der Heilige.'

Line 27: *Advocatum Roma ploret.* A common designation of the head of the Holy Roman Empire was 'Protector (*advocatus*) of Rome.' In a famous poem of Walther von der Vogelweide, addressed, nearly 200 years later, to Frederic II (Lachmann's ed. 28, 1), the poet calls the Emperor: *Von Rôme vogt, von Pülle künec* (King of Apulia).

14. *Nenia in funebrem pompam Heinrici II Imperatoris.*

MS. fol. 434rb ll. 6-40.—pp. 27 (sub 8) and 51.—Jaffé, pp. 460-1 (on whom the text of the present edition is based). Du Méril, pp. 286-7, has some useful notes. See the notes to the preceding poem (No. 13). The poem has been preserved only in the Cambridge Manuscript.

Line 17 proves that the poem was written for the funeral of the Emperor at Bamberg. The cathedral, founded by Henry, and dearly loved by him, is asked faithfully to preserve his body. See Siegfried Hirsch (—Harry Bresslau), *Jahrbücher des deutschen Reiches unter Heinrich II*, Vol. III (1875), 300. As to the author see the note to No. 17. The long and solemn refrain of this song should be specially noticed.

15. *Cantilena in Conradum II factum Imperatorem.*

MS. fol. 432ra l. 7–432rb l. 23.—pp. 27 (sub 2) and 51-52.—Jaffé (who has some good notes and used some emendations proposed by Fröhner in *H. Z.* XI, 12. The present text is based on that of Jaffé), pp. 361-2.

NOTES

The date of this poem, which, like Nos. 13, 14, 16, is preserved only in the Cambridge MS., is March 26, 1027. The author of it may well be Wipo, although it cannot be proved with certainty. See Wilhelm Arndt, *Die Wahl Conrad II*, Göttingen, 1861. On pp. 46–52 there is an Excurs III *Über den sogenannten Krönungsleich in Conradum Salicum* (based on Fröhner, *H. Z.* XI, 12 sqq., as Jaffé's edition was not yet available). Arndt leaves it undecided if the poem was composed, by a clergyman, before or after the coronation. He makes it very probable that Wipo was the author of this song and fitly refers to Pertz's essay on Wipo published in the *Abhandlungen der Kgl. Akad. d. Wissenschaften zu Berlin*, 1851, p. 222. Jaffé, p. 462, is sceptical as to Wipo's authorship, while Wattenbach, *Geschichtsquellen*, [6]II, 13 accepts it. On Conrad's election cp. the fine passage, spoken by Werner, in the second act of Uhland's tragedy *Ernst, Herzog von Schwaben*.

The first stanza (*Melos cuncti*...) probably belongs to some other poem. The Manuscript has in Stanza 2 (*Voces laudis humane*...) a new big coloured initial such as is only used by the scribe to denote the beginning of a new song. Stanza 11 refers to July 13, 1024; Stanza 12 to Sept. 8, 1024; and Stanza 14 to March 26, 1027.

16. *Cantilena in Heinricum III anno* 1028 *regem coronatum.*

MS. fol. 436rb l. 38–436va l. 37.—pp. 27 (sub 15) and 52–53.—Du Méril, pp. 289–90, has some useful notes.— Jaffé (who made use of some emendations by Fröhner, and on whom the present text is based), pp. 462–4. The poem was also printed by F. L. v. Soltau, *Einhundert deutsche historische Volkslieder*, Leipzig, 1836, p. 31. See the account of the Coronation given in Wipo's *Vita Cuonradi Salici* in Pertz, *Monumenta Germaniae*, XI (1854), pp. 267–8. It runs thus: 'Anno Domini MXXVIII, indictione XI, imperator Chuonradus filium suum Heinricum, magni ingenii et bonae indolis puerum, aetate XI annorum, principibus regni cum tota multitudine populi id probantibus, a Pilegrino, archiepiscopo Coloniensi, in regalem apicem apud Aquisgrani palatium sublimari fecerat. Tunc in principali dominica paschae consecratus et coronatus, paschalem laetitiam triplicavit.'

The poem occurs only in the Cambridge Manuscript. It is a song, possibly written by Wipo himself, for the coronation of the Emperor Conrad's promising eleven-year-old son Henry, as King of Burgundy; in 1039 he succeeded his imperial father as Henry III. The coronation took place, amid much pomp and ceremony, at Aix-la-Chapelle (*ad Aquasgrani*, line 5) on April 14, 1028, where the prince was crowned by the Archbishop Piligrim of Cologne (lines 25–26). The 'Krönungshymnus' may well have been sung during the celebrations at Aachen. See Harry Bresslau, *Jahrbücher des deutschen Reiches unter Konrad II*, Vol. I (Leipzig, 1879), 240–2. Bresslau printed the Coronation Song in his school edition of *Wiponis Opera*, p. 80. See also W. Arndt, *Die Wahl Conrad II*, p. 51, and W. Wattenbach, *Deutschlands Geschichtsquellen im Mittelalter*, [6]II (Berlin, 1894), 13, who both consider it likely that Wipo was the author.

The whole of the first stanza serves as a refrain that was repeated after each stanza, probably by a chorus of singers, different from the one singer or the chorus that sang Stanzas 2 to 13. The short and popular metre is similar to that used in *Heriger* (No. 26), *Alfrâd* (No. 29) and *St Victor of Xanten* (No. 10).

Line 13: *agni sponsa* is the Church. l. 19 refers to Easter Sunday, March 26, 1027. l. 22 refers to the Coronation day, April 14, 1028. l. 25, *die predicto* (see l. 19), refers to Easter Sunday, 1028.

17. *Nenia de Mortuo Conrado II Imperatore.*

MS. fol. 440ra ll. 7–36.—pp. 27 (sub 32) and 53.—Du Méril, pp. 290–2, gives some useful notes.

The four stanzas of the Cambridge Manuscript are only the beginning of a longer poem, by Wipo, on the death of Conrad II, who died on June 4, 1039, at Utrecht. The whole poem is printed, in a critical edition, at the end of Wipo's Life of the Emperor, in the *Monumenta Germaniae*, Vol. XI (1854), pp. 274–5. The text of the present edition follows the text of the Monumenta ('Versus pro obitu Chuonradi imperatoris').

The poem has been twice translated into German. The first translator was P. Anselm Schubiger in his book *Die Sängerschule St Gallens vom achten bis zum zwölften Jahrhundert*, Einsiedeln und New-York, 1858, pp. 91–92. After a short introduction Schubiger translates the whole poem, printing the nine stanzas, Latin and German, side by side. The first lines run thus:

> Wer laut vermag zu singen, der singe dieses Lied
> Vom jammervollen Jahre, das Schmerz und Weh beschied.
> Es klagt das Volk im Freien, es klagt in jedem Haus,
> Spricht wachend durch die Nächte zu Gott den Seufzer aus:
> Herr, wer da lebt, bewahre; der Toten dich erbarme!

The second translator was W. Pflüger, who translated Wipo's Life of the Emperor Conrad, from the *Monumenta Germaniae*, in the Collection *Die Geschichtschreiber der deutschen Vorzeit*, Berlin, 1877. Second ed. Leipzig, 1888. Vol. 41, pp. 83–84. The first stanza of Pflüger's translation runs thus:

> Wen ziert der Stimme Klang, der singe diesen Sang
> Vom Jahr, da klaget manche Brust, vom unaussprechlichen Verlust,
> Um den ein jeder wird verzehrt im Schmerze draußen wie am Herd.
> Das Volk um seinen Herren klagt zur Nachtzeit, wie wann's wieder tagt.
> Schütze, die leben, o Herre Gott! Habe Erbarmen mit denen, die tot!

On the Burgundian Wipo, who was a confidential Chaplain and the biographer of Conrad II, see Wattenbach, *Deutschlands Geschichtsquellen im Mittelalter*, ^{6}II, 10–16, also the essay by Pertz quoted among the notes to No. 15, and Wattenbach's article in the *Allgemeine Deutsche Biographie*, Vol. XLIII (1898), 514. There is no doubt that this deeply-felt lament on the death of a beloved Emperor was composed by Wipo himself, although, at the end of Chapter 37 of his *Vita Chuonradi imperatoris* ('Monumenta Germaniae,' XI, 274), he only modestly says *pro quo quidam de nostris cantilenam lamentationum fecerat, quam postea filio suo Heinrico regi in Constantia civitate praesentavit*. Wipo more than once speaks of himself as *quidam de nostris*; he presented his lament to Henry III at Konstanz in April 1048. Wipo wrote a number of Latin poems which have come down to our times. He is also the author of the famous Easter sequence *Victimae paschali laudes*, which is still sung in German churches. Cp. K. S. Meister, *Das katholische deutsche Kirchenlied*, I, No. 179, pp. 347–53, and K. Simrock, *Lauda Sion*, Stuttgart, 1868, p. 182.

Line 11: *Gunnild regina*, or Chunehildis, Chunhilda, was the daughter-in-law of the Emperor, the young wife of his son King Henry, and daughter of Cnut the Dane. Conrad's wife was the Empress Gisela.

Line 12: *Herimannus* (in a spurious line) is Duke Heriman of Swabia, the step-brother of King Henry, the son of the Empress Gisela by her first marriage to the Duke of Swabia. He was a gallant youth of whom great hopes were entertained at the Imperial Court.

With regard to the contents of the second and third stanzas Chapter 37 of the *Vita Chuonradi imperatoris* (Mon. Germ. XI, 273) should be compared, where Wipo writes of the pestilence that decimated the German army in Italy in July 1038: 'Eo tempore propter nimium calorem nimia contagio pestilentiae exercitum invasit, neque aetatibus neque personis pepercit. Ibi regina Chunehildis, coniux Heinrici regis, 15^g Kalendas Augusti quasi in limine vitae, ingressu mortis occubuit, relinquens tantummodo solam filiolam de rege, quam postea pater Christo desponsans, in abbatissam consecrari fecit. Filius imperatricis Herimannus dux Alamannorum, iuvenis bonae indolis et in rebus bellicis strennuus, eadem peste gravatus inter manus peritissimorum medicorum 5. Kalendas Augusti non sine magno detrimento imperii obiit. Eodem mense atque sequenti maxima multitudo exercitus morbo contacta periit. Corpus reginae tenerum et delicatum, aromatibus conditum cum rege et imperatrice ductum ad Germaniam, in praepositura Lintburg sepultum est. De duce statutum fuerat, ut in Constantiam civitatem Alamanniae duceretur; sed calore nimio obstante, in Tridento sepelitur.' See also Harry Bresslau, *Konrad II*, Vol. II, 318, notes 1 and 2.

NOTES

With regard to the authorship of the poems Nos. 13 to 17, it is clear that Wipo must be considered to be the author of at least the last one. He was very probably also the writer of No. 16. About the other three poems all that can be said is that it is possible that they were written by him, but that no direct evidence of his authorship can be adduced. This was stated as early as 1851 by Pertz in his paper published by the *Berliner Akademie der Wissenschaften* in 1852, pp. 215 sqq.

18. *Gratulatio reginae a morbo recreatae.*

MS. fol. 441ra l. 22–441rb l. 14.—pp. 27 (sub 40) and 54.—Jaffé, p. 465 (on whom the text of the present edition is based).

With regard to the charming trochaic metre of fifteen syllables in which this poem is composed compare Nos. 21, 31, the note to No. 8, and also Grimm, *Lat. Ged.* Introd. xlvii–xlix. It is to be noted that all the lines have the same ending, viz. -a (as also in No. 31). The same easy metre of fifteen syllables, with a break after the eighth, but without rime, occurs in earlier Latin literature, e.g. in the 'Pervigilium Veneris' (*Cras amet qui nunquam amavit, quique amavit cras amet*), and in the delightful poem by Tiberianus (*Amnis ibat inter arva valle fusus frigida*). See Emil Baehrens, *Unedirte lateinische Gedichte*, Leipzig, 1877, pp. 34 sqq.

This poem, which is found only in the Cambridge Manuscript, seems to be the composition of a literary lady at the Imperial court. The exact occasion for which it was written is unknown.

l. 21. *nonnulla...sidera.* Should the reading not be *deus, nulla non qui semper scandit super sidera? nulla non...sidera* meaning 'all the stars'? The *non* was perhaps omitted in the original manuscript and subsequently put above *nulla* from where the Canterbury copyist placed it by mistake in front of *nulla* instead of after it.

19. *Cantilena in Heribertum Archiepiscopum Coloniensem.*

MS. fol. 433va l. 3–433vb l. 35.—pp. 27 (sub 9) and 54–55.—Jaffé, pp. 456–8 (on whom the text of the present edition is based. He made several emendations of the text and added some useful notes).

The poem occurs only in the Cambridge Manuscript. It is composed in the form of a sequence and is a song of praise in honour of Heribert, who was Archbishop of Cologne from 999 to 1021. It is provided with a refrain. The song seems to have been composed soon after his death on March 16, 1021. Heribert was a distinguished priest and politician under Otto III (whose Chancellor he became in 998) and Henry II.

See Lantberti *Vita Heriberti*, in the 'Monumenta Germaniae,' SS. IV; Fröhner, *H. Z.* XI, 22 note; W. Wattenbach, *Deutschlands Geschichtsquellen im Mittelalter*, ^{8}I (1893), 327 note 3, and ^{6}II (1894) 136–7; and the article in the *Allgemeine Deutsche Biographie*, XII (1880), 110–11, at the end of which the present poem is mentioned. Heribert founded the Benedictine Monastery at Deutz on the right bank of the Rhine opposite Cologne. He was buried at Deutz in the Church of St Mary (see Stanza 9), and the present Katholische Pfarrkirche possesses a *tumba* of St Heribert dating from the year 1147. In poem No. 9 another religious foundation at Cologne is referred to; poem No. 10 refers to Xanten, No. 20 to Treves (Archbishop Poppo), and No. 21 probably to Mayence (Archbishop Willem)—all persons and places of importance on the Middle and Lower Rhine, where the collection of songs was originally made. See pp. 23, 30, 40.

With regard to the metre see Fröhner, *H.Z.* 20, and Bartsch, *Lat. Seq.* pp. 30 sqq. The repetition of the refrain *Pater, nate, spiritus sancte*, etc. after each stanza proves that the poem was destined to be sung.

The words *in huius* in the refrain were added by Jaffé, as there is a blank in the Manuscript between *corde* and *vite* in which another hand put the word *pius*. See note to Stanza 5.

Stanza 4 contains an allusion to Matthew xxv. 21.

Stanza 5. See Matthew xx. 1, 2, 9.—The words *tertii Ottonis* were added by Jaffé. A space was left in the Manuscript by the monk who copied the original and who was perhaps unable to read the words which he omitted. In fol. 433vb l. 27 he had written *fecerat*, which in the margin he corrected to *fecit*. This refers to the events of the year 998. For *scandit dextram note viam Pithagorice*, see on page 100 the note to Poem No. 42, Stanzas 6–8, and also du Méril, p. 279 note 3.

Stanza 6. *Post non magnum temporis curriculum*, viz. on July 9, 999; the *summus pontifex* was Pope Silvester II.

Stanza 7. *gerit*. Should it be *gessit*?

Stanza 8. *consolatur*. Should it be *consolatus (est)*?

Stanza 9. See the previous page, also Fröhner, *H.Z.* xi, 22 note, and Lantberti, *Vita Heriberti* ('Monum. Germ.' SS. iv, 746), 'iubens in Divitensi castro monasterium exstrui,' and p. 753, 'translatum est autem corpus eius et illatum sanctae dei genetricis, quod ipse fundavit, coenobio.' Castrum Divitense, or Tuitiense, is the present town of Deutz. Heribert died on March 16, 1021.

Stanza 10. *fecit*. Jaffé, and also Piper, print *fecerat*, but the *cit* in the margin shows that *fecerat* which the scribe had first written should be altered into *fecit*.

20. *Ecclesie Trevirensis nomine scripti ad Popponem Archiepiscopum versus.*

MS. fol. 438rb l. 23–438va l. 11.—pp. 27 (sub 24) and 55.—Jaffé, pp. 464–5 (on whom the text of the present edition is based. He added a number of useful notes. For the sake of the metre I have added *nunc* before *iubent* (l. 13) and have written *muniat* instead of *premuniat* (l. 21)).

The poem of welcome, addressed on behalf of the Church of Treves (*sponsa*) to her new Archbishop Poppo (*sponsus*), is only preserved in the Cambridge Manuscript. Poppo, the son of Leopold I, Margrave of Austria, who was first Provost of Bamberg Cathedral, and subsequently made Archbishop of Treves by the Emperor Henry II at a time when conditions at the see of Treves were specially difficult, was a learned and energetic man who fully justified the Emperor's confidence. He was Archbishop from 1016–47. See Harry Bresslau, *Jahrbücher des deutschen Reiches unter Heinrich II*, Vol. iii (1875), 27–32; the *Allgemeine Deutsche Biographie*, xxvi (1888) 431–4; and especially Friedrich Lesser, *Erzbischof Poppo von Trier* (1016–47), Leipzig, 1888, pp. 22 sqq., where the conditions are discussed under which Poppo came to Treves, the work he did there, and throughout which this poem is referred to.

The poem was probably written between 1028–35 (see the note to ll. 24–26). The metre is the same as that of the poems No. 27 (*De Iohanne abbate*) and No. 28 (*Sacerdos et lupus*). The caesurae and the end rime, each half-line has eight syllables, the rhythm is iambic. In this popular metre many medieval Latin hymns were written. See *M.S.D.*[1] (1864), p. 317, and Grimm, *Lat. Ged.* Introd. pp. xliv sqq. Grimm calls attention to the great popularity of this metre in early Medieval Latin poetry, giving instances, and adds 'Die Weise scheint besonders in Deutschland und namentlich in lothringischem, niederländischem Gebiet, lange Zeiten hindurch, beliebt. Docen (*Misc.* ii, 191) führt aus Trierischer Gegend folgenden Anfang eines Liedes, vermutlich des dreizehnten Jahrhunderts an:

> Sol solis in stellifero
> Stellas excedit radio,
> Sed unica quam diligo
> Mihi placet et populo.

Hierher gehört nun auch das merkwürdige neulich von Leo entdeckte Berliner Bruchstück des lateinischen *Gregorius*....' The same metre is also found in the capital story *Unibos* (Grimm, *Lat. Ged.* pp. 354–80), translated by Heyne (pp. 1–44) in the metre of the original under the title 'Gevatter Einochs.'

NOTES

l. 5. *quod fusca sim.* Cp. Cantic. I, 5: *Nolite me considerare, quod fusca sim.* See also l. 16: *qui me fuscam illuminat.*

l. 6. For the facts referred to in these lines see Jaffé, *l.c.*, who quotes parallel passages from the *Gesta Treverorum* ('Monum. Germ.' SS. VIII, 171 sqq.). The Cathedral is a very old building, one of the oldest churches of Germany. It had several times been partially destroyed, especially by the Normans, and it was renovated and enlarged by Poppo and his successors.

l. 7. *uritat.* Should it be *quaeritat*? (Sir John Sandys).

l. 14. *Simeon tuus* refers to a Greek monk Simeon, whom Poppo had brought with him from the Holy Land and who lived for seven years in the Eastern tower of the fine old Roman gate (*the Porta Nigra*) between 1028 and 1035. The *Porta Nigra*, or *Römertor*, is for this reason also called *Simeonstor*.

From l. 16 it follows that the poem was written during Simeon's lifetime, hence between 1028 and 1035.

21. *De Willelmo.*

MS. fol. 441va ll. 1-13.—pp. 27 (sub 42) and 56.—Jaffé, p. 466 (on whom the text of the present edition is based).

The poem is fragmentary, as after l. 8 one or more lines must be missing although there is no gap in the manuscript. It is uncertain who the Willem praised in this song is. In Songs Nos. 19 and 20 the Archbishops of Cologne and Treves are celebrated, and it seems very probable that this poem refers to the great Archbishop of Mayence (954-68), the highly-gifted natural son of the Emperor Otto I, who during his father's reign played a very important part in the spiritual and political life of Germany. He was elected Archbishop on Dec. 17, 954, and died on March 2, 968. See the *Allgemeine Deutsche Biographie*, Vol. 43 (1898), 115-17. There is no other Willem to whom this poem can be taken to refer with equal probability. If it does refer to him it is one of the oldest, if not the oldest, of the historical poems included in the Goliard's Song book. See the note to No. 11 (*De Heinrico*).

The poem was intended to be sung by a singer (*cantor*, l. 3) to the accompaniment of a lyre played by another musician (*magister*, l. 2).

With regard to the metre of this poem, see the note to Poem No. 18. All the lines end in *-e* (except ll. 1, 5, and 2).

ll. 7-8. In 964 the Archbishop Wilhelm of Mayence was appointed by the Emperor Otto head of the Imperial Chancery, and during his father's absence in Italy Wilhelm governed the German lands with a firm hand.

l. 12. *zabulon subtrahite. zabulon* stands for *diabolum.* The substitution of *z* for *di* in *zabulus* = *diabolus* is very frequent in Medieval Latin manuscripts. Many instances are given in Hermann Rönsch, *Italia und Vulgata*, Marburg, ²1875, p. 457. Similarly *zacones* is written for *diacones*, *zebus* for *diebus*, etc.

22. *Modus Liebinc.*

MS. fol. 435vb l. 29-436rb l. 9.—pp. 27 (sub 13) and 56.—Jaffé, pp. 472-4.—*M.S.D.* ³I (1892), 44-45 and ³II, 114-17. Meyer, *F.B.* pp. 175-6 (critical text). The sequence has come down to us in three MSS., W, C, and a Vatican Codex utilized by W. Meyer. The text here given is mainly based on that in the latest edition of *M.S.D.* (which is critical and generally follows the readings of W), but occasionally the text as given by Meyer in *F.B.* (in ll. 8 and 13) has been adopted. The readings of C can easily be ascertained from the transcript. On the sparing use made of rime in the *Modus Liebinc* and *Modus Ottinc*, see Bartsch, *Lat. Seq.* p. 163.

NOTES

Du Méril₁, pp. 275–6, prints the song under the mistaken heading 'Chanson sur l'air de l'amour' and adds a few useful notes. The title *Modus Liebinc*, which is given to this facetious poem in W, means 'Poem sung to the air of the Song on Liebo.' On Liebo see the note to *M.S.D.* ³II, 116–17. On the term 'Modus' cp. p. 29, note 1, of this book. These Latin songs were often written to well-known and popular tunes.

For discussions of the sequence later than *M.S.D.* ³II see J. Kelle, I, 204, 206, 381.—Kögel₁, 254–5, and Kögel₂, p. 134. Philip Schuyler Allen, in *Modern Philology*, v, 3 (Jan. 1908), 429.—Reinhold Köhler, *Kleine Schriften*, Berlin, 1900, II, 564.—See also Dunlop-Liebrecht, *Geschichte der Prosadichtungen*, Berlin, 1851, pp. 41, 499 (note 374ᵃ), 522, 542; H. Kurz, note to Burkhard Waldis's *Esopus*, IV, 71; and Willi Splettstösser, *Der heimkehrende Gatte und sein Weib in der Weltlitteratur*, 1898. W. P. Ker, *The Dark Ages*, London and Edinburgh, ²1911, p. 227, says: 'In the Middle Ages, Germany is ahead of France in a kind which is reckoned peculiarly French; the earliest Fabliaux are in German Latin, with Swabians for comic heroes.'

The poem has been translated into rimeless verse by Heyne, *Spielmannsgedichte*, pp. 59–63, under the title 'Der Sang von Liebo'; and in rimed verse, with some imitation of the metrical structure of the sequence, by Winterfeld, pp. 213–15 (discussion p. 441), under the more appropriate title 'Das Schneekind.' August von Platen treated the subject in capital stanzas at the end of the second act of *Der romantische Ödipus*.

Heyne's rendering begins thus:

> Hört an, ihr Leute, einen lächerlichen Schwank,
> Und vernehmet, welcher Art
> Einst ein Schwabenweib den Mann betrog und er's ihr heimgab.
>
> Ein Schwäblein war von Konstanz und ging übers Meer,
> Schatzbeladen war sein Schiff;
> Seine nur zu geile Frau ließ er daheim im Hause.

The same lines are rendered by Winterfeld in the following way:

> Hört zu und merkt
>   Treulich alles Volk den tollen Schwank,
>   Wie's des Schwaben Frau gelang,
>   Trügen ihren Mann,
>   Und wie er Gleiches ihr getan.
>
> Von Konstanz fuhr
>   Einst ein Schwäble hin wohl übers Meer,
>   Waren tauschen hin und her;
>   Derweil schuf sein Weib
>   Daheim sich guten Zeitvertreib.

Meyer, *F.B.* p. 176, rightly observes: 'Dies Gedicht hat mit dem Modus Ottinc (our No. 12) so große Ähnlichkeit der Formen, daß beide Gedichte von demselben Verfasser um das Jahr 1000 geschrieben oder richtiger gesungen sein müssen. Denn die Formen dieser Gedichte sind so krystallklar und so klangschön, daß sie von einem Meister geschaffen sein müssen, der des Gesanges und des Harfenspiels mindestens so kundig war als der schönen Rede. Die Melodie ist uns leider nicht erhalten: aber schon der gleiche rythmische Bau aller Strophenschlüsse...bezeugt, daß die so verschiedenartigen Strophen alle in dieselbe Schlußmelodie ausliefen....'

The story of the 'snow-child' or 'ice-child,' which is very widely spread over the literatures of Europe (see the references given above and in *M.S.D.* ³II, 115) may possibly be of Indian origin. See Felix Liebrecht, *Zur Volkskunde*, Heilbronn, 1879, p. 101. The story was early sung in Germany by mimes; it was one of the subjects sung by a mime before a rich lord as told by Sextus Amarcius. See p. 40, note 1, also Winterfeld, p. 490. Four other Latin versions (2 long and 2 short) are given by W. Wattenbach, under the heading 'Das Schneekind,' in Haupt's *Zeitschrift für deutsches Alterthum*, XIX (1876), 119 sqq., 240 and 498. The shortest version, an epigram of but one distich, was printed by Gaston Paris in the *Romania*, v (1876), 232. For

a recent free treatment of the old subject in German verse by Johannes Ninck see the Zürich periodical *Wissen und Leben*, VIII (August 1915), 736-7.

W. P. Ker, *l. c.* p. 227, rightly remarks: 'The malice of the *Snow-Child* is something different from anything in vernacular literature till the time of Boccaccio and Chaucer; the learned language and the rather difficult verse perhaps helping to refine the mischief of the story. It is self-conscious, amused at its own craft: a different thing from the ingenuous simplicity of the French "merry tales," not to speak of the churlish heaviness of the worst among them.'

The seven lines printed in brackets after line 30 (Stanza III, C) are not found in MSS. V(aticanus) and W; they were added in C and are justly called by Meyer 'diese gereimte und doch ungereimte Strophe.'

l. 47. *Sic perfidam Suevus coniugem deluserat* is the original reading of the poem as given in the MSS. V and W, while in C the bad reputation of the Swabians with the neighbouring tribes is reflected in the altered reading *Sic perfidus Suevus coniugem deluserat*. See *M.S.D.* ^{3}II, 115, and Kelle, 204. A wily Swabian is also the hero of the *Modus Florum* (our No. 25), which in the Cambridge Manuscript follows immediately (fol. 436rb 10) after the *Modus Liebinc*. See L. Uhland, *Schriften zur Geschichte der Dichtung und Sage*, III, 223.

23. De Proterii filia.

MS. fol. 439rb l. 1–439vb l. 9.—pp. 27 (sub 29) and 57.—Jaffé, pp. 467-9 (who made several emendations in the text of the manuscript and on whom the text of the present edition is based). In one or two cases Jaffé's reading of the manuscript must be corrected.

The poem is only found in the Cambridge Manuscript and it differs in form essentially from the other sequences. It was intended to be sung. See Stanza 1. Stanzas 2 and 4 are provided with neum-accent notation. There are rimes in each stanza occurring at irregular intervals.

Stanzas 1 and 2 are merely introductory, the real story begins with Stanza 3.

This poem is a very old, but not absolutely the oldest, instance of a man's compact with the Devil in German literature. See Kögel$_1$, 247 note.

The origin of this story is very probably not German. See Kögel$_1$, p. 260, and Kögel$_2$, p. 135, § 121.

In the first stanza every word begins with a *c*. Such playing with words, especially with words beginning with a *c*, is not unusual in Medieval Latin literature. Compare fol. 432ra lines 5-6, which are obviously corrupted (see the note on Poem VII on p. 73). The most amusing instance is perhaps a poem addressed by the monk Hugbald to the Emperor Charles the Bald, and called *Ecloga de laudibus calvitii*, which consists of 141 hexameter verses in which every word begins with a *c*. The first and the last lines of this whimsical production run thus:

> Carmina, clarisonae, calvis cantate, camaenae......
> Completur claris carmen cantabile calvis.

This poem is preserved in another portion of the Cambridge MS. Gg. 5. 35 and is printed in the publication by the Rev. Dr John Allen Giles, *Anecdota Bedae, Lanfranci et aliorum*, London, 1851, pp. 71-76, and also, with some critical notes, in Migne's *Patrologia*, Vol. 132 (1853), pp. 1041-7.

24. De Lantfrido et Cobbone.

MS. fol. 433ra l. 19–433va l. 2.—pp. 27 (sub 5) and 58.—Jaffé, pp. 470-1.—*M.S.D.* ^{3}I, 48-50 (on which the text of the present edition is based), and ^{3}II, 121-7 (with a valuable discussion, by Scherer, of the various kinds of 'Freundschaftssagen'). The poem is only found in the Cambridge Manuscript, but a Latin metrical treatment of the same subject, the text of which is in a corrupt state, was first published by Gaston Paris in *Le Moyen Age*, Vol. I (1888), pp. 179-84, and subsequently printed, with emendations by himself and others, by

Steinmeyer in *M.S.D.* ³II, 124–5. See also H. Patzig's reconstruction and discussion in *Romanische Forschungen*, Vol. VI (1891), 424.

Of later literature see Kelle, I, 203, and especially Kögel₁, 255–60 (who treats the subject-matter very fully and gives many bibliographical references), and Kögel₂, p. 134, sub 3. See also M. Landau, *Die Quellen des Decamerone*, Stuttgart, ²1884, pp. 267 sqq.

The relation of the Parisian metrical version of this often treated motif of true friendship ('Freundschaftssage') to the rhythmical version of C has not yet been clearly established if it ever can be determined with any degree of certainty. The matter has been carefully discussed in the notes to *M.S.D.* and by Kögel. Steinmeyer considers the rhythmical version to be the older, while Kögel thought that there must have been a common source for C and P. The source to which all the different versions may ultimately be traced back was probably Greek and not Oriental. See Wilhelm Grimm, Introd. to his *Athis and Prophilias*, pp. 52 sqq.

With the beginning of this piece compare the very similar passage in Isidore, *Origines*, Book III, Chapter XVIII, p. 116: *De triformi musicae divisione*: '1. Ad omnem autem sonum, qui materies cantilenarum est, triformem esse constat naturam. Prima est harmonica, quae ex vocum cantibus constat. Secunda organica, quae ex flatu constitit. Tertia rhythmica, quae pulsu digitorum numeros recipit. 2. Nam aut voce editur sonus, sicut per fauces; aut flatu, sicut per tubam vel tibiam; aut pulsu, sicut per citharam, aut per quodlibet aliud, quod percutiendo canorum [sonorum *vulg.*] est.' After this Chapter XIX deals with 'De prima divisione musicae quae harmonica dicitur'; Chapter XX 'De secunda divisione quae organica dicitur'; Chapter XXI 'De tertia...quae rhythmica nuncupatur.' In this chapter on the string instruments the 'rota' is not yet mentioned. See the note on p. 96.

For the words *alicubi pretermittam absque me* after l. 72 (fol. 433va ll. 1–2) see *M.S.D.* ³I, 50 (note). Does it mean in the Latin of the scribe 'the rest I will pass over'?

25. Modus Florum.

MS. fol. 436rb ll. 10–37.—pp. 27 (sub 14) and 59.—Jaffé, pp. 471–2.—*M.S.D.* ³I, 42–43 (on which the text of the present edition is mainly based), and ³II, 112–14.

The poem is found in two manuscripts, W and C. In C it follows immediately after the story of the 'snow-child.' Both are stories of clever Swabians, but in both cases C has altered the original text in order to introduce an uncomplimentary remark to the Swabians. In l. 34 C reads *falsa gener regius est arte factus*. See the note to the 'Modus Liebinc' on p. 83.

See also Kelle, I, 204–5, 207. Kögel₁, 252–4, and Kögel₂, p. 133, § 119 (1). Meyer, *F.B.* p. 177. Carl Müller-Fraureuth, *Die deutschen Lügendichtungen bis auf Münchhausen*, Halle, 1881, pp. 3 sqq. and 86.

The poem has been translated twice into German verse. The first rendering is by Müller-Fraureuth, pp. 3–4, and the beginning runs thus:

> Ein Lügenlied will ich euch singen,
> Das soll euch wohl zum Lachen bringen.
> Es war ein König, der sein Töchterlein,
> So kündet' er, dem Manne wollte frei'n,
> Der also Meister wär' im Lügen,
> Daß sich der König ihm müßt' fügen.

The other version is written in very humorous and colloquial German by Winterfeld (pp. 220–1) under the title 'Vom König, der alles glaubte,' and the corresponding lines are rendered in the following manner:

> Ich weiß ein Schelmenliedchen fein,
> Das üb' ich gleich den Kindern ein,
> Daß alles sie zum Lachen bringen,
> Wenn sie die Schelmenverse singen.

NOTES

> Ein König eine Tochter hätt',
> War wohlgestalt und zier und nett;
> Der macht' in seinem ganzen Land
> Ein feierlich Gebot bekannt,
> Wer die Prinzessin freien wollte,
> Daß der ein Ding erfüllen sollte:
> 'Kommt vor mein Angesicht ein Mann,
> Der also grausam schwindeln kann,
> Daß ich ihn selber strafe Lügen,
> Dann soll er meine Tochter kriegen.'

The 'mendosa cantilena' was fitly to be recited 'modulos per mendaces' and, as appears from the opening lines, was probably originally composed for the youthful pupils of a monk in the Monastery School. Kelle says (p. 205) 'Wahrscheinlich wurden die "Lügenweisen" an einem Schulfeste, bei denen es damals namentlich in den Domschulen mitunter schon recht lustig herging, wirklich vorgetragen....Und wie die Geschichte von dem wundersamen Hasen mag manche andre, die im Volke umlief, für die Klosterschüler, zum Teil von den Klosterschülern, in lateinische Verse gebracht worden sein. Wahrscheinlich sind in den Klöstern solche Lügenmärchen...auch erfunden worden.' W. P. Ker, *l. c.* p. 227, calls it *How the Swabian made the King say 'That's a story.'*

The story of the Wonderful Hare, sung in the 'Melody of the Flowers,' is the oldest German 'Lügenmärchen' that has come down to our times. With it may be compared the fragments of another hunter's story, in a St Gallen Manuscript of the eleventh century, the lines on the terrible wild boar (see *M.S.D.* ³I, 56 and ³II, 131, and J. Baechtold, *Geschichte d. deutschen Lit. in d. Schweiz*, p. 15), in which capital use has been made of the form of poetic hyperbola. Similar amusing poems of the same or a somewhat earlier time are *Tres iuvenes fratres* (Dümmler, *Poetae*, II, 474; translated by Winterfeld, pp. 172-4, under the title 'Der Wunschbock') and the capital *Unibos* (Grimm, *Lat. Ged.* pp. 354-80; transl. by Heyne, *Lat. Spielmannsgedichte*, pp. 1-44, under the title 'Gevatter Einochs'), *Heriger* (our No. 26), and others.

With regard to the style of the 'mendosa cantilena' which, on account of its being devoid of rime, must not be later than the very beginning of the eleventh century, W. Meyer says: 'Das Gedicht ist sicher eine Sequenz, allein vergeblich müht man sich, die Form klar zu erkennen. Man muß sich mit der Eingangsstrophe zufrieden geben:

> Mendosam, quam cantilenam ago   puerulis commendatam dabo:
> quo modulos per mendaces risum   auditoribus ingentem ferant,

d. h. das Schelmenstück wird auch in Schelmenversen dargestellt....Die Sequenzenform ist bereits völlig die Form der weltlichen feinen Lyrik geworden.' (*Fragm. Bur.* p. 177. Reprint 1, 45-46.)

l. 26. *totidem pisarum* 'as many peas.' Uhland, *S.G.D.S.* III, 223, and Müller-Fraureuth, p. 3, translate *pisarum* by 'Goldstücke,' 'Goldfüchse'; but Du Cange in his *Glossarium Med. et Inf. Lat.* VI (1886), p. 333, shows that *pisa* was sometimes used instead of *pisum*. He quotes several instances to which the present may be added.

26. *Heriger*.

MS. fol. 438ʳᵃ l. 30-438ʳᵇ l. 22.—pp. 27 (sub 23) and 59-60.—Du Méril₁, pp. 298-302 ('Chanson sur les fausses visions,' with numerous notes).—Jaffé, pp. 455-6.—*M.S.D.* ³I, 53-55 and ³II, 128-9 (on which the text of the present edition is based). The poem has only been preserved in the Cambridge Manuscript.

Heriger was Archbishop of Mayence from 913-27, but the humorous and satirical story with which his name is connected in this poem was probably coupled with it at a much later date than the early tenth

century. It seems very likely, as was pointed out by Grimm, *Lat. Ged.* pp. 373-4, that our poem is a retelling in Latin Adonic riming couplets of a favourite subject that was originally treated in vernacular German popular song. In it the old merry tale of the cunning Swabian who stole and ate the liver was combined with the story of an impostor who was punished by Archbishop Herigêr. See also Allen, *Mod. Phil.* v, 3 (Jan. 1908), pp. 429-30; Kögel$_1$, pp. 263-4, and Kögel$_2$, p. 135 (sub 2). A similar metre is found in Poems Nos. 3 and 10, and the same occurs in No. 29. For the metre and style see Bartsch, *Lat. Seq.* (in various places), *M.S.D.* ^{3}II, 127, and note W. Wackernagel's observation (*Geschichte d. deutschen Litteratur* (ed. E. Martin), ^{2}I (Basel, 1879), p. 94) with regard to this 'schwankhafte Erzählung': 'es wird eine Rückwirkung der deutschen Dichtkunst sein, daß diese Form nun auch der lateinischen zur Darstellung unkirchlicher Stoffe dient.'

With regard to the treatment of the subject-matter see Grimm, *l.c.* pp. 343-4; Scherer in *M.S.D.* ^{2}I, 129, and in his *Geschichte der deutschen Dichtung im elften und zwölften Jahrhundert*, Strassburg, 1879, p. 7, where he very fitly compares our poem with the sixteenth-century 'Schwänke' of Hans Sachs. He says: 'Auch vor komischer Behandlung des Heiligen schrickt man nicht zurück, wie Rosviths Dulcitius und das Lied vom Erzbischof Heriger beweisen, welches letztere sich unmittelbar mit Hans Sachsischen Legenden vergleicht.' Gustav Gröber, in his *Grundriß der romanischen Philologie*, Vol. II, 1 (1902), p. 179, rightly says with regard to Nos. 22, 25, and 26: 'Allen diesen Schwänken eignet ein wirksamer sachlicher Witz und eine seine Wirkung befördernde schlichte Darstellung.'

The poem was translated into popular German metre by Heyne, pp. 50-53, the first stanza of which runs:

> Heriger, der da hat
> Bischofssitz in der Stadt
> Mainz, gab einmal Gehör
> Einem, der sprach, er wär'
> Einst in die Höll' entrückt,
> Hätt' sich drin umgeblickt.

Stanza 6 is not given in the Cambridge Manuscript, and there is no indication that anything is missing. Thomas Wright was the first to point out this omission by writing 'there appears to be here a verse wanting, in which Peter was mentioned as *magister cocorum*.' See p. 33.

Lines 33-36. Jaffé refers to Luke i. 13-15: 'Et vocabis nomen eius Ioannes...et vinum et siceram non bibet.'

l. 66. The manuscript ends with *cave ne furtum facias*. Jaffé added *esum*, Grimm *tetrum*. The addition of *spurcum* was fitly suggested by Max Rödiger in Haupt's *Zeitschrift f. deutsches Alterthum*, 33, 417.

27. *De Iohanne abbate.*

MS. fol. 441rb ll. 15-40.—pp. 27 (sub 41) and 60.—Du Méril$_1$, pp. 189-90 (under the heading 'Légende par saint Fulbert' with some notes).—Jaffé, pp. 469 and 560.—Winterfeld (on whom the present edition is based) gave a critical text, pp. 430-1.

This humorous poem has been preserved in two manuscripts the readings of which are in some cases widely different. Apart from C it has come down to us in a Parisian Codex (P), printed in C. de Villiers' edition of *Fulberti Carnotensis opera varia*, Paris, 1608, page 183. See Winterfeld, p. 430. Winterfeld based his critical edition mainly on P. The readings of C can easily be ascertained on fol. 441.

With regard to the popular metre see the note to Poem 20; also du Méril$_1$, p. 190. Winterfeld calls the verses 'etwas freigebaut'; instead of riming couplets the rimes are occasionally intermittent.

The author of this merry tale was Saint Fulbert, Bishop of Chartres, who died in 1029, but who probably wrote the poem as a young 'clerk' long before he was elevated to the see of Chartres. Hence the poem may have been composed in the opening years of the eleventh century.

NOTES

The 'hübsche Erzählung eines französischen Spielmanns' (Winterfeld, p. 430) was translated, from his own emended text, by Winterfeld (p. 211) under the title 'Der Einsiedel.' The first lines run thus:

> Es war einmal ein Mönch Johann,
> Der hoher Tugend Ruhm gewann,
> Ob zwar er klein nur an Gestalt;
> Der lebt' selbzweit im wüsten Wald.
>
> Er sprach: 'Den lieben Englein gleich
> Will leben ich im Himmelreich,
> Nicht Speise kennen noch Gewand,
> So zubereitet Menschenhand.'

The beginning of the ditty was thus rendered in English by Ph. Schuyler Allen, *Mod. Phil.* v, 3, p. 468:

> A monk named John, of stature small,
> But in the virtues straight and tall,
> Thus to the older brother spoke,
> Who dwelt with him mid hermit-folk:
>
> 'I fain would live like those above,'
> He said, 'secure in Heaven's love,
> No raiment wear, no viands take,
> Such as the hands of men do make.'

l. 5. *Iohannes abba.* Winterfeld (p. 431) remarks, 'Das bedeutet aber hier nicht den Abt, sondern, weil es sich um Heilige der ägyptischen Wüste handelt, die selbzweit zusammen hausen, so ist *abba* nur als der ihnen vom Volke willig zugestandene Ehrentitel zu nehmen, wie der Mönch *pater* genannt wird.' In C Iohannes is called *minor* and the older hermit *maior*.

l. 14. *incepti.* Would it be preferable to read *inepti*?

l. 43. *intentus ad crustula.* See Winterfeld, p. 431. John is so famished that the simple hermit's food seems delicious to him and he munches it with the keenest pleasure regardless of all the mockery of his 'maior.'

28. *Sacerdos et Lupus.*

MS. fol. 440rb l. 16–440va l. 34.—pp. 27 (sub 34) and 61.—Grimm, *Lat. Ged.* pp. 340-2 (from a copy sent by J. M. Kemble) and 345.—Du Méril₁, pp. 302-9 (with numerous notes).—*M.S.D.* First ed. (1864), pp. 37-40 and 317-8 (with useful notes; the poem was omitted from the later editions because most probably it is of French origin. The text of the present edition is based on *M.S.D.*).

The poem has come down to us in two manuscripts, C, and a manuscript of Fulda (F) made known by E. Dümmler in Haupt's *Zeitschrift für deutsches Alterthum*, xv (1872), 452. Dümmler merely gave the various readings of F as compared with the text of C (reproduced in *M.S.D.*).

The poem is called at the beginning a 'iocularis cantio.' It was evidently intended to be sung, and the metre is the same as that in which it was customary to compose popular church-hymns, viz. stanzas of four short lines, each of which consisted of eight syllables. See the note to Poem No. 20. The present poem is a merry tale, a 'Schwank,' but not a true animal fable. The same story (of 'un prestre dant Martin') is told in the short eighteenth 'branche' of the *Roman de Renart* (E. Martin's ed. Vol. II (1885), pp. 243-7), where it is obviously based on the present Latin poem which, in l. 103, is referred to as an 'escripture.' (See Grimm, *Reinhart Fuchs* (Berlin, 1834), Introd. cxxiv, 12 and Gröber's *Grundriß*, II, 1 (1902), § 275, p. 410.) On the French origin of the story see also Ernst Martin, *Göttinger Gelehrte Anzeigen*, Vol. 160, 571, and *Observations sur le Roman de Renart*, Strasbourg, 1887, pp. 91-92; Kögel₁, pp. 264-7, and Kögel₂, p. 135, § 121.

The poem was translated by Heyne, pp. 45–49, who rendered the beginning in the following way:

> Wer seinen Sinn auf Possen kehrt
> Und Schnurren gern erzählen hört,
> Der höre die Geschichte an,
> Die ich als wahr verbürgen kann.
>
> Auf einem Dorf ein Pfarrer war,
> Schon schwach von manchem Lebensjahr;
> Er lebte, seiner Herde froh:
> Das ist ja auf dem Dorfe so.
>
> Die Mühe, die er um sie trug,
> Die hätte sich belohnt genug,
> Wär' gier'ger Wölfe Aufenthalt
> Gewesen nicht im nahen Wald.

29. Alfrâd.

MS. fol. 437va l. 24–437vb l. 24.—pp. 27 (sub 19) and 62.—Grimm, *Lat. Ged.* pp. 337–40 (*Alveradae asina*), and 344–5.—*M.S.D.* ³I, 51–53, and ³II, 127–8 (on which the text of the present edition is based). The poem is only preserved in the Cambridge Manuscript.

The riming couplets of short lines of five syllables are the same as occur in *Herigêr*, and the poem was certainly intended to be sung to the tune of a popular melody. See the note on No. 26.

It is a satirical poem on the old maid's affection for her pet she-ass. It may well be based on some actual occurrence. M. Haupt perhaps overstates its importance when he says (*Altdeutsche Blätter*, p. 395), 'Es sieht fast wie ein allegorisches Spottgedicht aus.' See also Kögel₁, p. 261–3, and Kögel₂, pp. 134–5, § 120, sub (1). The scene of action is laid in Thuringia; the nunnery referred to is Homburg on the Unstrut, near the town of Langensalza.

This humorous tale was translated by Heyne, pp. 54–58. The first two stanzas of his rendering run thus:

> Einen Ort kenne ich,
> Hohenburg nennt er sich:
> Weidend erging sich drin
> Alfrades Eselin,
> Kraftvoll und klug dabei,
> Und ihrer Herrin treu.
>
> Wie sie von dort aus
> Streift in das Feld hinaus,
> Sieht sie, daß voller Gier
> Her läuft ein Wolf zu ihr,
> Und sie verkreucht sich,
> Nur ihr Schwanz zeigt sich.

30. Carmen Estivum.

MS. fol. 438ra ll. 6–29.—pp. 27 (sub 22) and 63.—Jaffé, pp. 491–2 (who utilized several emendations proposed by M. Haupt, added some of his own, and on whom the text of the present edition is mainly based). The song seems to occur only in the Cambridge Manuscript.

The poem is written in the form of a Sapphic ode. This metre was very much used by medieval poets, even for hymns (see Cl. Blume, *Analecta Hymnica medii aevi*, Vol. LI (1908), 61 sqq., 101 sqq. (also rime), 106,

112 sqq., 115 sqq., 134 sqq., 135 sqq. (rime and assonance), 137 sqq., 142 sqq., 153 sqq., 167 sqq., 171 sqq., 188 sqq. (rime), etc.). A counterpart to this poem is found in an early medieval Sapphic ode (seventh century) by Eugenius, a Benedictine monk, who subsequently became Bishop of Toledo, on the excessive heat of a summer. It was printed by du Méril$_1$, p. 241, note 1, who rightly observes, 'Si la forme en est antique, l'esprit descriptif et pittoresque est entièrement moderne.' For the voices of birds in Latin see du Méril$_2$, p. 213, n. 2, and E. Baehrens, *Poetae Latini Minores*, v, 364 sqq. (poems LXI and LXII).

Stanza 6. *que talem tipum gerit*, the MS. reads *que talem gerit tipum*. On bees and birds see A. B. Cook's interesting paper *The Bee in Greek Mythology* in the 'Journal of Hellenic Studies,' Vol. XV (1895), pp. 1 sqq., and on bees as birds, *ibid.* p. 9, note 65. The idea that the bee is a type of chastity was probably derived from the fact that 'apium...coitus visus est numquam' (Pliny, *N.H.* XI, 16). See Walter Robert-Tornow, *De apium mellisque apud veteres significatione et symbolica et mythologica*, Berlin, 1893, pp. 12 sqq., who also refers to Petronius, p. 878; Quintilian, *Decl.* XIII, 16; and to Virgil, *Georg.* IV, ll. 197 sqq., where we read:

> Illum adeo placuisse apibus mirabere morem,
> quod neque concubitu indulgent nec corpora segnes
> in Venerem solvunt aut foetus nixibus edunt;
> verum ipsae e foliis natos, e suavibus herbis
> ore legunt....

See also A. B. Cook, *l.c.* p. 13, note 102. Du Cange, *Glossarium*, I (1884), 312, says: 'apis significat formam virginitatis sive sapientiam, in malo, invasorem,' and he quotes, 'Cecilia, famula tua, Domine, quasi apis tibi argumentosa deservit.' In medieval divinity the bee is not infrequently mentioned as the symbol of chastity and in this way connected with the Virgin. Thus in Aldhelm's treatise *De laudibus virginitatis* (Migne's *Patrologia* LXXXIX, Chapter v, pp. 106-7) we read: 'Apis, inquam, propter peculiaris castimoniae privilegium pudicissimae virginitatis typum et ecclesiae portendere speciem indubitata scripturarum auctoritate astipulatur. Quae florentes saltuum cespites ineffabili praeda depopulans, dulcia natorum pignora, nesciens conjugii, illecebrosa consortia fetosa quadam suavissimi succi concretione producit.' In the *Defensorium inviolatae virginitatis*, first printed at Saragossa, in 1470 (reprinted, with a valuable introduction, Weimar, 1910), those who refuse to believe in the immaculate conception and the virgin-birth are blamed because they must admit and do admit just as wonderful miracles in the animal world:...'quod concedere non verentur de avium et aliorum animalium communi natura. Qualiter inter apes sine patribus fetus matrum tantummodo crescunt.' In the old Easter services, at the blessing of the Easter candle, made of beeswax, a curious praise of the bee was inserted partly based on the above-quoted passage from Virgil, which is, however, no longer in use in the present service of the Roman Catholic Church. The bee was praised as being chaste and fecund like the Holy Virgin and as offering in its mode of generation a symbol of the origin of the Word from the mouth of the Father. See L. Duchesne, *Origines du Culte Chrétien. Étude sur la liturgie latine avant Charlemagne*, Paris, ^{2}1898, pp. 242-5. He says: '"Voici ce passage dans la formule "Deus mundi conditor" du sacramentaire gélasien: "Apes vero sunt frugales in sumptibus, in procreatione castissimae....Partus non edunt, sed ore legentes concepti foetus reddunt examina, sicut exemplo mirabili Christus ore paterno processit. Fecunda est in his sine partu virginitas....Apis caeteris quae subiecta sunt homini animantibus antecellit....[245] O vere beata et mirabilis apis! Cuius nec sexum masculi violant, foetus non quassant, nec filii destruunt castitatem. Sicut sancta concepit virgo Maria: virgo peperit et virgo permansit."' A much fuller discussion of the same topic is found in the remarkable book on the bees, with theological explanations, called *Bonum universale de apibus*, by Thomas Cantipratanus (printed Duaci, 1597, Book II, Chapters 29-31); there is also an interesting paragraph in Petrus Berchorius, *Reductorium morale de rerum proprietatibus* (Coloniae Agrippinae, 1730, Vol. II, Book X, Chapter 6, § 6).

In medieval poetry and folk-lore there is likewise a connexion between the bee and the Virgin Mary. In l. 3 of the Old High German bee-charm ('Lorscher Bienensegen,' *M.S.D.*, No. XVI), we read:

> sizi, sizi, bîna: inbôt dir sancte Maria,

and in a note to this passage, *M.S.D.* ³II, 92, an old Latin bee-charm is quoted in which the bees are addressed *vos estis ancille domini, vos faciatis opera domini*, and among other popular literature a sixteenth-century 'Spruch,' the beginning of which is: *Maria stand auf eim sehr hohen berg, sie sach ein swarm bienen kommen phliegen. sie hub auf ihre gebenedeite hand, sie verbot ihm da zuhand....*

The sixth stanza, which praises the chaste bees after five stanzas have celebrated the delights of the birds in the summer, imparts to the poem a kind of moral conclusion.

l. 23. *nisi que Christum baiulavit alvo.* This emendation was suggested to me by Dr James, Provost of King's College. In the original text, which was copied at Canterbury, *Maria* was probably put over *que*, and *portavit* over *baiulavit*; the copyist put *Maria* before *que* into the line and replaced the original *baiulavit* by the commonplace *portavit*. Compare the hymn *De beata virgine* in Karl Simrock, *Lauda Sion*, Stuttgart, ²1868, p. 244:

> Quem terra, pontus, sidera
> Colunt, adorant, praedicant,
> Trinam regentem machinam
> Claustrum Mariae baiulat.

31. *De Luscinia.*

MS. fol. 434va ll. 1–434vb l. 30.—pp. 27 (sub 9) and 63.—Du Méril₁, pp. 278–9 (with some notes).—Jaffé, pp. 490–1 and 560 (on whom the text of the present edition is mainly based).

This charming song has been preserved in two manuscripts, viz. in C and in a French Manuscript (F); reprinted in the *Opera varia* by St Fulbert, Bishop of Chartres (ed. Ch. de Villiers, Paris, 1608, p. 181). See the note to Poem 27 (*De Iohanne abbate*). Apart from a number of minor discrepancies between the two manuscripts, the lines 22–33, which occur in C, are absent in F, which thus has only 28 lines.

J. A. Symonds (in *Wine, Women and Song*, p. 16) refers to this fine 'specimen of thoroughly secular poetry' and says, 'such are the sapphics of the spring, which, though they date from the seventh century, have a truly modern sentiment of Nature.' 'This poem is perhaps identical with that panegyric of the nightingale which, according to Sextus Amarcius, was sung by a mime before a German nobleman, together with three other songs, the subjects of which are mentioned by him. Of these four poems, three seem to have been preserved in C (Nos. 22, 31, 42). The lines in Amarcius (*Sexti Amarcii Galli Piosistrati Sermonum Libri IV* (ed. M. Manitius, Leipzig, 1888), Liber I, lines 438–43), following after the description of the arrival and the artistic preparations of the mime, run thus:

> Ille fides aptans crebro diapente canoras,
> Straverit ut grandem pastoris funda Goliath,
> Ut simili argutus uxorem Suevulus arte
> Luserit utque sagax nudaverat octo tenores
> Cantus Pythagoras et quam mera vox Philomelę
> Perstrepit....

See also W. Scherer, *Gesch. d. deutschen Dichtung im 11–12 Jahrhundert*, p. 16; Winterfeld, p. 490; and L. Traube in the *Anzeiger für deutsches Alterthum*, xv (1889), pp. 195 sqq., especially p. 200. See No. 42, note.

It is an interesting fact that in an earlier portion of the same Cambridge MS. (on fol. 369) is found another poem on the nightingale, written in elegiac metre and consisting of 14 distichs, which begins:

> Sum noctis socia, sum cantus dulcis amica;
> Nomen ab ambiguo sic philomela gero....

This poem must have been very popular. It was first published, from the Cambridge Manuscript, by the Rev. Dr J. A. Giles in *Anecdota Bedae, Lanfranci et aliorum*, London, 1851, pp. 69–70, and E. Baehrens printed the poem from six other manuscripts in his *Poetae Latini Minores*, Vol. v (Leipzig, 1883), 368–70.

NOTES

There was also a poem in praise of the cuckoo ('versus de laude cuculi') on the now lost fol. 45o of the Cambridge Manuscript. See R. Priebsch, *Deutsche Handschriften in England*, I, 21. In the earlier Latin poetry of the Carolingian period there are verses *De cuculo* attributed to Alcuin, and the *Carmen philomelaicum* of Paulus Albarus. See on these Allen, *Mod. Phil.* v, 3, 464.

On the metrical form see the note to No. 18 and No. 22. All lines except l. 17 (*catervulas*) end in -*a*.

A facsimile and German translation of part of this poem (ll. 29–42) are given in Anselm Salzer's *Illustrierte Geschichte der deutschen Literatur von den ältesten Zeiten bis zur Gegenwart*, Vol. I (1912?), p. 100.

32. *Verna femine suspiria.*

MS. fol. 441ra ll. 1–21.—pp. 27 (sub 39) and 64.—Jaffé, pp. 492–3. An emended text of this touching song was given by Winterfeld, p. 446, who discussed it on pp. 445–7, and gave a metrical German rendering of it, under the title 'Frühling,' on p. 219. The text of the present edition is based on Winterfeld. The poem has been preserved only in C, the text of which is not free from corruptions.

Is this song a 'planctus monialis' written by a woman? For nuns' complaints in medieval poetry and in folk-songs of the xvth and xvith centuries, see Allen in *Modern Philology*, v, 432–5, and on 'Frauenstrophen' in Old German lyrics, *ibid.* vi, 395. The question whether this poem was composed by a girl or by a goliard for a girl cannot be decided; but it is quite possible that a love-sick or disappointed maid herself wrote these heart-stirring lines which we may call 'Des Mädchens Klage.' W. Scherer, in his *Gesch. d. deutschen Dichtung im xi. und xii. Jhd.*, p. 8, says: 'Naturgefühl und Liebesgefühl gehen Hand in Hand...und besonders die schönen Frühlingsklagen einer Frau atmen tiefes Gefühl. Ihnen reiht sich der volkstümliche Liebesgruß im Ruodlieb würdig an.' On this latter see p. 40 of this book. This 'Complaint of a Maid' is a true forerunner of the finest poems of the early German Minnesong. G. Gröber, in his *Grundriß d. roman. Phil.* II, 1, p. 417, calls it 'das liebliche älteste Frauenlied.' Winterfeld's view, 'Die Heimat des Liedes ist wohl Frankreich' (p. 527), is not supported by any convincing arguments; it may just as well have been composed on the banks of the Rhine. He added, with more justice it would seem: 'Das Naturgefühl, das sich in dem Gedicht ausspricht, mutet ganz modern an,' an opinion which Ph. Schuyler Allen, who translated the poem into English prose, took pains to contradict (see *Mod. Philology*, v, 431). Another important early medieval love-poem in Latin stanzas is given by Allen in *Mod. Philology*, IX, pp. 428–9; it was translated into German by Gertrud Stockmayer, *Über Naturgefühl in Deutschland im x. und xi. Jahrhundert*, Leipzig und Berlin, 1910, p. 18.

The first two and the last two stanzas in Winterfeld's rendering run as follows:

> Mit lindem Hauch der Westwind weht,
> Die Sonne warm am Himmel steht,
> Und ob dem Feld in blauer Luft
> Der Ackerkrume würz'ger Duft.
>
> Es kam der Lenz in Herrlichkeit,
> Er trägt sein festlich buntes Kleid,
> Nun sprießen neu das Laub im Wald,
> Der Wiese Blumen mannigfalt....
>
> Ich Ärmste sitz' in Einsamkeit
> Versonnen da mit meinem Leid,
> Und hebe ich das Aug' empor,
> Ist blind mein Auge, taub das Ohr.
>
> Erhöret Ihr das Flehen mein,
> Herr Mai, in Gnaden seht darein;
> Die ganze Welt in Blüten steht,
> Indes mein darbend Herz vergeht.

33. *Invitatio amice.*

MS. fol. 438va l. 25–438vb l. 15.—pp. 27 (sub 26) and 64.—The poem has been largely erased in C, as the monks of St Augustine obviously objected to it, although they did not destroy it quite as effectively as the following poem which they not only erased but blacked with a tincture of galls. Jaffé does not print it, but refers to M. Haupt, who published the song (from a better text, in a Viennese MS. (V) of the tenth century) in his *Exempla poesis latinae medii aevi*, Vindobonae, 1834, pp. 29–30. Du Méril$_2$, p. 196, reproduced Haupt's text, adding a few useful notes and emendations. A third MS. is P, a Parisian Codex of the tenth century, which was published, in 1852, by E. de Coussemaker, *Histoire de l'harmonie*, pp. 108–9. He gave photographic reproductions of the MSS. V and P in both of which the text is provided with neum-accent notation. The present edition is mainly based on V, which offers, on the whole, the best text. The three MSS. differ a good deal, more especially at the end. The readings of C agree more frequently with P than with V. C is shorter than either V or P; it has only 32 lines, as the last two stanzas of V are missing (ll. 33–40); they are also missing in P which adds a stanza that occurs neither in V nor in C. It runs: 'Iam nix glaciesque liquescit; | Folium et herba virescit; | Philomela iam cantat in alto; | Ardet amor cordis in antro.' The order of the lines is not exactly the same in the three manuscripts. The text of C, as far as it can be read, is inferior to that of V, e.g. l. 16 spoils the rime (*puella:*) *bella* by putting *pulchra* (P does the same), and also by omitting *tibi* (P has *ibi*) which makes the line too short. In line 20, instead of *pigmentatis* (a conjecture proposed by du Méril) V has *pinguitatis*, P has *universis*, and in C the corresponding word is missing.

The poem may have been composed originally in France; *dulcis amica* is the same as the common French appellation *ma douce amie*, while in German the equivalent would be *mîn* (*vil*) *liebez liep*. In several medieval poems the nightingale is addressed as *dulcis amica*. See E. Baehrens, *Poetae Latini Minores*, Vol. v, 363: 'Dulcis amica veni, noctis solatia praestans.' See also p. 90: 'Sum cantus dulcis amica.'

The poem has been discussed by Allen in *Mod. Philology*, III, 4, 424–5 and V, 3, 473.

The dainty amorous song has been well translated into English by John Addington Symonds in his charming collection *Wine, Women and Song* (reprinted in 'The King's Classics,' No. 35, London, 1907), on pages 14–15. The opening stanzas are rendered by him in the following manner:

> Come therefore now, my gentle fere,
> Whom as my heart I hold full dear;
> Enter my little room, which is
> Adorned with quaintest rarities:
> There are the seats with cushions spread,
> The roof with curtains overhead;
> The house with flowers of sweetest scent
> And scattered herbs is redolent...

Symonds calls it 'a curious secular piece of the tenth century' which 'shows how wine, woman and song, even in an age which is supposed to have trembled for the coming destruction of the world, still formed the attraction of some natures. What is more, there is a certain modern, as distinguished from classical, tone of tenderness in the sentiment' (*l.c.* p. 14).

34. *Magister puero.*

MS. fol. 441vb ll. 16–34.—pp. 27 (sub 47) and 65.—Jaffé, pp. 493–4. The poem has come down to us in two manuscripts, in C and in V, a Vatican Manuscript in Longobardic script of the late eleventh century, which was originally published by G. B. Niebuhr in the 'Rheinisches Museum,' III (1829), 1 sqq. A critical edition of this curious and much discussed poem was given by Ludwig Traube in 1891, in his fine essay on this and another poem of similar structure from which he took the title *O Roma nobilis*. This essay was published in the 'Abhandlungen der philosophisch-philologischen Klasse der kgl. Akademie der Wissenschaften zu München,

Band XIX, Abteilung II, 1891, pp. 299–309; pp. 304 sqq. refer to *O admirabile Veneris idolum*. In his essay Traube gave a translation of the poem into German prose and added photographic reproductions of both manuscripts. This was all the more welcome as the neumatic notations that are found in both manuscripts had not been reproduced by Niebuhr, du Méril, and Jaffé. Two of the three stanzas are provided with neum-accents in the Cambridge Manuscript, while in V only the first stanza has a musical notation. The text of the present edition is mainly based on Traube's edition but, for the sake of uniformity, the usual spelling of C has been adhered to. The poem is also printed in Alexander Riese's *Anthologia Latina*, Vol. II, p. xl, Leipzig, 1870, and in the popular collection of medieval secular Latin lyrics called *Gaudeamus. Carmina vagorum selecta in usum laetitiae*, Leipzig, 1879, pp. 96–97. An English rendering, based upon the restoration of Traube, was given by Allen, *Modern Philology*, V, 3 (Jan. 1908), pp. 471–2, who discussed this passionate appeal to a runaway boy by a Veronese schoolmaster in the same paper on pp. 431, 456 and 471.

The nature of the poem has often been misunderstood. It is neither the expression of artistic enthusiasm on the part of an old Roman who had dug up a beautiful statue of Venus which he was obliged to give up (Niebuhr) nor the fervent plea of a girl to a boy (Jaffé gave it the title 'Feminae amantis gemitus'). Allen, *l.c.* p. 471, calls this poem 'the first medieval example of any worth of the pederastic verse so popular in the Middle Ages,' and Traube concludes his essay with the words: 'Wenn dies Gedicht heidnisch ist [Niebuhr had called it 'heidnisch'], dann gibt es gar viele heidnische Gedichte aus christlicher Zeit. Ich finde in ihm nur die gespreizte Gelehrsamkeit des Schulmeisters, der seine Glossare und Handbücher nicht nur kannte, sondern auch verwerten wollte. Da es ihm aber an wahrer Empfindung doch nicht ganz gebrach und seine Zeit ein offnes Ohr gerade für den hier angeschlagenen Ton hatte (vgl. die Stelle aus Ivo von Chartres bei Dümmler, 'Zeitschrift f. d. Alterthum,' XXII, 258), so wird man sich nicht wundern, neben andern beliebten und gern gehörten Stücken auch unser Lied in dem Textbuch jenes ältesten Goliarden wiederzufinden, das uns die Cambridger Liederhandschrift überliefert' (p. 307). See also A. F. Ozanam, *Documents inédits pour servir à l'histoire littéraire de l'Italie depuis le viiie siècle jusqu'au xiiie, avec des recherches sur le moyen-âge italien*, Paris, 1850, pages 18–19. The vice to which this poem refers is very frequently discussed or alluded to in Medieval European literature. It is sometimes represented by the figure of Ganymede, and a classical example of a literary treatment of this unsavoury subject is afforded by the rhythmus *Altercatio Ganymedis et Helenae* (67 stanzas of 4 lines, all having but one rime), that was apparently specially addressed to the clergy. This rhythmus was printed by W. Wattenbach in the 'Zeitschrift f. d. Alterthum,' XVIII (1875), 124–36. In the same volume of the same periodical (pp. 457–60) the rhythmus *Iupiter et Danae* (27 stanzas, by the author of Ganymede and Helena?), in which the same vice is alluded to in stanza 15, was published by Wattenbach. See also E. Dümmler's essay *Zur Sittengeschichte des Mittelalters* in Haupt's 'Zeitschrift f. d. A.' XXII (1878), pp. 256–8; Traube, *O Roma nobilis*, p. 308, (2); Allen, *Mod. Philology*, V, 3, p. 456, note 1. The poem must be looked upon as an early Italian παιδικόν that was written by a schoolmaster at Verona some time between the ninth and the eleventh century. Traube (p. 306) says 'Zweisilbige Assonanz mit dem Streben, sich zum reinen Reim durchzuarbeiten, ist für das zehnte Jahrhundert passend. Verona ist in der Zeit vor und nach Bischof Ratherius eine Hauptstätte geistigen Lebens und Strebens in Italien.'

l. 3. *Archos* 'the Lord.' Traube remarks: 'Archos ist mittelgriechisch häufig,' and refers to *Poetae aevi Carolini*, II, 397 L.

l. 6. *quae baiulat colum*. This was taken, according to Traube, from the well-known verse on the Parcae: Clotho colum baiulat, Lachesis trahit, Atropos occat.' See E. Baehrens, *Poetae Latini Minores*, V, 388.

l. 7. *Saluto*. Traube conjectures *Saluato*, and renders the line '*Erhalte dem Knaben das Leben!*' *fleh' ich nicht im Scherzspiel.*

l. 11. *fluvium Tesim* 'the river Adige.' Niebuhr suggested the alteration of *Tesim* into *Athesim* which Traube adopted. But both manuscripts have only the shorter form, viz. *Thesim*, V, *Tesim*, C, which seems to be a popular form of the name of the river. The substitution of the learned *Athesim* makes the line too long by

one syllable; *fluvium* must be read as a trisyllabic word, as is clearly shown by the neum-accents. Traube makes the note: 'Die Veroneser kannten folgende Etymologie von Athesis: "Athesis fluvius interpretatur"... "sine positione," i.e. "instabilis," nam "a" privativa dictio est, "thesis" dicitur "positio"; est autem "rapidissimus amnis." Commentar der *Gesta Berengarii* ad Vers 148 ed. Dümmler S. 89.'

Our rhythmus (as well as the religious poem *O Roma nobilis* which is found together with it in the Vatican MS. and which may have been written in imitation of it, as it has the same metrical form) consists of three stanzas, two of which have six lines. Each line has twelve syllables, and the lines of the same stanza are kept together by the same assonance of the last two syllables. The neum-accent notation of the second stanza is a variation of that of the first, and the additional line gives this middle stanza a character of its own. The third stanza has no neumes put over the words which means that the melody of the first stanza was to be repeated.

The first stanza is rendered thus by Traube (p. 307):

> O wunderbares Abbild der Liebesgottheit,
> An dessen Leib auch nicht der kleinste Makel ist,
> So möge der Herr dich schützen, der Sterne und Himmel
> Schuf und Meer und Festland gestaltete.
> Nicht durch die List des Lebens-Diebes sollst du tückisches Leid erfahren;
> Nein, liebend schonen möge dich Clotho, die den Rocken dinset!

The second stanza is rendered by Allen (*l.c.* p. 471) in the following way:

> Preserve the boy, I pray not in jest
> To Lachesis, but with my whole heart,
> To the sister of Atropos, lest she abandon thee.
> May'st thou have as guides Neptune and Thetis
> When thou farest across the river Adige.
> Why doest thou flee, pray, when I love thee?
> Unhappy what shall I do when I see thee not?

35. *Clericus et Nonna.*

MS. fol. 438vb l. 16–439ra l. 8. The poem, which unfortunately has only come down to us in the Cambridge Manuscript, has been most effectively obliterated and blacked by the use of *tinctura gallica*. See my transliteration on pp. 16–17 and in Haupt's 'Zeitschrift für deutsches Alterthum,' xxx (1886), 190–1. A little more can be read in the manuscript than appears on the photographic reproduction. The transliteration gives in such cases everything that can be made out, and dots have been placed under the letters the reading of which is specially uncertain. The photographs will show how much space is available for supplying missing words.

There is some discussion of this interesting fragment in *M.S.D.* ^{3}II, 106 (Steinmeyer combating Scherer's views). See also Kögel$_1$, p. 136 sqq., and Kögel$_2$, p. 128, § 112; Wolfgang Golther, *Die deutsche Dichtung im Mittelalter*, Stuttgart, 1912, p. 71; Hans Naumann, *Althochdeutsches Lesebuch* (in the 'Sammlung Goeschen,' No. 734), 1914, pp. 127–8; and Philip Schuyler Allen, *Mod. Phil.* v, 3 (Jan. 1908), 433–4. Some of Kögel's ingenious conjectures cannot be upheld in view of the space available in the manuscript.

Scherer supposed the poem to be a hymn to the Virgin, but there can be little doubt that it is an erotic poem in the form of a dialogue between a monk and a nun, and that on account of its amorous nature it was destroyed by the monks of St Augustine although apparently the *carissima nonna* unhesitatingly rejected all the fervent pleadings of the enamoured monk. This poem is the oldest document of German love-poetry in which German words occur and at the same time the earliest specimen of macaronic love-poetry. See also Gertrud Stockmayer, *Über Naturgefühl in Deutschland im x. und xi. Jahrhundert*, Leipzig und Berlin, 1910, p. 29. The love-greeting in *Ruodlieb* should also be compared. See p. 40 of this book. Many macaronic poems of an erotic kind are found in the *Carmina Burana* and in later German literature. See H. Hoffmann von Fallersleben's anthology *In dulci jubilo*, and Emil Henrici, *Sprachmischung in der älteren Dichtung Deutschlands*, Berlin, 1913.

NOTES

36. *'In languore perio.'*

MS. fol. 441vb ll. 35–40. See my transliteration on p. 22 and in Haupt's 'Zeitschrift f. deutsches Alterthum,' Vol. xxx (1886), 191, and cp. *ibid.* 189.

The poem is a fragment, and we cannot say how much may be missing. It is not macaronic. It was obviously a poem of passionate longing, such as Nos. 32, 33, 34, and the leading motif was probably 'Come (*Ueni*) my love...I am consumed with longing.' The title has been made up by me from the only line that is fairly legible.

37. *V.......*

MS. fol. 440vb ll. 24–40. See my notes in Haupt's 'Zeitschrift f. d. A.' Vol. xxx (1886), 189 and 191.

This is a fragment of a poem and again, as in the case of No. 36, it is impossible to say how much may be missing. It contained at least six stanzas of three lines each. vi, 3 is missing, and possibly more. See p. 24 of this book, and Robert Priebsch's very plausible remarks which are quoted on that page.

38. *Lamentatio Neobule.*

MS. fol. 441va l. 32–442vb l. 2.

The manuscript offers a somewhat corrupt text of the well-known Horatian ode. See Q. Horati Flacci *Carmina*, III, 12. The mistakes of C have been corrected, but the spelling of the MS. (*Ebri* for *Hebri*, etc.) has been left. See the note on *orto = horto*, Poem I, Stanza 3, p. 71. This is another poem of lamentation. See p. 73.

39. *Admonitio iuvenum.*

MS. fol. 436vb l. 40–437rb l. 26.—pp. 27 (sub 17) and 66–67. See also pp. 24–25.—Jaffé, pp. 484–7 (on whom the text here given is mainly based, although it seems doubtful if his numerous transpositions of words are all really necessary).

These 'versus de contemptu mundi' have come down to us in two manuscripts beside C. One is a Viennese MS. (V), referred to, but not published, by Denis in his *Catal. Codd. theol.* I, 3, p. 2932. He did not think much of the poem. The other is a manuscript from the beginning of the ninth century, written by an Anglo-Saxon scribe, which originally was the property of the Chapter of Cologne Cathedral. In 1794, when a French invasion of Germany was feared, the Cologne manuscripts were sent for safety further south-east, and this manuscript, together with others, was for a long time kept at Darmstadt. Consequently in earlier editions it is always called the Darmstadt Manuscript (D). In 1867 the manuscripts were returned from Hessia to Cologne and, in 1874, they were indexed and described by Jaffé and Wattenbach, in their publication *Ecclesiae Metropolitanae Coloniensis Manuscripti*, Berolini, 1874. On p. 43, sub cvi (= Darmstadt, No. 2106) of this publication the manuscript is dealt with and described in the following way: 'Membranaceus saec. ix, forma maxima, foliorum 74, quem variae manus exaraverunt, in his etiam manus Anglo-saxonicae. fol. 17–17^v: Versus de contemptu mundi: Audax es vir iuvenis.' D was first printed (with the addition of numerous notes) by F. J. Mone in his *Lateinische Hymnen des Mittelalters*, Vol. I (Freiburg, 1853), under No. 288, on pp. 395–7. This text was reprinted by H. A. Daniel in the *Thesaurus Hymnologicus*, Vol. IV (1855), pp. 132–3, who, referring to Mone, also repeated some of his predecessor's notes. D offers frequently a better text than C.

This didactic poem is a so-called *Hymnus alphabeticus*, in which each stanza begins with a different letter of the alphabet, running through all the letters from *a* to *z*. Each stanza has four short lines with riming couplets. Each stanza is followed by the same refrain of two slightly longer lines from which it appears that the poem was intended to be sung on Ash-Wednesday (see Daniel, IV, 134). Another alphabetical hymn is printed in du Méril$_2$, pp. 297–300, and another by E. de Coussemaker, *l.c.* pp. 116–18.

The metre is not always well observed in either C or D. The writer of C wrote the poem as prose in the prose order of words. Some lines are one syllable short, others too long by one syllable (e.g. 19, 1; 20, 3), most lines contain eight syllables, but not a few have only seven syllables, the first unaccented syllable of the line being suppressed. Each line has four accents. The rimes are often at best mere assonance (lines 3–4, 7–8, 17–18, 67–68, 87–88), and sometimes they are not put in couplets but are intermittent (stanzas 9, 11, 19); sometimes the rimes are altogether corrupt.

A facsimile, transcription and translation of part of the poem are given in Anselm Salzer's *Illustrierte Geschichte der deutschen Literatur*, Vol. I (no date, 1912?), p. 101. See note to No. 31.

An Old High German poem of the eleventh century, which is very similar in tendency and attacks the 'vil ubeler mundus,' is called *Memento mori* and printed in M.S.D. ³I, No. xxx[b], and in Braune's *Althochdeutsches Lesebuch*, under No. XXXXII. There are also Latin poems *de contemptu mundi* written in the eleventh century by Anselm of Canterbury (*Opera*, ed. Gerberon, I, 277). See Mone, *l.c.* p. 396. For notes on the text of our poem Mone should be consulted.

Stanza 18. Mone (p. 397) explains *venia* to mean 'remission of sins' (*Sündenvergebung*), and *indulgentia* 'indulgence,' 'remission of temporal punishment' (*Nachlaß der zeitlichen Strafen, Ablaß*).

Stanza 22. The Manuscript D reads *Ydei*. There is naturally a great difficulty in beginning a Latin stanza with the unusual letter Y. May we take *Ydei* to stand for *Y dei*, i.e. *Y* (= *I* 'go'), *Dei quaere gratiam*? C has substituted *Fides* and differs altogether.

40. De Musica.

MS. fol. 441va ll. 24–31.—pp. 27 (sub 44) and 67.—Jaffé, p. 489. See also the note in M.S.D. ³II, 121. The poem has been preserved only in the Cambridge Manuscript, the text of which is disfigured by several corruptions.

The rhythm of the lines is as follows:

Róta módos ártè | pérsonémus músicá

and the poem is thus in structure very similar to two stanzas of four long lines as they occur in certain hymns.

l. 1. *rota*. The rota is a musical instrument of the violin class, which stands half-way between a harp and a fiddle. The instrument is several times mentioned in Old High German literature and is called *rota, rotta, hrota* (in later German *rotte, rote*). As early as in the second half of the ninth century Otfrid von Weissenburg mentions the *rotta* by the side of the *harpha*, 'harp.' In describing the wonderful music that is made in the heavenly kingdom he mentions the instruments used (v, 23, 197 sqq.), and says:

Sih thar ouh ál ruarit,   thaz órgana fuarit,
líra joh fídula   joh mánagfaltu suégala,
Hárpha joh rótta,   joh thaz io gúates dohta.

The original form of *rota* in German was probably *hrotta*, which is an early Germanic adaptation of the word recorded in the sixth century, by Venantius Fortunatus, as the Breton *chrotta* (*chrotta britanna placet*, Corin. liber VII). The instrument was of Celtic origin and was called *crwth*. See the full discussion by Ferdinand Wolf, *Über die Lais, Sequenzen und Leiche*, Heidelberg, 1841, pp. 244–8. Karl Weinhold, *Die deutschen Frauen in dem Mittelalter*, ²I (Wien, 1882), 156; Alwin Schultz, *Das höfische Leben zur Zeit der Minnesinger*, ²I (Leipzig, 1889), 554; E. G. Graff, *Althochdeutscher Sprachschatz*, II, 487–8; Benecke, Müller and Zarncke, *Mittelhochdeutsches Wörterbuch*, II, 773[b], 12 sqq. (where much literature is given); M. Lexer, *Mittelhochdeutsches Wörterbuch*, II, 509; *New English Dictionary*, under *rote*, Vol. VIII (1910), 807[b]; *The Century Dictionary*, Vol. V (1890), 5237[c], under *rote*; La Curne de Sainte-Palaye, *Dictionnaire Historique de l'ancien langage François*, Vol. IX (1881), p. 269[b].

NOTES

See also the very interesting chapter, 'Rote and Harp,' in Francis W. Galpin, *Old English instruments of music, their history and character*, London (1910), pp. 1-19 (with illustrations). From this it appears that the *rota* was a bowed stringed instrument, not round in shape, but a long oblong, with rounded corners. It took the place of the harp when the art of the old minstrels passed into the hands of the joculatores, mimi and goliardi and when the use of the harp became less common. See W. Wackernagel (-E. Martin), *Geschichte der deutschen Litteratur*, ²1 (Basel, 1879), p. 99.

modus is 'melody,' 'lay.' See p. 29, note 1.

ll. 3 and 4. See No. 42, Stanzas 4 and 5, and the notes to them.

l. 6. The manuscript has *quarum fit celestis musica numerorum normula*. *musica*, which can be inferred from *celestis*, was probably added by the scribe. *normula* occurs again in Stanza 5 of No. 42.

l. 8. This line runs in the manuscript: *rex mirandus pantokrator nos reget per secula*, which makes the line longer than all the others. In omitting *mirandus* the rhythm of the first half line would be *réx pántokrátòr*, i.e. the Latin line would have to be read in the German way, in which an unaccented syllable between the first and the second stressed syllable (Hebung) could be omitted. *pantokrator* (παντοκράτωρ) is not uncommon in Biblical Greek. See Wilke-Grimm's *Clavis Novi Testamenti*, translated, revised and enlarged by Joseph Henry Thayer under the title *A Greek-English Lexicon of the New Testament*, Edinburgh, 1886, p. 476. There occur some other Greek terms in the Cambridge Songs, e.g. *pneuma* (No. 1. 1), *athanatos* (No. 14. 21), *melos* (No. 31. 5), *sophie* (No. 42. 2), etc.

41. *De Mensa Philosophie*.

MS. fol. 440vb ll. 6-13.—pp. 27 (sub 36) and 67.—Jaffé, p. 489.

The last three lines of this piece differ in their metrical structure from the first and their contents do not correspond well with the opening lines. It seems very doubtful that they belong to the beginning. The idea of a richly spread table of Philosophy, or of an invigorating well of Philosophy, occurs in other Medieval Latin poems. The most interesting instance is the insertion of a song on 'the well of Philosophy' into an old Christmas-play (*Ludus scenicus de Nativitate Domini*) in the *Carmina Burana* (ed. Schmeller, No. CCII, p. 92, ll. 47 sqq.). The beginning of it (with the exception of the reading *fontem* instead of *mensam*) is exactly the same as in C. The poem, as it appears in this early thirteenth-century collection, has six more lines of fifteen syllables than the Cambridge Manuscript (Schmeller prints twelve half lines), three of which are in each case bound together by the same rime. They continue the idea *fontem Philosophie* and run thus:

> quem Pythagoras rimatus   excitavit physice,
> inde Socrates et Plato   honestarunt ethice,
> Aristoteles loquaci   desponsavit logice,
>
> ab his secte multiformes   Athenis materiam
> nacte hoc liquore totam   irrigarunt Greciam,
> qui redundans infinite   fluxit in Hesperiam.

This song is sung in the Christmas-play by the followers of the King of Egypt. In a work of the twelfth century by Alanus ab Insulis (Alain de Lille), *Anticlaudianus* (ed. Thomas Wright in his 'Minor Anglo-Latin Satirists and Epigrammatists of the 12th Century,' London, 1872, Vol. II, p. 320), we read the line:

> 'mensam Pythagorae, quae menti pabula donat.'

The idea of a large table spread first for the few, then for the many, and ultimately for all, has been worked out in a splendid poem called *Alle* ('Es sprach der Geist: "Sieh auf!" Es war im Traume') by Conrad Ferdinand Meyer, in his *Gedichte*, Leipzig, ²1902, p. 256.

With regard to the metre of the first half of this poem, see the notes on Nos. 18, 21 and 31.

98 NOTES

l. 4. *gramma* stands for *grammatica*. See Du Cange, *Glossarium*, IV (1885), 96. *gramma prima* would mean 'the rudiments of grammar.'

poetica ydra does not make any sense, and *(h)ydra* seems to be a mistake of the scribe. R. A. Nicholson suggests the emendation *rima*, which, if spelt *rhyma*, would make good sense and explain to some extent the mistake of the copyist.

l. 6. *Mantuana fistula* denotes bucolics after the manner of Virgil. Perhaps lines 4–6 were originally a sestet of short and rugged lines somewhat of the following shape:

> Hinc fluit gramma prima,
> Hinc poetica rhyma,
> lanx hinc satiricorum,
> plausus hinc comicorum,
> letificat convivia
> Mantuana fistula.

42. *De simphoniis et de littera Pithagore.*

MS. fol. 435rb ll. 12–32.—pp. 27 (sub 11) and 67–68.—Jaffé, pp. 488–9 (who gives an emended text and some useful notes and on whom the present edition is mainly based). See also the note in *M.S.D.* ^{3}II, 121.

This poem consists of two main portions (Stanzas 4–5 and 6–8) which are preceded by an introduction (Stanzas 1–3) and followed by a partial repetition and adaptation of the opening stanza (Stanza 9). Jaffé's title *De littera Pythagore*, viz. the letter Y, refers only to Stanzas 6–9. This poem setting forth, among other things, in what way the wise Pythagoras had found the Octave was perhaps one of those which, according to Sextus Amarcius (I, 441–2), were sung by a 'mimus' to a 'luxuriosus' (Book I, Ch. 5 deals with 'De diversis luxuriae illecebris'). See the notes to Nos. 22 (p. 82) and 31 (p. 88); also Winterfeld, p. 490.

Stanza 2. *Veritatem*, viz. *Christum*.

Stanza 3. *metapsicosis* for *metempsychosis*.

Euforbium for *Euphorbum*. *Euphorbus*, the son of Panthus, was a brave Trojan whose soul Pythagoras asserted had descended to himself through the process of transmigration. See Ovid, *Metamorphos.* xv, ll. 161 sqq.

Stanza 4. The story of the ingenious way in which Pythagoras first found out the proportion and concord of sounds one to another, i.e. the Octave, the Perfect Fifth, and the Perfect Fourth, observing how they were produced by the different-sized hammers in a blacksmith's forge, is told, with more or less detail, by many ancient writers. See the accounts of Macrobius, *Commentarii in Somnium Scipionis*, II, 1, 8–25 (pp. 572–6 in the Teubner edition); Boethius, *De institutione musica*, I, Chapter 10 (p. 197 in the Teubner edition, and pp. 1176–8 in J. P. Migne, *Patrologiae cursus completus*, Vol. 63, Paris, 1847); Nicomachus, *Harmonices manuale* (ed. Meibom), Book I, pp. 10–14; Iamblichus, *in Nicom.* 171 sqq.; and others. See also No. 40, l. 3. The chapter in Thomas Stanley's *History of Philosophy*, 2nd ed., London, 1687, Part IX, Section II, Chapter VI, pp. 532 sqq., is mainly based on Nicomachus, but see on this chapter the useful corrections of E. W. Naylor in his paper *Music and Shakespeare* contributed to 'The Musical Antiquary,' April 1910, pages 144–6. With regard to the whole question of the finding of the Octave by Pythagoras see now Eduard Zeller, *Die Philosophie der Griechen in ihrer geschichtlichen Entwicklung*, ^{5}I (Leipzig, 1892), pp. 401 sqq. (in the English translation, by S. F. Alleyne, *A history of Greek Philosophy*, London, 1881, Vol. I, pp. 431–2).

Stanza 5. This stanza offers many difficulties. For the elucidation of it Jaffé rightly refers to Martianus Capella, *De Nuptiis Philologiae et Mercurii*, Book II, § 107 (page 29 in F. Eyssenhardt's edition, Leipzig, 1866). See below.

NOTES

With regard to the terms used in this stanza it should be noted that

simphonias are 'concords,' i.e. perfect intervals, such as the unison, the octave, the fourth and the fifth. Cp. Vitruvius, *De Architectura* (ed. H. Müller-Strübing, Leipzig, 1867), Book v, Chapter 4, p. 113: 'Concentus quos natura hominis modulari potest, graeceque συμφωνίαι dicuntur....' In Poem No. 40, l. 4 the writer mentions *quattuor consonantias*, 'the four concords' or 'the four harmonies.' In the old musical system, which knew only a single octave, the three simphoniae called *diatessaron*, *diapente* and *diapason* were especially important. They were recognised as 'perfect' by the medieval harmonists. See E. W. Naylor, *l.c.* p. 146. See also No. 43 and the note on it.

diatesseron = a fourth musical interval, a perfect fourth, 'quarta.' The term is short for ἡ διὰ τεσσάρων χορδῶν συμφωνία and is consequently as a rule written *diatessaron*; but the form *diatesseron* is sometimes found instead of it (always in the Cambridge Manuscript, and also in Notker. See p. 97), and, at the end of a hexameter verse, even *diatesron*. See Du Cange, *Glossarium*, III (1884), p. 99.

diapente = a fifth musical interval, a perfect fifth, 'quinta.'

diapason = the whole octave (ἡ διὰ πασῶν χορδῶν συμφωνία), a consonance through all the tones of the diatonic scale, the concord of the first and the last notes, the interval of an octave.

On *simphonias tres* cp. Martianus Capella, *l.c.* Book IX, § 934: 'Ex sonis qui et singulis et omnibus tropis rite conveniunt, symphoniae tres, quarum est prima διὰ τεσσάρων, quae Latine: ex quatuor; alia symphonia quinaria est et dicitur διὰ πέντε, atque constat sonis quinque: tertia διὰ πασῶν, quae ex omnibus octo sonos recipit.' In the passage quoted above Vitruvius, writing at a time when the musical system had extended to two octaves, says: 'Concentus...sunt sex: diatessaron, diapente, diapason, et disdiatessaron et disdiapente et disdiapason....'

quaternarium = *quaternarium numerum*. The expression seems in this case to denote the number 10, and to be a Latin equivalent of the Greek τετρακτύς, the number comprising in it the first four numbers. See the extract from Martianus Capella quoted below.

armoniam, harmonia (ἁρμονία) is a name for the octave. See Eduard Zeller, *Die Philosophie der Griechen...*, p. 358, note 2, who quotes Nicomachus, *Harmonic.*, Introd. 1, 16: 'οἱ παλαιότατοι...ἁρμονίαν μὲν καλοῦντες τὴν διὰ πασῶν.'

ma ten tetraden, 'by the tetrad!' which has here the meaning of swearing by the quaternary number (viz. the sum of the first four numbers, i.e. the number 10). This number (made up from 1 + 2 + 3 + 4) was considered by Pythagoras and his followers to be the most perfect number, the root and fountain of the eternal nature. It was introduced by the Pythagoreans into their most solemn oath, the oath by the τετρακτύς, in which, out of respect for their master, and forbearing to mention his name, they swore by the name of the person who communicated the τετρακτύς to them.

τετράδην stands here, as it sometimes does, for τετρακτύν. For the literature on this oath in which Pythagoras was celebrated as the revealer of the τετρακτύς, see E. Zeller, *l.c.* p. 398, note 5 (Engl. transl. p. 428, note 3), and Thomas Stanley, *l.c.* pp. 526-7. The Cambridge Manuscript has, instead of *ma ten tetraden* the words *matente traden traden*. The second *traden* (fol. 435va l. 1) was by mistake repeated by the scribe from the last line of the preceding page (fol. 435rb l. 40), and he wrote *matente traden* as he obviously did not understand the meaning of the Greek words μὰ τὴν τετράδην.

The passage from Martianus Capella (Liber II, § 107) to which Jaffé rightly refers as the probable source of this part of the poem runs thus: 'An aliud illa senis deieratio, qui μὰ τὴν τετράδα non tacuit, confitetur nisi perfectae rationis numerum? quippe intra se unum secundum triademque ipsumque bis binum tenet, quis collationibus symphoniae peraguntur. nam tres ad quattuor epitritus vocitatur arithmetica ratione ac diatessaron perhibetur in musicis. item intra eum iacent tres ad duo, quae hemiolios forma est symphoniamque secundam, quae diapente dicitur, reddunt. tertia symphonia diapason in melicis perhibetur diplasioque conficitur hoc est uno duobus collato. igitur quaternarius numerus omnes symphonias suis partibus perfectus absolvit omniaque

mela harmonicorum distributione conquirit'.... In this important passage the Pythagorean oath is called μὰ τὴν τετράδα, but in Book VII, § 734 (ed. Eyssenhardt, p. 259) Martianus Capella has: *Quid tetradem dicam?* Hence it is probable that the compiler of the song book and commonplace book which is preserved for us in C used a manuscript of M. Capella which in § 107 read *tetraden*.

Stanzas 6–9. See Poem 19, Stanza 5 (end). Jaffé refers to Lactantii *Institut.* VI, c. 3, 6 opp., ed. Bünemann, p. 708, note n. Compare also Isidori Hispalensi episcopi *Etymologiarum libri XX*, ed. F. Lindemann, Leipzig, 1833. In Book I, Chapter 3 ('De literis communibus') a paragraph (§ 7) is devoted to the Pythagorean letter, Y. It runs thus: 'Y literam Pythagoras Samius ad exemplum humanae vitae primus formavit; cuius virgula subterior primam aetatem significat, incertam quippe et quae adhuc se nec vitiis nec virtutibus dedit. Bivium autem, quod superest, ab adolescentia incipit: cuius dextera pars ardua est, sed ad beatam vitam tendens: sinistra facilior, sed ad labem interitumque deducens. De qua Persius [*Sat.* III, 56] sic ait:

    Et tibi quae Samios diduxit littera ramos,
    Surgentem dextro monstravit limite callem.'

Apparently the idea of the Pythagorean Y was that on the right-hand side the stroke went straight up in direct continuation of the lower part of the letter, while the left arm which branched off was longer and less steep (Υ). In Stanzas 7 and 8, however, the Christian idea of the narrow and the wide gate and the straitened and the broad way has supplanted the original idea of Pythagoras of the steep and the easy way. Cp. St Matthew vii. 13–14: 'Introite per angustam portam: quoniam lata est porta, et spatiosa via, quae abducit in exitium, multique sunt qui introeunt per eam. Quia angusta est porta, et stricta via, quae ducit ad vitam; et pauci sunt qui inveniant eam,' and St Matthew viii. 12: 'filios vero regni ejectum iri in tenebras illas extimas: illic erit fletus, et stridor dentium.' See also John Connington in his edition of the Satires of Persius (Oxford, ³1896), p. 61 (note on III, 56–57).

43. *Diapente et Diatesseron.*

MS. fol. 437vb ll. 25–29.—pp. 27 (sub 20) and 68.—Jaffé, p. 451.

For these detached lines on the concords of the Perfect Fifth and the Perfect Fourth see the note to Stanza 5 of the preceding piece.

intensa et remissa. Cp. Iamblichus (ed. Sam. Tennulius), p. 171: 'Narrant vero chordarum intensiones et remissiones, quae sunt secundum dictas rationes, primum Pythagoram inter se commensurasse.' *intensa et remissa...consonantia* apparently refers to the tightening and slacking of the strings, and the former seems to denote the higher pitch of the concord of the fifth (*diapente*), and *remissa* the lower concord of the fourth (*diatesseron*). Cp. Christian August Brandis, *Geschichte der Entwickelungen der griechischen Philosophie und ihrer Nachwirkungen im römischen Reiche*, Part I, Berlin, 1862. On p. 171 he says: 'Der Harmonie sollte die Oktave entsprechen und diese in Quarte und Quinte zerfallen, als deren Unterschied der Ton betrachtet wird.' The same view that the octave is made up by adding up a fourth and a fifth was held by Philolaos, a Pythagorean philosopher. See August Boeckh, *Philolaos des Pythagoreers Lehren, nebst Bruchstücken seines Werkes*, Berlin, 1819, pp. 68 sqq. Boeckh says on p. 68: 'Des Philolaos Angaben gründen sich auf das alte hellenische System von einer Oktave.... Die Größe der Harmonie, sagt Philolaos, ist συλλαβὰ und δι' ὀξειᾶν. Συλλαβὴ ist nemlich der alte Name der Quarte (διὰ τεσσάρων), weil sie die erste Zusammenfassung konsonierender Töne ist (πρώτη σύλληψις φθόγγων συμφώνων); δι' ὀξειῶν aber ist die Quinte (διὰ πέντε), weil sie der Quarte nach dem Hohen zu folgt (ἐπὶ τὸ ὀξὺ προχωροῦσα). So lehrt Nikomachos.... Da nun eine Quarte und eine Quinte die Oktave umfassen..., so sagt Philolaos συλλαβὰ und δι' ὀξειῶν sei die Größe der Harmonie.' This is worked out in full by Boeckh.

The same idea is found at the end of the tenth and the beginning of the eleventh century in the

writings of Notker of St Gallen and his pupils. See Paul Piper, 'Die Schriften Notkers und seiner Schule,' Vol. III (Freiburg, 1882), pp. 854-6 (from an Appendix, *De Musica*). On p. 854, 23-27 we read: 'Tíu dríu alphabeta sínt tánne nôte sô gelîh . dáz án îogelîchemo sî diapason . únde dárána diatesseron . unde diapente . únde án diatesseron sîn drî únderlâza tonus tonus semitonium . únde án diapente fîere . tonus tonus semitonium tonus.' On p. 855, 21 sqq.: 'Án dîen octo modis . íh méino ypodorio . ypofrigio . ypolidio . dorio . frigio . lidio . mixolidio . ypermixolidio . sínt úns keóuget octo species . diapason simphonię . án dîen uuír fíndên ûfstîgendo fóne demo níderôsten ze demo óberôsten díse sîben úndarskéita . tonum . tonum semitonium tonum tonum semitonium tonum . Pe díu líutet tíu óberôsta uuárba . duplum gagen dero níderôstun....'

44. *Umbram Hectoris videt Eneas.*

MS. fol. 440ra l. 37-440rb l. 15.—pp. 27 (sub 33) and 68.

These lines are an extract from Virgil's *Æneid*, II, ll. 268-83.

This extract, as well as the two following ones, shows clearly what kinds of passages from the ancient poets the goliard considered to be of principal interest to his hearers. He selected invariably pathetic addresses, outpourings of sorrow and of passionate tenderness. See also Nos. 8, 32, 38.

45. *Hipsipile Archemorum puerum a serpente necatum plorat.*

MS. fol. 439vb ll. 10-24.—pp. 27 (sub 30) and 69.

These lines are an extract from a very pathetic episode of the *Thebaid* (P. Papini Stati *Thebaidos*, Liber V, ll. 608-16). Will. Lillington Lewis, who translated the *Thebaid* of Statius into English verse (Oxford, 1767, 2 vols.), says with regard to this passage (I, 232): 'Upon the whole, we may conclude this oration to be a masterpiece in the pathetic way. That of Eurialus *his* mother in the ninth book of the Æneid, and of Andromache in the twenty-second of the Iliad, are the only ones that can stand in competition with it.'

The text here given is taken from Postgate's *Corpus*, IV, 336^b. The English rendering of Hypsipyle's lament by Lewis is given *l.c.* Vol. I, p. 231, ll. 863-76.

46. *Argie lamentatio maritum Polinicem a fratre interfectum invenientis.*

MS. fol. 439ra ll. 9-40.—pp. 27 (sub 28) and 69. Another extract containing almost entirely the same passage occurs on the same leaf, fol. 439vb ll. 25-440ra l. 6.—pp. 27 (sub 31) and 69.

These most pathetic lines are another extract taken from (the twelfth book of) the *Thebaid*. The former comprises lines 325-48 and the latter lines 322-35. In the present edition (the text of which is taken from Postgate's *Corpus*, IV, 381) the two extracts are given in one combined text beginning with *Hunc ego te, coniunx* (l. 322). The three opening lines are in the second extract put right at the end (fol. 440ra ll. 1-6) after the longer extract beginning with *Huc adtolle genas* (fol. 439ra l. 9 and 439vb l. 25).

The English rendering, by Will. Lillington Lewis, is found in Vol. II, page 589, lines 470-508.

47. *Nisus omnigeni.*

MS. fol. 440vb ll. 14-23.—pp. 27 (sub 37) and 69.—Jaffé, p. 453.

Most of these six unconnected lines are more or less well-built dactylic hexameters. They are isolated lines, and some do not make any sense. They seem to be mere metrical experiments, and the title has been made from l. 3. Jaffé rightly calls the whole an *unverständliches Stück*.

CHAPTER VII

A Contested Passage in 'De Heinrico[1]'

AMONG the scanty fragments of shorter Old High German poems which have come down to our times few surpass the political ballad *De Heinrico* in interest and difficulty. Its peculiar North Middle Franconian dialect[2], its metre and style, at once popular and learned, especially the mixture of Latin and German which we meet here for the first time in Old German poetry[3], are no less interesting than the investigation of the historical circumstances to which the poem refers and in which it was written in the second half of the tenth century. This important 'leich' has not been preserved in any other manuscript.

Up to fairly recent times it was considered to refer to one of the several reconciliations of the German Emperor Otto I, the Great (936–73), with his rebellious brother Henry I, Duke of Bavaria. About the time and place of the particular reconciliation different scholars held different views, but all agreed that a friendly meeting of the brothers was celebrated by a learned poet whose sympathies were with Henry, who was anxious to praise the Duke's wise rule and his love of justice, and to make as little as possible of the very serious offences of which he had been guilty, in his earlier years, towards his brother and the Empire[4]. In regard to the different views that have been advanced concerning the time and place of this meeting of the brothers, as to which no agreement has so far been arrived at, the chronological bibliography at the end of this chapter will give full information.

All conjectures as to the historical background of our poem were until recently based on the

---

[1] Part of the present chapter was first published in *The Modern Quarterly of Language and Literature*, I, 1 (March 1898), 42–46. In a few cases the repetition of facts mentioned in previous chapters could not be altogether avoided. See page 29, note 2, pages 31 and 33 of the present book.

[2] There is still a difference of opinion as to the dialect in which the 'Song of Henry' was originally composed. See Wilhelm Seelmann in the *Jahrbuch des Vereins für Niederdeutsche Sprachforschung*, XII (1886), 75 sqq. and XXIII (1897), 99 sqq.; H. Meyer, *ib.* XXIII (1897), 81 sqq.; Rudolf Kögel, *Geschichte d. deutschen Litt. bis zum Ausgange des Mittelalters*, I, 2 (1897), 127 sqq.; P. Habermann, *Die Metrik der kleineren althochdeutschen Reimgedichte*, Halle, 1909, pp. 72 sqq.

[3] For the only other specimens of this kind of macaronic poetry in Old High German literature (*Clericus et Nonna*, and the love-greeting from *Ruodlieb*), see page 40.

[4] See Rudolf Köpke and Ernst Dümmler, *Kaiser Otto der Grosse*, Leipzig, 1876, p. 120: 'Unter dem Eindruck der hervorragenden Stellung, die Heinrich in späterer Zeit einnahm, trat die Erinnerung an die verbrecherischen Pläne seiner früheren Jahre in den Hintergrund. Schon bei der höfischen Dichterin Hrotsvith erscheint seine Schuld sehr abgeschwächt und es wird vorzüglich die Rührung des Lesers für die reuige Unterwerfung des Büssenden erweckt; in einem halb deutschen, halb lateinischen Leich endlich ist dieser Bussakt fast in einen Triumphzug verwandelt, und ehrenvoll steht Heinrich neben dem Könige.'

three lines which follow immediately on the introductory stanza of four lines, in which the learned poet implores the help of Christ for the composition of a song in praise of 'a certain Duke, Lord Henry, who had gloriously protected (i.e. ruled over) the realm of the Bavarians.' From this it appears that the hero of the 'leich' was no longer alive when it was composed. The following three lines run thus in all the editions of our poem previous to 1892:

> *Intrans nempe nuntius,*   then keisar manoda her thus:
> *'Cur sedes,' infit, 'Otdo*   ther unsar keisar guodo?
> *hic adest* Heinrĭch,   bruother hera kuniglĭch.

If the reading of the last line should prove to be doubtful or incorrect, of course all speculations as to the historical events referred to must be carefully reconsidered. Grave doubts as to the correctness of the reading *bruother kuniglĭch* '(thy) royal brother,' i.e. Henry, have arisen of late, and consequently it is of the greatest importance to have this question definitely settled, if possible, before the historical investigation can be proceeded with.

The writing of by far the greater portion of the poem is very clear and does not admit of the slightest doubt; the dark ink still shines in most places as if it had been used but yesterday, instead of nearly 900 years ago. Unfortunately, however, the very words that are of paramount importance for the historical explanation of the whole are now partly gone[1]. The most important line is the fifth from the bottom of the page, the third of those given above, and examination of the manuscript shows that the ending of each of the last lines on this folio has become either dimmed or quite obliterated, probably through the action of the fingers in turning over the leaf. In these places the parchment is now almost completely worn off, and its former yellowish tint has become whitish-grey[2].

As a basis for the following observations the last eight lines in the second column of fol. 437ʳ are here printed exactly as they stand, so far as they are now distinctly legible, in the manuscript:

> Intranſ nempe nuntiuſ then
>   keiſar namoda her thuſ cur ſed*es*
> infit otdo. ther unſar keiſar
> guodo. hic adeſt heinrich brı
> her hera kuniglich. dignum ti*bi*
> fore thir ſelue moze fine.
> Tunc furrexit otdo ther unſa*r*
>   keiſar guodo. prex̄ illi obuiā.

Thus it appears that the all-important word *bruother* does not really stand in the MS. if, indeed, it ever stood there[3].

When, in 1885, I collated[4] and transcribed from the Cambridge MS. all the poems which had

---

[1] In the case of four other poems the text cannot be determined, or is at best most doubtful, because at a very early date the lines were intentionally erased or blacked out by the use of chemicals. The effacement of the particular words in *De Heinrico* was, however, not intentional. Mistakes of the scribe, which are not infrequent in other poems, are by no means absent from *De Heinrico* and must be considered quite possible here. The last editions of the *Denkmäler* (1892) and of Braune's *Althochdeutsches Lesebuch* (⁷1911) give in every case trustworthy information as to the emendations that have been proposed.

[2] See pages 23–24, and the photographic facsimile of the passage in question on fol. 437ʳᵇ, ll. 33–38.

[3] The final *es* in *sedes* is almost completely rubbed out, and the final *bi* in *tibi* is nearly gone. But both are just legible, being, though faint, more distinct than anything that followed after *brı*. See p. 26, note 2.

[4] See pages 32–33.

been printed in the *Denkmäler*, I did not fail to call Scherer's attention to the very doubtful reading of the manuscript in this important passage. When, after Scherer's premature death, Steinmeyer brought out (in 1892) his excellent new edition of the *Denkmäler*, he had been for some time in possession of all my collations and transcripts. In the notes to the text (Vol. II, 106) Steinmeyer consequently made an ingenious conjecture, proposing the substitution of br⟨ingit⟩her for the traditional br⟨uot⟩her. I turned at once to the manuscript again to ascertain whether this conjecture was confirmed by any faint traces of letters; but in spite of repeated efforts I was unable to come to any definite conclusion as to the true reading of the obliterated word.

In 1894 Robert Priebsch, who was at that time collecting in Cambridge materials for his admirable book *Deutsche Handschriften in England* (Part I, Erlangen, 1896), naturally bestowed a great deal of time and attention upon our manuscript, especially upon the leaves on which the songs are written; and one day, with the help of a chemical reagent, he read quite clearly, not indeed *bringit*, but *bringt*, the *t* being joined to the preceding *g* by a ligature[1]. He hereupon inserted a preliminary notice of his discovery in the *Anzeiger für deutsches Alterthum*, XX (1894), 207, and subsequently discussed the passage at greater length and with much critical acumen in regard to its now altered political significance in his *Deutsche Handschriften in England*, I, 25 sqq. When a few days after Priebsch's discovery, of which he had immediately informed me, I examined the manuscript once more, the passage seemed as illegible as ever, if not more so; and, when I was anxious to repeat the application of a chemical, the Librarian, Mr Francis Jenkinson, shrank from allowing a second use of the reagent. It was, however, applied two years later, in 1896, in the presence of the Librarian and Sir E. M. Thompson, the widely experienced Keeper of the Manuscripts of the British Museum. Neither Sir E. M. Thompson nor I could on that day see anything distinct after *bri*, but Mr Jenkinson thought he could detect part of the tail of an Old English ʒ followed by a very faint *t*.

In the mean time, partly owing to the publication of Steinmeyer's conjecture and Priebsch's confirmation of it, partly owing to the preparation, for the *Monumenta Germaniae*, of a comprehensive edition of the minor Old German historical poems[2], German scholars had begun to investigate the poem afresh. Wilhelm Braune adopted the new reading *bringit* in the fourth edition of his widely used *Althochdeutsches Lesebuch* (Halle, 1897), while Rudolf Kögel took pains to defend the older reading *bruother* in his learned and suggestive *Geschichte der deutschen Litteratur bis zum Ausgange des Mittelalters* (I, 2, 132 sqq., Strassburg, 1897). During the twelve years between 1897 and 1909 a number of articles have been published, partly dealing with the reconstruction of the text, with the dialect and the metre, and partly with the historical bearings of the poem. No general agreement having been reached so far on any of these points, it may be useful to examine once more, with the help of the photographic reproduction of fol. 437, what conjectures may or may not be based on the actual reading of the manuscript.

Most of the writers who have so far discussed the passage, and have often materially contributed to the emendation and the proper understanding of the text, have not been able to consult the manuscript for themselves.

[1] There occur indeed a few ligatures after *n* in the case of *nt* and *ns* (e.g. fol. 432rb l. 9 quereba*nt*, fol. 433ra l. 21 su*nt*, fol. 434ra l. 28 sumperu*nt*, fol. 433rb l. 15 uaca*ns*), but in no place have I come across a *t* joined in this way to a preceding *g*; in fact the writing of coniu*ngit* (on fol. 438rb l. 34) seems rather to speak in favour of reading bri*ngit* for which longer form the available space would just suffice.

[2] The very desirable publication of these poems, originally undertaken, but subsequently abandoned, by H. Meyer, had not yet been carried out in July 1914, as far as I am aware.

A CONTESTED PASSAGE IN 'DE HEINRICO'

Johann Georg Eccard, who, in 1720, edited *De Heinrico* for the first time[1], had no access to the manuscript itself. He published the poem in his *Veterum Monumentorum Quaternio* (pp. 49–52) with a few additional remarks under the title 'Poema in Henricum Palatinum Rheni,' adding 'ab anonymo Lotharingo.' On p. 51 Eccard informs the reader that the poem had been sent to him (*ex codice membranaceo Cantabrigiensi transmissum*). Unfortunately he does not mention when and from whom he received it, or when the transcript was made[2]. Eccard's text is most untrustworthy and unfortunately contains no statement as to any doubt or difficulty in the reading of the manuscript. He prints simply (without any regard to the true division of the lines):

> Intrans nempe nuntius
> Then Kaisar namoda,
> Herthas, cur sedis, infit, Otdo
> Ther unsar Kaisar guodo
> Hic.........adest Heinrich
> Bruother, hera Kuniglich
> Dignum tibi fore
> Thit selve more.

On this most unsatisfactory text the editors of the poem who succeeded Eccard had for a long time to base their discussions and emendations. One's first thoughts would be to suspect that before 1720 the letters making up the word *bruot/her* could still be pretty plainly read in the manuscript, for it would seem rather unlikely that an Englishman unacquainted with Old German, as the rest of the transcript proves him to have been, would have imagined this word. Or are we to suppose that it was Eccard himself who pieced together the *bru..* and *her* of the copy sent to him in order to obtain the word *bruother* which seemed to make such good sense, and that he did not call attention to the real reading of the manuscript[3]?

Wackernagel, Lachmann and Schade, who did so much for the improvement and explanation of the text[4], had not themselves inspected the manuscript; neither did Hoffmann von Fallersleben, who printed Wackernagel's improved version (*Fundgruben*, I, 340–1), nor did Jacob Grimm, who intended to publish the 'leich[5],' endeavour to obtain a new collation. At the end of the sixties

---

[1] See page 30.

[2] It is difficult to guess who may have transcribed it for him, together with the eight purely Latin poems which Eccard published from the same manuscript. See the table on p. 27. The influence of George Hickes and his friends seems to be noticeable. Hickes himself, it is true, had died in 1715, but one might think of Humphrey Wanley, Christopher Rawlinson, and especially of John Smith who published at Cambridge, in 1722, his edition of the Old English Bede. The University Librarians were: 1712–18 P. Brooke, B.D., of St John's College, and 1718–21 T. Macro, M.A., of Gonville and Caius College. The valuable manuscript had not been long at Cambridge when the poems were copied from it for the use of Eccard. It was acquired for the Library, probably soon after 1670, out of Bishop Hacket's bequest. See *University Library MS.* Oo. 7. 52, p. 83, where it is mentioned under No. 213. John Leland, who just before the middle of the sixteenth century made his great antiquarian tour through England, saw it still at St Augustine's Abbey, Canterbury, and enumerated some of its contents. See Leland, *Collectanea*, London, 1770, IV, 7. How much longer it remained at Canterbury we do not know; many of the manuscripts were dispersed during Leland's lifetime.

[3] Eccard does not inform us on this important point. With regard to the line which he prints 'Hic...adest Heinrich,' he says: 'Suppleo: Hic *nam* adest,' while he has no note on the reading 'Bruother' with which he begins the next line. As a matter of fact there is no space whatever between 'hic' and 'adest' and the next line does not begin with 'Bruother' but with 'her.' See p. 13 (fol. 437rb, lines 36–37).

[4] See page 31.

[5] See Jac. Grimm und Andr. Schmeller, *Lateinische Gedichte des x. und xi. Jahrhunderts*, Göttingen, 1838, p. 343.

Jaffé came to Cambridge, went carefully through the part of the manuscript containing the songs, and published the result of his labours in a most valuable article in the *Zeitschrift für deutsches Alterthum*[1]. But, strangely enough, he has not (on p. 451) a single word of doubt as to the correctness of the reading *bruot/her*, although he sets right several trifling mistakes that he noticed in the first edition of the *Denkmäler* (1864). This looks as if Jaffé accepted the reading *bruot/her*, the importance of which he certainly realised. After him Braune (*Althochd. Lesebuch*) and Piper (*Die älteste deutsche Litteratur bis um das Jahr* 1050) printed the text, without apparently having had recourse to the original or to a fresh collation of the text.

When, in the spring of 1885, I went over the same ground again, and could not find any distinct trace of letters after the *bri*, I asked my late friend, Henry Bradshaw, then University Librarian and one of the greatest authorities in all matters concerning medieval manuscripts, to look with me at the passage. We repeated our readings several times on the brightest days of May and June, but neither he nor I could· decipher any more. Certainly *bruother* could not be read; but when I asked Bradshaw to allow me the use of a reagent he felt unable to do so, as he was afraid of the damage it might do to the manuscript[2]. In 1894, as stated before, Robert Priebsch, with the permission of the new Librarian, Francis Jenkinson, applied a reagent and was thus able to decipher *bringt her*, while Paul Piper, in 1895, still accepted the old reading *bruother*, in spite of a tracing of the passage which I had placed at his disposal and in spite of Priebsch's article in the *Anzeiger für deutsches Alterthum* (XX (1894), 207). In order to enable scholars in Germany to judge from autopsy, I twice sent good photographic reproductions of the passage in question to several *Germanisten* (in 1895 and 1902)[3].

To sum up, several scholars who, in former years, were able to consult the manuscript, read *bruot/her*. Priebsch, however, has no doubt that, with the help of the reagent, then applied for the first time, he actually saw *bringt*[4]. At present only *bri* can be read for certain, even with the help of a fresh reagent and a good magnifying glass. It is scarcely to be hoped that, after the repeated treatment with chemicals, the manuscript will ever disclose to our eyes the few strokes on which so much depends for the interpretation of the poem.

In the circumstances, it is difficult to arrive at a satisfactory decision. It cannot be denied that the fact that *bruot/her*, a form not likely to be guessed by an Englishman transcribing the poem in the early eighteenth century, was the earliest published reading, and was not challenged by scholars so careful as Pertz (1827) and Jaffé (1868), would seem to speak in favour of adhering to the old reading. Again, in spite of Priebsch's able arguments, it seems very doubtful whether we ought to admit in so early a poem the form *bringt* instead of *bringit*[5]. Braune consequently prints *bringit* in the later editions of his *Althochdeutsches Lesebuch*. It cannot be doubted that the available space would well allow the room required for the longer form *bringit*; it will be seen, too, from an inspection of the photographic reproduction that some words (*sedes*, *tibi*, and others) are

---

[1] See page 32.

[2] When I informed Scherer of my unsuccessful attempts he wrote on May 21, 1885, 'Wie schade, dass kein Reagens angewandt werden darf. Eine künftige Zeit wird es gewiss tun und dann wissen, was da verborgen liegt.'

[3] See page 34, note 1.

[4] Elias Steinmeyer, in Richard Bethge's *Ergebnisse und Fortschritte der Germanistischen Wissenschaft im letzten Vierteljahrhundert*, Leipzig, 1902, p. 230, claims as 'ein sicheres Ergebnis' that 'die Handschrift (Zeile 7) nicht *bruother*, sondern *bringt* liest.' But see the following observations.

[5] Priebsch has now for many years considered *bringt* to be a mere clerical error instead of *bringit*.

more than once put close to the margin, and the same would be possible in the case of *bringit*. A very much greater difficulty, as far as space goes, is caused by the impossibility of allowing a complete *n* to have found room before the *g*[1]. The *r* in *brı* is clearly an Old English ꞃ, not the continental ꭇ, and consequently the second smaller stroke which still belongs to the ꞃ must not be mistaken for an *i* which would then allow the present *i* to be taken for the first part of an *n*. ꞃi and ꞃo look very different in heinꞃiche (l. 31) and thero beiaꞃo ꞃiche (l. 32) in the preceding line, while the ꞃ in heinꞃich (l. 36) and heꞃ (l. 37) is the same as the ꞃ in bꞃı which stands between them. On the other hand, a very faint Old English ᵹ, which I do not remember having seen in 1885, is now very dimly recognisable in the manuscript and also in the photographic reproduction of the passage. But even if one reads an Old English ᵹ immediately before the *t*, the difficulty still remains that it is hardly possible to find sufficient room for an *n* before the spread out ᵹ. After the *brı* there is clearly only room for one more stroke before the ᵹ begins. It would be amply sufficient to make *bru-o*, but would not quite suffice for *brin-g*, even if the *n* was put quite close to the ᵹ[2]. This is quite clearly seen if one looks at the space required for *nig* in *kuniglich* (l. 37); *nig* would occupy the same space as *ing*.

But if most of these points are nearly as much in favour of the reading *bruot/her* as of *bring(i)t her*, another point, not mentioned by Priebsch, seems to tell against *bruother* and strongly supports the reading *bringit*. If we look at the way in which the words are divided in our manuscript, we find in *De Heinrico* alone the following: *fau/tor*, *be/thiu*, *sco/ne*, *miche/lon*, and in the purely Latin pieces for instance *athana/thos* (fol. 434rb l. 38), *rith/micam* (fol. 435rb l. 37), *simpho/nie* (fol. 434rb l. 39), *pro/phete* (fol. 432va l. 25), from which it appears that the division of words is carried out intelligently and that the letters in *th* and *ph* are never separated. Everywhere in the manuscript a proper division of the words, German or Latin, is made by the scribe or scribes. The most instructive instance is *be/thiu*, 'both,' which proves that the two letters (*th*) which denote but one sound were not separated by the scribe who himself spoke the voiced spirant sound which once, in l. 20, he rendered by the proper Old English Runic letter þ[3]. If he had wished to divide the word *bruother*, he would in all probability have written *bruo/ther*. This fact, taken together with Priebsch's deliberate statement, seems to me a very strong argument for abandoning the reading *bruother*, and consequently I have printed *bringit* in the text on page 48 (No. 11, line 7).

[1] Attention was first called to this fact in my note printed in the *Anzeiger für deutsches Alterthum* XXIV (1898), 59 which had been sent to the editors as early as January 1896.

[2] The omission of one stroke of the *n* may, however, well be a scribe's mistake. Compare on fol. 441rb, l. 40 *angelis* instead of *angelus*.

[3] It has often been pointed out that in the part of the Cambridge Manuscript which contains the 'Cambridge Songs' many letters occur indiscriminately, now in the English and now in the continental form. It is worthy of notice that nowhere in the ten folios 432–41 is this more the case than on fol. 437 which contains the 'leich' *De Heinrico*. Again, while there are throughout the folios double forms of *a* and *d* and of the capital *H*, and while the Old English *t* is commonly used, and the Old English *r* at least is met with on many of the folios, the other Old English symbols are exceedingly rare and only occur once in the case of þ and p, and three times in the case of ꝼ (in the same poem), and nearly all on the same folio (fol. 437va). The Old English ᵹ is also of very rare occurrence throughout the manuscript except on the very folio (437) on which the other Old English letters occur. This seems to point to the fact that this part of the songs was written by a scribe whose habits were different from those of the writer or writers of other folios. There are many pages on which no Old English ᵹ occurs (on others neither an Old English ᵹ nor even an Old English ꞃ), while on fol. 437rb l. 36 *guodo* is spelt with a continental *g*, and l. 40 *guodo* with the Old English ᵹ; in l. 37 *kuniglich dignum* show the two *g*'s, and l. 32 *riche beuuarode* the two *r*'s side by side. See also p. 25.

But if from the reading of the manuscript it is no longer necessary to assume that the 'leich' *De Heinrico* dealt with the meeting of two brothers, and that consequently the Duke Henry of Bavaria must be Henry I, the rebellious brother of the Emperor Otto I, it does not follow that our poem may not for all that celebrate the famous final reconciliation[1] of the brothers and the solemn investment of Duke Henry with great authority at the hands of the Emperor himself. On the other hand, there is no longer any reason why scholars should not search in the German history of the second half of the tenth century for some other important state function at which an Emperor Otto showed great honour to a Duke Henry of Bavaria. If the poem does not refer to Otto I and Henry I, it can only be taken to refer to Otto III and Henry II[2]. Again, it may or may not have been composed immediately after the meeting of the princes. Even if it was written much later than the events to which it refers, it may still celebrate Henry I, the brother of the Emperor Otto I, and may have been composed with a special political purpose[3]. The views of scholars on these points are still widely different, as it is most difficult and precarious to build any theory on the few and elusive lines of our poem, especially as this contains several expressions that have not as yet been elucidated beyond all doubt[4]. After careful consideration of the various arguments that have been set forth with much ingenuity, though their propounders are sometimes, no doubt, erecting imposing edifices on exceedingly unsafe foundations, I do not feel able to propose a new and better or a definite solution of the many difficulties that stand in the way of assigning to this fascinating poem a date that would be free from all objections.

On the whole I am inclined to believe, with Meyer and Seemüller, that the persons whose meeting is so graphically described in the 'leich' are the Emperor Otto I and his brother Henry I, and that the event referred to is Otto's handing over of the Duchy of Bavaria to Henry in 948 as a fief to be held under the Emperor. The poem, however, seems to have been written at a considerably later date, probably just before the diet of Frankfurt, at the beginning of 985, when Henry II, the son of Henry I, definitely made his peace with the young Emperor Otto III, and by doing so secured for himself the Duchy of Bavaria. The situation was very similar[5] to that which had existed in 948, and the poem, in which the honour shown and the well-rewarded confidence given to Henry I by the great Otto was celebrated in emphatic terms, was perhaps composed by

---

[1] Lachmann's assumption that the 'leich' referred to Otto's meeting with his brother Henry I at Christmas 941 has now probably been given up by the majority of scholars. It was apparently maintained for the last time by W. Wilmanns in the *Göttinger Gelehrte Anzeigen* of 1893, p. 434.

[2] See Elias Steinmeyer in the third edition of the *Denkmäler*, II (1892), 106, and R. Priebsch, *Deutsche Handschriften in England*, I (1896), 26–27. Both assume it to refer to the expedition of Henry II to Brandenburg, in 992, in order to reinforce the Emperor Otto III. In that case the poem would have been composed at the end of the tenth century by someone at the court of Henry III.

[3] See the articles by Heinrich Meyer and Joseph Seemüller enumerated in the Bibliography under the years 1897 and 1898, also the one by Eugen Joseph (1898) the conclusions of which are, however, less plausible. Seemüller and Meyer (the latter with certain qualifications) are of opinion that the 'leich' celebrates the reconciliation of Otto I with his brother Henry and the bestowal upon him of the Duchy of Bavaria as a fief from the Emperor, but that it was not written until 984 or 985, and was, perhaps, intended by its author to be sung at the diet of Frankfurt.

[4] Such as *hera kuniglich* (l. 7) and *ambo vos equivoci* (l. 13).

[5] Already Ludwig Uhland remarked: 'Ereignisse und Situationen, die sich so, selbst unter gleichen Namen, von Generation zu Generation in der deutschen Kaisergeschichte erneuerten konnten auch in der Sage fortwährend denselben Typus anfrischen).' See his *Schriften zur Geschichte der Dichtung und Sage*, VII, 581.

some learned goliard in the service of the Imperial party with the intention to influence Henry II, the son of Henry I, in favour of coming to terms with the Emperor[1].

If we may thus still hold that the political events described in *De Heinrico* refer to the reconciliation of the Emperor Otto I with his ambitious brother Henry, however much the real facts may have been disguised by the learned and strongly biassed author of the macaronic 'leich,' it is an interesting fact that the historical self-humiliation of Henry and the magnanimity of Otto have formed the subject of two modern German ballads. The famous Christmas service of 941, at which Henry, escaping from prison, threw himself, in a penitent's garb, at his brother's feet and implored his forgiveness, has inspired, nearly 990 years after the *De Heinrico*, two ballads that are very different in style and in the treatment of their subject[2]. One was written by H. von Mühler, who subsequently became Prussian Minister of Education; this ballad proceeds slowly, in the stately metre of the later Nibelungen stanza. The first stanza runs thus:

> *Zu Quedlinburg im Dome   ertönet Glockenklang,*
> *Der Orgel Stimmen brausen   zum ernsten Chorgesang,*
> *Es sitzt der Kaiser drinnen   mit seiner Ritter Macht,*
> *Voll Andacht zu beginnen   die heil'ge Weihenacht.*

The other poem is one of the finest ballads of the great Swiss writer, Conrad Ferdinand Meyer. It is called *Der gleitende Purpur* and is highly dramatic. Its opening stanzas are:

> *'Eia Weihnacht! Eia Weihnacht!'*
> *Schallt im Münsterchor der Psalm der Knaben.*
>   *Kaiser Otto lauscht der Mette,*
> *Diener hinter sich mit Spend' und Gaben.*
>
> *Eia Weihnacht! Eia Weihnacht!*
> *Heute, da die Himmel niederschweben,*
>   *Wird dem Elend und der Blöße*
> *Mäntel er und warme Röcke geben.*
>
> *Hundert Bettler stehn erwartend—*
> *Einer hält des Kaisers Knie umfangen*
>   *Mit den wundgeriebnen Armen,*
> *Dran zerrißner Fesseln Enden hangen....*

---

[1] It is true that in this case the term *hera kuniglich* causes considerable difficulty, but it seems to me to be less great than the difficulties that arise if the meeting between Otto and Henry is taken to refer to the Brandenburg expedition of 992.

[2] Both are easily accessible in the valuable collection of German ballads by H. Benzmann, *Die deutsche Ballade*, Leipzig, 1913, 2 volumes. Heinrich von Mühler's *Otto I und Heinrich* is given in Vol. II, 188; Conrad Ferdinand Meyer's *Der gleitende Purpur* in Vol. II, 89. The original version of Meyer's ballad did not include the present stanza 8 (*Wehe mir, da du dich kröntest, Hat des Neides Natter mich gebissen, Mit dem Lügengeist im Bunde Hab' ich dieses deutsche Reich zerrissen!*) that is so full of meaning. See *Gedichte* von C. F. Meyer, Leipzig, Haessel, 1882, pp. 259–61. In its final form the poem appears in Meyer's *Gedichte*, 60th ed., Leipzig, 1912, pp. 312–14, and in Benzmann, *l.c.*, and in other anthologies.

CHRONOLOGICAL BIBLIOGRAPHY

1720. J. G. ECCARD, Veterum monumentorum quaternio. Leipzig, 1720. No. III, pp. 49 sqq.

1819. JACOB GRIMM, Deutsche Grammatik, I, p. lx (reprinted in the 'Kleinere Schriften,' VIII, 76). (Directed against Eccard's 'unbegreiflichen Missgriff' in dating the poem as late as 1209.)

1823. B. J. DOCEN, in Hormayr's 'Archiv für Geschichte, Kunst und Litteratur,' p. 532. (Also controverting Eccard's dating of the poem.)

1829. KARL LACHMANN, Über die Leiche der deutschen Dichter des zwölften und dreizehnten Jahrhunderts, in the 'Rheinisches Museum,' III, pp. 430–3. Reprinted in his 'Kleinere Schriften zur deutschen Philologie,' I, 335–9. See p. 31, note 1 of the present book.

1830. WILHELM WACKERNAGEL gave the first critical text of the poem in H. Hoffmann's 'Fundgruben für Geschichte deutscher Sprache und Litteratur,' I, 340–1.

1830–1. LUDWIG UHLAND, now in 'Schriften zur Geschichte der Dichtung und Sage,' I, 382, 473–5 and VII, 578–81 (differed from Lachmann with regard to the explanation of the historical allusions).

1833. KARL LACHMANN, Über Singen und Sagen. Paper read in the Berlin Academy on Nov. 26, 1833. Reprinted in his 'Kleinere Schriften,' I, 464 sqq.

1837. F. J. MONE, in the 'Anzeiger für Kunde des deutschen Mittelalters,' Vol. VI, 317.

1838. KARL LACHMANN, critical text in L. Ranke's 'Jahrbücher des deutschen Reiches,' I, 2, p. 97, with an examination of the historical facts referred to by R. A. Köpke. See p. 31, n. 3 of the present book.

1860. OSCAR SCHADE, Veterum monumentorum decas. Weimar. No. II, pp. 5–8. Reprinted in Heinrich Hoffmann's 'In dulci jubilo,' pp. 3 sqq. and 27–29.

1861. WILHELM WACKERNAGEL, text in his 'Altdeutsches Lesebuch.' 4th ed. Basel. pp. 109–12.

1862. OSCAR SCHADE, 'Altdeutsches Lesebuch.' Halle. pp. 60–61.

1864. WILHELM SCHERER, in the 'Denkmäler deutscher Poesie und Prosa aus dem VIII–XII Jahrhundert.' Berlin. No. XVIII, pp. 25–26 (text), 304–7 (notes).

1869. PHILIPP JAFFÉ, in the 'Zeitschrift für deutsches Alterthum,' XIV, 451 sqq.

1872. R. WINTER, Heinrich von Bayern. Inaugural-Dissertation. Jena. pp. 76–78.

1873. WILHELM SCHERER, in MSD², No. XVIII, pp. 27–28 and 324–8.

1875. WILHELM BRAUNE, Althochdeutsches Lesebuch. Halle. p. 144.

1876. ERNST DÜMMLER, Kaiser Otto der Große. Leipzig, 1876. p. 120.

1880. PAUL PIPER, Lesebuch des Althochdeutschen und Altsächsischen. Paderborn. p. 189.

1885. KARL BREUL, in the 'Zeitschrift für deutsches Alterthum,' XXX, 187–92. See also MSD³, II, 100 and 160.

1886. WILHELM SEELMANN, in the 'Jahrbuch des Vereins für niederdeutsche Sprachforschung,' XII, 75–89. (See also under 1897; and see Joh. Kelle, Geschichte d. d. Lit. (1892), I, 376–7.)

1887. ADOLF EBERT, Allgemeine Geschichte der Literatur des Mittelalters im Abendlande. Leipzig. Vol. III, 347–8.

1892. ELIAS STEINMEYER, in MSD³, No. XVIII, I, 39–40 and II, 99–106 (Scherer's edition revised and enlarged). See pp. 32–33 of the present book.

JOHANN KELLE, Geschichte der deutschen Literatur von den ältesten Zeiten bis zur Mitte des XI Jahrhunderts. Berlin. I, 194 sqq. and 376–7.

1893. WILHELM WILMANNS, in the 'Göttinger Gelehrte Anzeigen,' p. 434 (in favour of Lachmann's dating and against Steinmeyer).

CHRONOLOGICAL BIBLIOGRAPHY

1894. ROBERT PRIEBSCH, in the 'Anzeiger für deutsches Alterthum,' xx, 207.
1896. ROBERT PRIEBSCH, Deutsche Handschriften in England. Erlangen. I, 25–27.
1897. RUDOLF KÖGEL, Geschichte der deutschen Literatur bis zum Ausgange des Mittelalters, I, 2, 126–36 and 360.
H. MEYER und WILHELM SEELMANN, in the 'Jahrbuch für ndd. Sprachforschung,' XXIII, 70–102.
1898. KARL BREUL, in the 'Anzeiger für deutsches Alterthum,' XXIV, 59 (written at the end of 1895 and sent in January 1896).
KARL BREUL, A contested passage in the Old High German poem *De Heinrico*, in 'The Modern Quarterly for Language and Literature,' I, 1 (March), 42–46.
ERNST MARTIN, in the 'Anzeiger für deutsches Alterthum,' XXIV, 58 (supporting Steinmeyer against Kögel).
JOSEPH SEEMÜLLER, Studien zu den Ursprüngen der altdeutschen Historiographie. Halle. pp. 61 sqq.
EUGEN JOSEPH, in the 'Zeitschrift für deutsches Alterthum,' XLII, 197 sqq.
PAUL PIPER, Nachträge zur älteren deutschen Litteratur (Vol. 162 of Kürschner's 'Deutsche National-Literatur,' pp. 221–2).
1899. ELIAS STEINMEYER, in 'Jahresberichte für germanische Philologie' (for 1898), pp. 73 sqq. (dealing with the views of Joseph, Seemüller, Meyer, Seelmann, Piper).
E. MAYER, Das bairische Herzogtum im Leich *De Heinrico*, in the 'Historische Vierteljahrschrift,' Vol. II, 517 sqq.
1900. ELIAS STEINMEYER, in 'Jahresberichte f. g. Phil.' (for 1899), p. 66 (on E. Mayer, and a few references).
1901. RUDOLF KÖGEL, in Paul's 'Grundriss der Germanischen Philologie,' Vol. II, §§ 110–11, pp. 126 sqq.
W. UHL, in the 'Zeitschrift für deutsche Philologie,' XXXIII, 247.
1902. ELIAS STEINMEYER, in R. Bethge, Ergebnisse und Fortschritte der germanistischen Wissenschaft im letzten Vierteljahrhundert. Leipzig. p. 230.
FRIEDRICH HOLTHAUSEN, in the 'Zeitschrift für deutsche Philologie,' XXXV, 89 (see E. Steinmeyer in the 'Jahresbericht' for 1902, pp. 63–64).
1903. G. EHRISMANN, in 'Paul und Braune's Beiträge zur Geschichte der deutschen Sprache und Literatur,' XXIX, 118–26 (see E. Steinmeyer in the 'Jahresberichte' for 1903, p. 86).
1904. FRIEDRICH HOLTHAUSEN, in the 'Zs. f. d. Philologie,' XXXVI, 483 (see E. Steinmeyer in the 'Jahresbericht' for 1905, p. 86).
1905. J. R. DIETERICH, in the 'Zs. f. d. Alterthum,' XLVII, 431–46 (see E. Steinmeyer in the 'Jahresbericht' for 1905, pp. 85–86).
1909. PAUL HABERMANN, Die Metrik der kleineren althochdeutschen Reimgedichte. Halle. pp. 65–77.
1911. WILHELM BRAUNE, Althochdeutsches Lesebuch, 7th ed., pp. 152–3 and 195–6.
1912. WOLFGANG GOLTHER, Die deutsche Dichtung im Mittelalter. Stuttgart. pp. 70–71.

A. ALPHABETICAL INDEX* OF

Manuscript Folio	First words (Chapter V)	Order in the MS.	Pages in Jaffé	Numbers in Jaffé	Pages in Piper	Numbers in this edition	Pages in this edition
440vb	Ad mensam Philosophie	36	489–90	xxvi	231	41	67
435vb	Advertite, omnes populi	13	472–74	xiv	217	22	56
436vb	Audax es, vir iuvenis	17	484–87	xxiii	220	39	66–7
434va	Aurea personet lira	9	490–91	xxvii	213	31	63
439rb	Caute cane, cantor care	29	467–69	x	226	23	57
441va	Chordas tange, melos pange	42	466–67	ix	233	21	56
437vb	Diapente et diatesseron	20	451	—	223	43	68
438va	Emicat o quanta pietate	25	484	xxii	225	9	46
437va	Est unus locus	19	a few notes: 451	—	222	29	62
441ra	Gaudet polus, ridet tellus	40	465–66	viii	232	18	54
432rb	Grates usie solvimus supreme	3	476–79	xvi	207	3	44–5
432ra	Gratuletur omnis caro	1	note on p. 461	not numbered	206	7	46
441va	Hec est clara dies	43	480	xviii	233	5	45
438ra	Herigêr, urbis Maguntiensis	23	455–56	i	223	26	59–60
439ra and ^{vb}	Huc attolle genas	28, 31		—	226; 228	46	69
438va	Iam, dulcis amica, venito	26	note on p. 494	xxxi	225	33	64
432va	Inclito celorum	4	474–76	xv	208	2	42–3
441rb	In vitis patrum veterum	41	469	xi	232	27	60
434rb	Iudex summe	8	460–61	iv	213	14	51
436va	Lamentemur nostra, socii, peccata	16	458–59	iii	219	13	50
441ra	Levis exsurgit Zephirus	39	492–93	xxix	231	32	64
434vb	Magnus cesar Otto	10	a few corr. 451	—	214	12	49
432ra	Melos cuncti concinentes	2	461–62	v	206	15	51–2
436rb	Mendosam quam cantilenam ago	14	471–72	xiii	218	25	59

* A very useful alphabetical Index of secular Latin Lyrics after the end of the xIth century was published, as early as 1872, by Wilhelm Wattenbach in Haupt's *Zeitschrift für deutsches Alterthum*, xv, 469–506 under the title 'Die Anfänge lateinischer profaner Rythmen des Mittelalters.' Wattenbach excluded from his list all the poems written before 1100 (thus excluding the 'Cambridge Songs'), also all the hymns proper (for which he referred to Mone) and the many learned imitations of classical Latin poetry in hexameters and elegiacs.

THE CAMBRIDGE SONGS

Manuscript Folio	First words (Chapter V)	Order in the MS.	Pages in Jaffé	Numbers in Jaffé	Pages in Piper	Numbers in this edition	Pages in this edition
441va	Miserarum est	45	—		233	38	65
437rb	Nunc almus assis filius ...	18	a few corr. 451	—	221	11	48
433vb	Nunc chorda pange	7	481–84	xxi	212	10	47–8
441vb	O admirabile Veneris idolum ...	47	493–94	xxx	234	34	65
439vb	O mihi deserte	30		—	228	45	69
433ra	Omnis sonus cantilene ...	5	470–71	xii	209	24	58
435va	O pater optime	12	479–80	xvii	217	1	42
436rb	O rex regum	15	462–64	vi	219	16	52–3
441vb	Pulsat astra planctu magno Rachel	46	481	xx	233	8	46
440rb	Quibus ludus est animo ...	34	a few corr. 452	—	229	28	61
440ra	Qui habet vocem serenam ...	32	p. 452 note.	—	229	17	53
433va	Qui principium constas rerum	6	456–58	ii	210	19	54–5
441va	Rota modos arte	44	489	xxv	233	40	67
438vb	S......	27	494–95	xxxii	225	35	65
437vb	Salve, festa dies...	21		—	223	4	45
440vb	Salve, vite norma	37	452–53	—	231	47	69
438rb	Sponso sponsa karissimo ...	24	464–65	vii	224	20	55
440va	Templum Christi, virgo casta ...	35	480–81	xix	230	6	46
440ra	Tempus erat, quo prima quies	33		—	229	44	68
440vb	V............	38	note on p. 453	—	231	37	65
441vb	Ven............	48	495	xxxiii	234	36	65
438ra	Vestiunt silve	22	491–92	xxviii	223	30	63
435rb	Vite dator, omnifactor deus ...	11	488–89	xxiv	215	42	67–8

Four poems are almost entirely erased (Nos. 33, 35, 36, 37 in this edition).

Otherwise every Latin poem known to him between 1100 and 1500 (roughly speaking) is mentioned in the alphabetical list of first lines together with brief indications of the place where it may be found. For the order in which the 'Cambridge Songs' are written in the manuscript, and for the enumeration of the most important older works in which some of them are printed, see the table on page 27.

B. SYNOPSIS OF THE CONTENTS OF

No.	Titles	Transliteration	Text	Notes
1	Carmen Christo dictum [*O pater optime*]	10ᵃ, 33	42	71
2	Modus qui et Carelmanninc [*Inclito celorum*]	4ᵃ, 31	42–3	71
3	Laudes Christo acte [*Grates usie*]	3ᵇ, 24	44–5	71
4	Hymnus Paschalis [*Salve, festa dies*]	14ᵇ, 30	45	72
5	Resurrectio [*Hec est clara dies*]	22ᵃ, 14	45	72
6	Ad Mariam [*Templum Christi, virgo casta*]	20ᵃ, 35	46	72
7	De Epiphania [*Gratuletur omnis caro*]	3ᵃ, 1	46	72–3
8	Rachel [*Pulsat astra planctu magno*]	22ᵇ, 3	46	73
9	De domo S. Cecilie Coloniensi [*Emicat o quanta*]	16ᵃ, 12	46	74
10	De S. Victore Carmen Xantense [*Nunc chorda pange*]	6ᵇ, 36	47–8	74
11	De Heinrico [*Nunc almus assis filius*]	13ᵇ, 27	48	75, 102–11
12	Modus Ottinc [*Magnus cesar Otto*]	8ᵇ, 31	49	75–6
13	Nenia de mortuo Heinrico II imperatore [*Lamentemur*]	12ᵃ, 38	50	76
14	Nenia in funebrem pompam Heinrici II [*Iudex summe*]	7ᵇ, 6	51	76
15	Cantilena in Conradum II factum imperatorem [*Melos cuncti*]	3ᵃ, 7	51–2	76–7
16	Cantilena in Heinricum III regem coronatum [*O rex regum*]	11ᵇ, 38	52–3	77
17	Nenia de mortuo Conrado II imperatore [*Qui habet vocem serenam*]	19ᵃ, 7	53	77–9
18	Gratulatio regine a morbo recreate [*Gaudet polus*]	21ᵃ, 22	54	79
19	Cantilena in Heribertum [*Qui principium constas rerum*]	6ᵃ, 3	54–5	79–80
20	Versus ad Popponem [*Sponso sponsa karissimo*]	15ᵇ, 23	55	80–1
21	De Willemo [*Chordas tange, melos pange*]	22ᵃ, 1	56	81
22	Modus Liebinc [*Advertite, omnes populi, ridiculum*]	10ᵇ, 29	56	81–3
23	De Proterii filia [*Caute cane, cantor care*]	17ᵇ, 1	57	83
24	De Lantfrido et Cobbone [*Omnis sonus cantilene*]	5ᵃ, 19	58	83–4

THE GOLIARD'S SONG BOOK

No.	Titles	Transliteration	Text	Notes
25	Modus Florum [*Mendosam quam cantilenam ago*]	11^b, 10	59	84–5
26	Herigêr [*Herigêr, urbis Maguntiensis antistes*] ...	15^a, 30	59–60	85–6
27	De Iohanne abbate [*In vitis patrum veterum*]	21^b, 15	60	86–7
28	Sacerdos et lupus [*Quibus ludus est in animo*]	19^b, 16	61	87–8
29	Alfrâd [*Est unus locus*]	14^a, 24	62	88
30	Carmen estivum [*Vestiunt silve*]	15^a, 6	63	88–90
31	De luscinia [*Aurea personet lira*]	8^a, 1	63	90–1
32	Verna femine suspiria [*Levis exsurgit Zephirus*]	21^a, 1	64	91
33	Invitatio amice [*Iam, dulcis amica, venito*]	16^a, 25	64	92
34	Magister puero [*O admirabile Veneris idolum*]	22^b, 16	65	92–4
35	Clericus et Nonna (largely erased)	16^b, 16	65	94
36	In languore perio (largely erased)	22^b, 35	65	95
37	V.... (erased)	20^b, 24	65	95
38	Lamentatio Neobule [*Miserarum est*]	22^a, 32	65	95
39	Admonitio iuvenum [*Audax es, vir iuvenis*]	12^b, 40	66–7	95–6
40	De musica [*Rota modos arte personemus musica*]	22^a, 24	67	96–7
41	De mensa Philosophie [*Ad mensam Philosophie*]	20^b, 6	67	97–8
42	De simphoniis et de littera Pithagore [*Vite dator*]	9^b, 12	67–8	98–100
43	Diapente et Diatesseron [*Diapente et Diatesseron*]	14^b, 25	68	100–101
44	Umbram Hectoris videt Eneas [*Tempus erat*]	19^a, 37	68	101
45	Hipsipile Archemorum plorat [*O mihi deserte*]	18^b, 10	69	101
46	Argie lamentatio [*Hunc ego te, coniunx*]	19^a, 1; 18^b, 25; 17^a, 9	69	101
47	Nisus omnigeni [*Salve, vite norma*]	20^b, 14	69	101

C. GENERAL INDEX

abba, in: Iohannes abba 87
abbreviations 25
accentual lyric poetry in Germany 36
admonitio iuvenum 66, 95
advocatus Romae 76
agni sponsa 77
Alanus ab Insulis 97
Albarus, Paulus 91
Alcuin 91
Alfrâd 29, 31, 62, 88
Allen, Ph. Schuyler 28, 34–7, 40, often in the Notes, 87, 91, 94
Alleyne, S. F. 98
alliteration in the Cambridge Songs 31
alphabetical poem 66, 95
Amarcius, Sextus 40, 82, 90, 98
Anglo-Saxon letters in the Manuscript 25
Anselm of Canterbury 96
Archipoeta 37
Archos 93
Argie lamentatio 69, 101
armonia, harmonia 99
Arndt, Wilhelm 77
Ash Wednesday, poem for 66, 95
Athesis fluvius 93
athleta dei, epithet of saints 74
Atkinson, Robert 73
authors, names of authors of C. S. known 39, 72, 76, 77, 86, 90

Baechtold, Jakob 85
Baehrens, Emil 79, 89, 90, 92
baiulare 90; colum b. 93
baldness, Hugbald's poem in praise of 83
Bamberg and Henry II 76
Bartsch, Karl 29, 32, 71, 81, 86
Bavonis mons 76
bee, its chastity 89–90; bee and Virgin Mary 89–90; bees and birds 89; bee-charm of Lorsch 89
Benediktbeuern, collection of songs 38

Benevento, sequences from B. 71
Benzmann, H. 109
Berchorius, Petrus 89
birds, voices of birds 89; bees and birds 89
Bithell, Jethro 37
Blume, Clemens 71, 72
Boeckh, August 100
Bömer, A. 38
Boethius 98
Bolte, Johannes 40
Bradshaw, Henry 32, 106
Brandis, Christian August 100
Braune, Wilhelm 29, 75, 96, 103–4, 106, 110–1
Bresslau, Harry 77, 78, 80
Breul, Karl 27, 32, 33, 103 sqq., 110–1
Burana, Carmina B. 37–8, 40, 97; Fragmenta B. 28, 38

c, stanzas in which every word begins with a c 83
Caecilia, de domo S. Cecilie Coloniensi 46, 74
calvus, de laude calvorum 83
Cambridge Collection of songs: where originally made 23, 30, 40, 79; its importance 36, 39, 40; names of authors 39, 72, 76, 77, 86, 90; variety of subjects and metrical forms 41
Canterbury Book 23, 30, 32
Cantipratanus, Thomas 89
Capella, Martianus 98, 99
Carelmanninc, Modus qui et C. 29, 42–3, 71
Carmina Burana 37–8, 40, 97
Carolingian Court poetry 35
Chevalier, U. 73, 74
Christ, poems on Christ 42 sqq., 71 sqq.
Christmas play (in the Carmina Burana) 97
Classical authors, extracts from C. A. in the Cambridge Collection 39, 40, 65, 68–9, 95, 101
clerici vagabundi 35–7
clericus et nonna 65, 75, 94, 102
Cobbo, Lantfrid et Cobbo 58, 83–4
Cologne 74, 79

GENERAL INDEX

confessio Goliae 37
Conrad II: made Emperor 51, 76; song on his death 53, 77
consonantia 99; intensa et remissa 100
contemptus mundi, versus de contemptu mundi 66, 95
contents of the Cambridge Collection, survey 27-9, 110-5
Cook, A. B. 89
Coussemaker, E. de 75, 92, 95
cuckoo, Latin poems on the cuckoo 91

Daniel, H. A. 72, 95
Deutz, Archbishop Heribert buried at D. 79, 80
Devil, compact with, *see* Proterii filia 57, 83
dialect of the German portions of the Cambridge Songs 23
diapason 99, 100
diapente et diatesseron 68, 99, 100
didactic poems of the Collection 40, 66-8, 95-101
Dieterich, J. R. 26, 111
Docen, B. J. 110
Dreves, G. M. 72, 74
Du Cange 85, 89, 98
Dümmler, Ernst 35, 72, 87, 93, 102, 110
dulcis amica 92
Du Méril, Edélestand 27, 31, 40, and often in the Notes
Dunlop-Liebrecht, 'Prosadichtungen' 82

Easter hymn 45, 72
Ebert, Adolf 35-6, 110
ecbasis cuiusdam captivi 36
Eccard 27, 30, 105, 110
Ehrismann, G. 111
Ellerton, John 72
emicat, at the beginning of songs 74
Eneas videt Hectoris umbram 68, 101
Epiphany hymn 46, 72
erased pieces in the Cambridge Collection 27, 39, 65, 94-5, 113
estivum carmen 63, 88-90
Euforbius, Euphorbus 98
Eugenius, Bishop of Toledo 89

Florum, Modus Florum 29, 59, 83-5
fons Philosophiae, mensa Phil. 97
Förstemann, E. 74

Frauenlyrik 91
Frederic (I) Barbarossa 37
Friendship legends, Lantfrid and Cobbo 58, 83-4
Fröhner, Chr. W. 27, 31, and often in the Notes
Fulbert, Saint F., Bishop of Chartres 86, 90

Galpin, F. W. 97
Ganymedes et Helena 93
Gautier, Léon 74
George, S. George (athleta dei) 74
Giesebrecht, W. 35
Giles, J. A. 83, 90
Glauning, Otto 40
Goedeke, Karl 29
Goliard 35-9; familia Goliae 35; the Goliard's Song book 38-41
Golther, Wolfgang 94, 111
Graff, E. G. 96
gramma for grammatica 98
Greek terms in the Cambridge Songs 97
Gröber, Gustav 86-7, 91
Gundlach, W. 36-7
Gunnild regina 78

h, initial h frequently omitted in the Manuscript 71, 95
Habermann, P. 102, 111
Hacket, Bishop Hacket's bequest 23, 105
Hec est clara dies 45, 72
handwriting of the Manuscript 25
Haupt, Moriz 31, 37, 88, 92
Hectoris umbram videt Eneas 68, 101
Heinrichsleich, De Heinrico 31, 33-4, 48, 75, 102 sqq.
Henrici, Emil 40, 94
Henry II, songs on the death of the Emperor 50-1, 76
Henry III crowned king 52, 77
Herdringen Manuscript of Latin lyrics 38
Heribert, Archbishop of Cologne 55, 79, 80
Herigêr 29, 31, 59, 85-6
Herimannus 78
Hertz, Wilhelm 29, 35
Heyne, Moritz 34, and often in the Notes
Hickes, George 105
Hipsipile Archemorum plorat 69, 101
historical poems in the Cambridge Collection 39, 48-56, 75-81

GENERAL INDEX

Hoffmann, Heinrich H. (von Fallersleben) 30-1, 40, 94, 105
Holthausen, Friedrich 111
Homburg on the Unstrut (Thuringia) 88
Horace, Ode of Horace 65, 95
Hrabanus Maurus 72
Hrotsvith of Gandersheim 36-7
Hubatsch, O. 35
Hugbald, ecloga de laudibus calvitii 83
Hugo of Orleans 37
humorous poems in the Cambridge Collection 39, 56-62, 81-8
Hûsen, Friderich von Hûsen 37
hymnus: alphabeticus 66-7, 95; h. paschalis 45, 72

Iamblichus 98, 100
Index: alphabetical index of the Songs of the Cambridge Collection 112-3; index of songs as they follow each other in the Manuscript 27
indulgentia 96
In languore perio 95
Invitatio amice 64, 92
Iohannes presbyter, I. abba 29, 60, 86; Christi pincerna 59, 86
Irish hymns 73
Isidore 84, 100
Iupiter et Danae 93

Jaffé, Philipp 27-8, 32, 39, often in the Notes, 105-6, 110
James, M. R. 90
Jenkinson, Francis 104, 106
Joseph, Eugen 108, 111

Kelle, J. 70, 82, 84-5, 110
Kemble, J. M. 24, 33, 34
Ker, W. P. 82-3, 85
Kögel, Rudolf 28-9, 40, often in the Notes, 94, 102, 104, 111
Krönungsleich Konrads 77

Lachmann, Karl 30-1, 37, 105, 108, 110
La Curne de Sainte-Palaye 96
Laistner, Ludwig 35, 37-8
lamentations: l. of a maiden 64, 91; l. of Neobule 65, 95; l. of Rachel 46, 73; lamentations of women in the Goliard's collection 73

Landau, M. 84
Lantfrid et Cobbo 58, 83-4
Latin lyrics (Medieval) in Germany 35-8
Leland, John 105
Lesser, Friedrich 80
Lewis, W. L. 101
Lexer, Matthias 96
Liebinc, Modus Liebinc 29, 56, 81-3
Liebrecht, Felix 82
Liersch, K. 40
ligatures in the Manuscript 104
littera Pithagore 98
Lorsch, bee-charm of Lorsch 89
love-greeting in Ruodlieb 40, 94
love-songs 39, 40, 64-5, 91-5; earliest specimen of a German love-song in which German words occur 94
Lügenlied, Lügenweise 84-5
Lundius, Bernhard 38
luscinia, carmen de luscinia 29, 63, 90

macaronic poems 36, 38, 40, 75, 94, 102
Macro, T. 105
Macrobius 98
magister puero 65, 92-3
Manitius, Max 37, 40
Manuscript: description 23 sqq.; transcript 26; probably more than one copyist 25; order of songs in the Manuscript 27; relation to Wolfenbüttel MS. 36
Mapes, Walter 36-7
Martin, Ernst 87, 111
Mary, hymn to the Virgin 46, 72; Mary and the bee 89
ma ten tetraden 99
Mayer, E. 111
Medieval Latin lyrics in Germany 35 sqq.
Medieval Renaissance in Germany 35
Meister, Karl Severin 72, 78
memento mori, Old High German poem 96
mendosa cantilena 85
mensa Philosophie 38, 67, 97
Merihilt 74
metre of songs 28 sqq., 40; 8 syllables 80; 12 syllables 94; 15 syllables 73, 79
Meyer, Conrad Ferdinand 97, 109
Meyer, H. 34, 102, 104, 108, 111

GENERAL INDEX

Meyer, Wilhelm 28, 36–8, and often in the Notes
mimes 36, 40, 75, 82
Minnesang: Minnesangs Frühling 37, 40; some poems in the Cambridge Collection are forerunners of the German Minnesong 40, 91
mixed prose 75
modus 29, 36, 97; M. qui et Carelmanninc 29, 42–3, 71; M. Florum 29, 59, 83, 84–5; M. Liebinc 29, 31, 56, 81–3; M. Ottinc 29, 31, 49, 75, 81–2
Mone, F. J. 95–6, 110
mons Bavonis 76
Moorsom, R. M. 72
Morel, Gall 72
Mühler, H. von 106
Müllenhoff und Scherer 27, 29, often in the Notes, 104
Müller-Fraureuth, Carl 34, 84–5
mundus, versus de contemptu mundi 66–7, 95–6
music: its threefold division 84
musica: carmen de musica 67, 96

Naumann, Hans 94
Naylor, E. W. 98, 99
Neobule lamentatio 65, 95
neum-accents, neumatic notation 26, 83, 93–4
Nicholson, Frank 37
Nicholson, R. A. 98
Nicomachus 98–9
nightingale 29, 63, 90
Ninck, Johannes 83
notes to the Goliard's Song book 39, 70–101; abbreviations used in the notes 70–1
Notker 75, 99, 101
novelistic poems in the Cambridge Collection 39, 56–62, 81–8

O admirabile Veneris idolum 65, 92–4
O Roma nobilis 92–4
Otfrid of Weissenburg 96
Ottinc, Modus Ottinc 29, 31, 49, 75, 81–2
Ottos, Latin literature under the Ottos 35

pantokrator 97
Paris, Gaston 36, 82–3
Paschalis hymnus 45, 72
Patzig, Hermann 83
personal poems (poems addressed to important persons) 39, 48–56, 75–81

Pertz, G. H. 30, 79, 106
Petrus magister cocorum 86
Petzet, E. 40
Pflüger, W. 34, 78
Philolaos 100
photographic reproductions of the Songs 34
Piper, Paul 27, 29, 33, 106, 110–1
pisa for pisum 85
Pithagoras: de simphoniis et littera P. 67, 98 sqq.; dextera via note Pithagorice 80, 100
Platen, August von 82
poems intended to be sung 75, 79, 81, 83, 87, 88, 95
poetae aevi Carolini 35
Poppo, Archbishop of Treves 55, 80–1
popular metres 29
Postgate, J. P. 101
Priebsch, Robert 23, 33, 91, 95, 104, 106, 108, 111
Prien, Friedrich 32
Primas (Hugo of Orleans) 37
Proterii filia 57, 83
punctuation 26
Pythagoras, see Pithagoras
Pythagorean; letter (Y) 100; solemn oath 99–100

quaternarium 99
queen restored from illness 54, 79

Rachel, her lament 46, 73; her 'soror improba' 73
Rawlinson, Chr. 105
refrain 72, 76, 77, 79, 95
Reginald of Dassel 37
Reich, Hermann 28, 71, 76
Reinaert, the Cambridge Reinaert fragments 32
religious poems in the Cambridge Collection 39, 42–8, 71–4
Renart, roman de Renart 87
resurrection, hymn on the resurrection 45, 72
Robert-Tornow, Walter 89
Rödiger, Max 86
Rönsch, Hermann 81
Roman de Renart 87
rota 84, 96–7
Ruodlieb 36, 40, 102

Sacerdos et lupus 29, 31–2, 61, 87
Sachs, style of Hans Sachs 86

salve, festa dies 45, 72
Salzer, Anselm 34, 91, 96
Sandys, Sir John 37, 81
Sapphic ode 88
Schade, Oscar 29, 30, 105, 110
Schelmenlied, Schelmenstück 84–5
Scherer, Wilhelm 29, 31–2, 40, 83, 104, 106, 110
Schmeidler, B. 37
Schmeller, J. Andreas 38, 105
Schönbach, Anton 36
Schröder, Edward 74
Schubiger, Anselm 34, 78
Schwank 86, 87
scribe or scribes of the Manuscript 25
Sedulius 72
Seelmann, Wilhelm 102, 110–1
Seemüller, Joseph 75, 108, 111
sequences 28, 36, often in Notes, 85
Simeon of Treves 81
simphonia 99
Simrock, Karl 72, 90
Smith, John 105
snow-child 81–3
Soltau, F. L. von 77
Specht, F. A. 35
spelling, inconsistencies 25–6, 107
Splettstösser, W. 82
spring and love, poems on these 39, 63–5, 88–95
Stanley, Thomas 98–9
Statius, extracts from the 'Thebaid' 69, 101
Steinmeyer, Elias 29, 33, often in the Notes, 84, 104, 106, 108, 110–1
Stockmayer, Gertrud 91, 94
Survey, tabulated s. of the Songs 27, 114–5
Swabians: bad reputation 83; wiliness 83–4, 86
Symonds, John Addington 34, 38, 90, 92

'Thebaid,' extracts from it 69, 101
Thesis, Tesis fluvius 94
Thompson, Sir E. M. 104
transcript of the Manuscript 3–22, 26
translations of the 'Cambridge Songs' 34
Traube, Ludwig 34–5, 40, 92
Treves, Trier 80

Troubadours 37

Uhland, Ludwig 75, 77, 83, 108, 110
Una 74
Unibos 80, 85
Uoda, Uuoda 74

Venantius Fortunatus 72, 96
venia 96
verna femine suspiria 29, 64, 91
Verona, poetry and intellectual life at V. 93
via dextra note Pithagorice 80, 100
Victor, S. Victor of Xanten 47, 74
Virgil, extracts from the 'Æneid' 69, 101; expressions borrowed from V. 75
Vitruvius 99
Vogt, Friedrich 34

Wackernagel, Philipp 72
Wackernagel, Wilhelm 29, 31, 86, 105, 110
Waltharius (manu fortis) 36
Walther von der Vogelweide 37, 76
Wanley, H. 105
Wattenbach, Wilhelm 35, 77, 78, 93, 95
Weinhold, Karl 96
Werner, Jakob 38
Willem, Archbishop of Mayence 56, 75, 81
Williram 75
Wilmanns, Wilhelm 28, 71, 108, 110
Winter, R. 110
Winterfeld, Paul von W. 28, 34–7, 40, often in the Notes
Wipo 77–9
Wolf, Ferdinand 96
Wolfenbüttel Manuscript 36
Wright, Thomas 31, 33, 36–7, 86
Wunschbock 85

Xanten, S. Victor of Xanten, 47, 74

Y, the Pythagorean letter 100

zabulon for diabulon, diabolum 81
Zeller, Eduard 98, 99
Zürich Manuscript of Latin lyrical poems 38

For EU product safety concerns, contact us at Calle de José Abascal, 56–1°,
28003 Madrid, Spain or eugpsr@cambridge.org.

www.ingramcontent.com/pod-product-compliance
Ingram Content Group UK Ltd.
Pitfield, Milton Keynes, MK11 3LW, UK
UKHW060049240426
12048UKWH00019B/1411